Martin Auferbauer, Gorda.
Arno Heimgartner, Liljana Rihter,
Roar Sundby (Eds.)

Social Development

Soziale Arbeit – Social Issues

herausgegeben von

Univ.-Prof. Mag. Dr. Arno Heimgartner
(Universität Graz)

und

FH-Prof. Mag. Dr. Maria Maiss
(Fachhochschule St. Pölten GmbH)

Band 22

LIT

SOCIAL DEVELOPMENT

Ways of Understanding Society
and Practising Social Work

edited by

Martin Auferbauer, Gordana Berc,
Arno Heimgartner, Liljana Rihter,
and Roar Sundby

LIT

Cover Image: Marko Vrdoljak

Supported by:
University of Zagreb, University of Ljubljana, Norwegian University
of Science and Technology, University College of Teacher Education
Styria, University of Graz, ICSD European Branch

Bibliographic information published by the Deutsche Nationalbibliothek
The Deutsche Nationalbibliothek lists this publication in the Deutsche
Nationalbibliografie; detailed bibliographic data are available on the Internet at
http://dnb.d-nb.de.

ISBN 978-3-643-91159-9 (pb)
ISBN 978-3-643-96159-4 (PDF)

A catalogue record for this book is available from the British Library.

© LIT VERLAG GmbH & Co. KG Wien,
Zweigniederlassung Zürich 2019
Klosbachstr. 107
CH-8032 Zürich
Tel. +41 (0) 44-251 75 05
E-Mail: zuerich@lit-verlag.ch   http://www.lit-verlag.ch
Distribution:
In the UK: Global Book Marketing, e-mail: mo@centralbooks.com
In North America: Independent Publishers Group, e-mail: orders@ipgbook.com
In Germany: LIT Verlag Fresnostr. 2, D-48159 Münster
Tel. +49 (0) 2 51-620 32 22, Fax +49 (0) 2 51-922 60 99, e-mail: vertrieb@lit-verlag.de
e-books are available at www.litwebshop.de

Content

Introduction

This editorial collection is a product of the papers that were presented at the 20th biennial symposium of the International Consortium for Social Development (ICSD). This international scientific conference took place in Zagreb from 7 to 11 July in 2017. It was a joint ICSD and ICSD European branch conference that brought together professionals and academics from many different disciplines. At the conference, 45 sessions were held, and 220 academics and professionals from 6 continents and 28 countries participated. This scientific symposium was centred around the academic and professional discussion of the role of multidisciplinary perspectives in order to realise social and economic prosperity while respecting the principles of human rights and social justice on the local, national and international levels.

Some of these topics are presented in these collected works, together entitled *Social Development – Ways of Understanding Society and Practicing Social Work.* All of the papers included have undergone a process of review.

Our experience and comprehension clearly shows us that our changing contemporary society brings many challenges related to understanding the various facets of social development. Different approaches, solutions and national strategies are being applied in order to provide an answer to current national and international social issues; this can be a challenge when it comes to the improvement of wellbeing and the ensuring of social rights for all. Social problems usually have diverse causes and impact various dimensions of people's lives. Therefore, corresponding professional responses on different levels, from micro to macro, are of great value.

The European continent has a long and interesting history of social problem resolution based on many differences, but also similarities, in terms of social, political, economic, educational, cultural and other contexts. Even today, these differing contexts generate intensive discussion. Sometimes feelings of fear, dread and insecurity arise, especially concerning conflicts and wars, for example the war in Ukraine, terrorist attacks in central Europe, and massive migration flows. These are considerable challenges for a modern Europe, and there are many theories that try to explain these situations. We know from previous experience that mutual respect as well as time and space for open discussion are crucial when making important decisions in order to provide for a peaceful and functional society.

From a broader perspective, this book focuses on different social groups because a rapidly changing society requires thorough reflection. Therefore, the content of the collection consists of several articles emphasising reflection and conceptualisation in relation to groups that are facing various social problems, possible measures that can be taken to improve lives and the role of social work in all of this.

Approaches to gain a deeper understanding of the context in which we are living are the concepts of post-truth in society (Ivan Svetlik) and a knowledge society in general (Lasse Skogvold Isaksen). To establish and maintain a system of social support, new economic structures are required (Hans Kolstad). Over the past few years, society and its social systems have been shaped by migrant movements that have led to a migrant crisis in some locations (Gordana Berc). The perception of the affected groups of refugees is of particular importance (Alma Pezerović, Jane McPherson & Marina Milić Babić). Unaccompanied children and adolescents can come to dominate the focus of social services (Sabine Klinger, Thomas Buchner & Ines Findenig). The third sector (Danijel Baturina, Jelena Matančević & Gojko Bežovan) greatly contributes to the welfare system and the development of a better society, in combination with an increased focus on intersectionality and gender disparities (Vjollca Krasniqi). Relatedly, an important element is the contribution of volunteers in many sectors of social support activities (Arno Heimgartner). As an additional future-related issue, social services for children and adolescents are covered. Youth information (Martin Auferbauer) as well as child and youth welfare (Geir Hyrve & Joachim Vogt Isaksen) are discussed, in particular in the context of changing needs and increased participation. Child and youth welfare are realms of governmental responsibility, with substantial contributions coming from private organisations. Therefore, questions of professionalisation and education for those taking on this role need to be discussed (Anne Grytbakk, Berit Skauge & Roar Sundby). The topics of risky sexual behaviour (Marijana Majdak & Zrinka Leko), relations between normativity and morality (Knut Magne Sten) and strategies to counter poverty (Maria Ozanaria da Silva e Silva) complete the content. In addition to the hermeneutic and empirical approaches, the content of this book is also deeply enriched by the different perspectives of its international contributors coming from Croatia, Slovenia, Bulgaria, Kosovo, Austria, Norway and Brazil.

As academics and professionals, we are called on to point out social and economic issues, to emphasise unrecognised and unresolved problems and to discuss possible solutions, as well as to give a voice to the most vulnerable groups, such as children, women, the elderly, poor and sick. Protecting and promoting human rights, wellbeing and social justice is always one of the basic topics of academic and professional communities; these issues should be highlighted in the spectrum of teaching, researching, providing services and advocating for the welfare of vulnerable groups. In that context, long-term goals should be focused upon, having an influence on policy makers and policy design processes, involving different disciplines, along with a dialogue with service users in order to improve the social development of contemporary society. We hope that this editorial collection is a fruitful contribution to this significant goal.

Special thanks to Anneliese Pirs (Office) and Nathan Ingvalson (Proofreading)!

The Editors

Ivan Svetlik (University of Ljubljana)

Social Inequality and Post-Truth Society

Abstract

Purpose: The purpose of this article is to draw the attention of researchers and the public to the close link between social inequality and the post-truth society, which could trigger highly undesirable social and political developments worldwide. It also intends to help clarify the relatively new discourse on post-truth.

Approach: The article is conceptual in nature and refers to noteworthy studies of social inequality and various sources focused on the post-truth society and politics.

Findings: Some indications reveal that social inequality has become part of post-truth politics and that it reinforces the post-truth society paradigm. Conditioning each other in the upswing of the post-truth and social inequality cycle represents a worrying development for modern society, resembling the situation 100 years ago. Post-truth politics finds fertile ground in several social phenomena, which do not necessarily represent a post-truth reality. Three criteria for identifying post-truth are proposed: self-evidence, scientific verification, and internationally recognised historical/civilisation achievements.

Social implications: The paper aspires to increase the awareness of those in power as well as the general public about likely social crisis and conflicts, and the need to avoid them.

Originality: The originality of the article lies in the explicitly shown link between social inequality and post-truth, and the proposed criteria for distinguishing post-truth and other phenomena.

Post-truth society

The Oxford English Dictionary defines post-truth as "relating to or denoting circumstances in which objective facts are less influential in shaping public opinion than appeals to emotion and personal belief" (Oxford dictionaries, 2017). In the last decade, the post-truth concept has mainly been applied to the field of politics (Roberts, 2010) where "campaigners continue to repeat their talking points, even if these are found to be untrue by the media or independent experts" (Wikipedia, 2017). The two most frequently cited events in which the post-truth approach was recently observed were the presidential election in the United States and the referendum on European Union membership held in the United Kingdom in 2016. However, there are other cases, demonstrating that the post-truth phenomenon is more complex than it might appear at first sight.

A less problematic example includes computer-generated imagery, television and Internet programmes that present fiction as reality or blur the distinction between them. This technology is often described as interesting, even fascinating. Yet such fascination becomes serious when young people exposed to such media find it difficult to distinguish reality and fiction in their everyday lives, lose the ability to cope with everyday problems, or even act out.

We encounter the denial of science-based medicine, refusal of medical treatment and vaccination and belief in so-called alternative medicine every day. We hear arguments that conventional medicine is all about the pharmaceutical industry making profit. The proponents of alternative medicine receive enormous sums of money through their alternative treatments. In 2009, Americans spent USD 34 billion on complementary and alternative medicine (NBC News, 2009). Moreover, with the support of top politicians, America's National Centre for Complementary and Integrative Health and its predecessors spent billions of dollars on the research and validation of alternative approaches without delivering any significant positive results (Brown, 2009). This approach puts in danger not only those who believe in alternative medicine but also their families and society at large. The reappearance of once eradicated infectious diseases is a good example. For instance, in 2017 Italy had to introduce the compulsory vaccination of children against infectious diseases for this very reason.

Hundreds of books and articles that offer evidence on trends and reasons for global warming have been published in recent decades (Wikipedia, 2017a; MacMilan, 2016; Selin, 2017; Sachs, 2015; Paris Climate Deal, 2015). It is now scientifically established that the ever more frequent climactic events, such as droughts, melting of polar ice, submersion of oceanic islands, dying out of animal and plant species, floods, landslides, frequent heavy storms and so on, are a consequence of global warming. The sources of global warming have been identified and programmes to reduce it described. However, some politicians still simply ignore such evidence, act in ways contrary to the international agreements to prevent global warming and promote political decisions that exacerbate the present situation. Instead of encouraging people and industry to change their day-to-day behaviour and production technology in favour of sustainable life on the Earth, they send out false messages.

Mankind has not yet eradicated the problem of starvation. Diseases that decrease human longevity and worsen the quality of life are ever changing. Science offers a promising tool to counter these problems. According to Nobel Prize laureate Sir Richard Roberts (Roberts, 2015), this tool is genetics. Yet, the scientifically unproven fear of genetic engineering seems to be stronger than people's hopes of surviving and improving their lives. Moreover, some governments, including European governments, have prohibited cloning in research laboratories. Referring to ethics, they prevent science from dealing with things that have been going on in nature from the outset.

The deep economic crisis of 2008 was largely caused by the financial sector, which invented so-called derivative financial instruments. It turns out that these instruments do not create significant added value in the economy and mainly serve to redistribute wealth in favour of financial elites. As pointed out by John Kay, the financial sector has become detached from the real economy, and financial organisations chiefly do business with each other (Kay, 2009). Nonetheless, governments and international economic organisations have failed to introduce the necessary regulatory changes. Business more or less continues as usual, running the risk of another crisis. In addition, new instruments like crypto currencies have emerged in the market.

Another example is the theory of evolution. It has been in place for over 150 years, since Charles Darwin published his famous research work On the Origin of Species (Darwin, 1859). Still, doubts surrounding evolution theory continue to be expressed by top public authorities in many countries, including the USA (Laats and Siegel, 2016). They advocate creationism and the theory of intelligent design as an alternative, while seeking to include it in the school curriculum. In some countries such as Turkey, the theory of evolution was recently removed from the school curriculum. This overlooks the fact that education based on creationism leads to misperceptions of both nature and society, and creates harmful beliefs and individual behaviours, among them ignoring man's impact on the natural environment. Such beliefs could mean that issues of environmental sustainability become unresolvable.

What do these examples tell us about post-truth? First, the post-truth concept should be defined in relation to the truth. There is not enough space in this article to present the entire scope of the understanding of truth. It should suffice at this point to refer to the most traditional correspondence theory, according to which truth means that thoughts and statements are in accord with fact or reality (Merriam-Webster, 2017), or correspondence with the actual state of affairs (Prior, 1969). With respect to this, facts, reality and the state of affairs might be self-evident, i.e. something that everybody can see or experience. Truth is also often scientifically proven and thus represents a second benchmark criterion of post-truth. This does not mean that science provides final truth but rather that correspondence with reality is consistently submitted to testing in the scientific community (Encyclopedia of Philosophy, 1969).

However, in the lives of individuals and societies, different individuals perceive numerous phenomena in differing ways. Everybody is sure of his/her own truth. Even scientific fields, particularly the social sciences, interpret the same 'facts' differently. Some see social inequalities as unavoidable and functional, while others see them as unnecessary and harmful (Crossman, 2017). Some interpret crypto currencies as an important social innovation, others as yet another trick to convince uninformed investors to part with their money. Beyond science there are ideologies, religions, value systems and personal interests. They are often regarded as the ultimate truth of individuals, groups and organisations, even though they are in absolute opposition to the truths of others. Moreover, their proponents seek to have them scientifically justified to give them social legitimacy. We have already referred to the example of creationism and intelligent design 'theory' (Laats and Siegel, 2016) or the justifications for derived financial instruments. This usually happens when emotion, religion, ideology and the subconscious are involved. In such cases, one cannot arrive at a benchmark for post-truth since everybody has the right to their own beliefs. Unfortunately, human civilisation has had quite bitter experiences with such phenomena, expressed in terms of the extinction of 'others', 'Wild West' practices, slavery, racism, religious wars, xenophobia, economic crises, world wars and the like.

As a consequence of such painful experiences, societies have developed some instruments to help find the correct balance between the differing or even opposing truths of various parties. When two individuals, organisations or states disagree, they can appeal to a court of law, which mediates between them. National and international legislation embodies codes of behaviour for individuals and organisations. There are also international organisations and international agreements, which codify human rights (United Nations), standards of wellbeing (World Health Organisation), rules of international trade (World Trade Organisation), labour standards (International Labour Organisation), sustainable development and so on. All of these achievements are invaluable in terms of helping to avoid historically disastrous human and societal costs. They represent the third benchmark of the truth apart from hard science and the self-evidence, historical experiences and achievements. In this case, a constructivist understanding of truth as something that depends on power relations and ideologies in the society should be referred to (Wikipedia, 2018).

Second, post-truth can form part of an individual's beliefs and behaviour, as well as aspects of social institutions. However, practising post-truth individually or collectively does not bring the same outcomes. Individuals are free to choose their beliefs and ways of living. Most people do not only live according to rational and scientific principles, just as was true in the past. They express their emotions, rely on intuition, are superstitious or religious, ignore the principles of healthy living, etc. This is their individual freedom, their choice and their right. Yet, it a difference comes into play when such individuals promote their lifestyles to others, organise themselves into networks and exert pressure on other citizens to follow their irrational and sometimes harmful life choices, and use public resources in such activities. It makes a big difference if politicians and other people who hold social power practise such behaviour, consciously or unconsciously, deliberately or unintentionally. It is worrying when political and other leaders engage in irrational discourse to gain power and popular support.

In other words, in contemporary societies ordinary people enjoy freedoms including the choice of what they believe in, what is true and important in their lives, how to behave, etc. so long as they do not impinge on the same freedoms of others. If they make a wrong choice, they are supposed to bear the consequences themselves. Yet it is not the same with a group, an organisation or a state. If these entities make wrong decisions, due either to their ignorance or their misuse of power so as to realise their short-term or particular interests, the consequences fall on the shoulders of group or organisational members and citizens. While 'post-truth' for ordinary citizens is a matter of personal freedoms and free choice, for leaders it amounts to the irresponsible use of power. Politicians who employ the post-truth discourse are ignoring the lessons of history and may be putting their own nations and the planet at risk. They are tempted, as was often the case in in the past, to not base their power on the truth, namely what corresponds to the scientifically or historically determined reality, but to enforce their power as an abstraction of truth.

Third, 300 years ago much less was known about the natural and social world that people were living in than today, whereas the influences of religion and mysticism were stronger. However, since the age of the Enlightenment, the primary sources of authority and legitimacy have been ideas centred on reason (History, 2017; Zafirovski, 2010; Gay, 1995). These ideas had a tremendous influence on social and economic developments. To mention just a few: the scientific revolution, scientific journals and dictionaries, the establishment of public schools and universities, a free market economy and liberal democracy based on natural rights to individual freedom and property, the technological and industrial revolutions, the separation of church and state, a modern nation-state and more. Unlike some modern political leaders, the rulers of that time, like Catherine II of Russia, Joseph II of Austria and Frederick II of Prussia, were eager to be advised by philosophers and scientists, such as Voltaire, Diderot, Rousseau, Hume, Smith, Kant and others. They were co-creators of the Age of Reason in which the truth was supposed to be in accord with factual reality.

In the course of history, there have been deviations and lapses in terms of mainstream developments, such as dictatorships, violation of human rights and wars. These events were based much more on subconscious thinking and emotion (nationalism, racism) and on understanding truth as power or faith (religion) than on rational reasoning. However, thus far societies have always returned to the prevalence of rationalism in the mainstream.

Fourth, post-truth politics is simply the tip of the iceberg. Beneath lies a social fabric composed of rational and emotional individuals experiencing various conscious and unconscious behaviours, thus providing fertile ground for post-truth politics, post-truth management, etc. Politics demonstrates its deep tendency toward bias by reverting to post-truth. One ought to question whether politics should directly reflect voters' minds, even if the politicians are directly elected. Political policy should instead bear responsibility for realising people's aspirations that they themselves cannot achieve individually. It should show individuals the right way to realise their long-term interests and it should not misuse their emotions and subconscious beliefs to strengthen the power of political, corporate and other elites as its main goal.

Based on this short analysis, we may conclude that society is made up of individuals who are not only rational but also emotional beings (Turner, 2009), and whose behaviour is often influenced by unconscious "reasoning" (McLeod, 2015). This is part of the true world we all live in. We are facing the post-truth when people in power, such as politicians, managers, other leaders and experts, exert their influence on citizens, employees and organisational members, telling them untruths or half-truths, or appealing to their subconscious and emotion, thus encouraging beliefs and behaviours inconsistent with self-evident or scientifically proven facts and/or historical experiences and human achievements (Suiter, 2016). Post-truth practices represent a definite breaking away from the Enlightenment rationality paradigm, thereby challenging the achievements made in the last three centuries (Jasanoff and Hilton, 2017).

Reasons for post-truth

At this point, one should ask: Which social processes are gradually eroding the rational and science-based societal paradigm, bringing about a shift to post-truth? What enables politicians to play a post-truth game? Why is this happening at a time in which the development of science and technology has reached unprecedented levels?

Harsin (2015) sees the primary reasons for the growing strength of post-truth in the changing nature and social position of the media. He stresses its fragmentation, the appearance of social media without safeguards to distinguish between facts, fiction and lies, the crisis of the news media seeking to ensure its survival through tabloid-style reporting where truth and facts have become objects of deliberate distortion and deception. Other authors (Drezner, 2016) add factors such as state-funded news agencies, which are losing credibility and changing their style so that equal emphasis is given to unsupported claims without challenging their factual basis (Suiter, 2016), social media where truth is measured by the number of views or followers rather than by researched facts. The post-truth political debate in the media reinforces rather than challenges people's existing biases, making it easier for misinformation to spread. These media are inclined to present content people are likely to agree with. They contribute to the emergence of self-reinforcing communities of like-minded people, which undermines the health of democracy. As Walter Quatrociocchi claims, "social media distort information" (World Economic Forum, 2017b).

It should be noted that the social sciences, such as psychology and communication science, might have their share of blame in the creation of post-truth. Their studies provide many potential techniques that may be used to influence individuals' cognition, emotions and behaviour. These techniques are used by marketing agencies when advising companies and politicians about how to better sell their products, services and claims. Producers therefore no longer sell cars, health products, cosmetics, and the like, but instead beauty, sex, power, happiness, comfort, adventure, etc. Politicians do not sell agendas based on civilisation's achievements and promote programmes focused on long-term prospects for all people on the globe, rather they sell nationalism, populism, fear of immigrants and terrorists, xenophobia, and a strict work ethic in order to gain the support of the masses. When in power, unfortunately, they are expected to keep their promises.

One could speculate about other reasons. One example is inadequate education that does not provide a strong enough emphasis on facts, history and science. Another is the fact that individuals are overburdened with work and family obligations, which does not allow them to stay well informed and reflect on what is presented in the media. Other examples include short-cuts to reduce the complexity of everyday life, the inadequate response of social institutions to address citizens' healthcare needs, social and other communal problems, aspirations of the political and economic elite to gain profits and power in organisations, unethical media and political practices, cases of science being misused thus decreasing its credibility, the short-term collective memory of societies which are inclined to repeat the mistakes of previous generations, etc. "In the post-truth era, collective memory seems to have lost touch with historical facts" (Saint-Laurent et al., 2017).

It is outside the scope of this paper to discuss all of the reasons for the growing appearance of post-truth in more detail. For this reason, in the following section I would like to focus on just one of them, i.e. increasing social inequality. Its meaning seems to be disputed in the social sciences and its historical role is often ignored. Moreover, it seems that social inequality is adding to the escalating role of post-truth politics.

Increasing social inequalities

Before linking social inequality with the post-truth society, I wish to briefly refer to two recently published comprehensive studies on social inequality. The first is Piketty's "Capital in the Twenty-first Century" (Piketty, 2014) and the second is Milanovic's "Global Inequality" (Milanovic, 2016). Both studies focus on long-term trends in wealth distribution between and within countries.

Piketty's detailed analysis shows that inequality within developed countries was growing until the 1910s, when it decline significantly and remained lower until the 1970s, then it started to rise again. He found that "Global inequality of wealth in the early 2010s appears to be comparable in the magnitude to the observed in Europe in 1900s–1910s. The top thousandth seems to own nearly 20 percent of total global wealth today, the top centile about 50 percent and the top decile somewhat between 80 and 90 percent" (p. 438). He claims that "… there is no natural, spontaneous process to prevent destabilizing, inegalitarian forces from prevailing permanently …" (p. 21). Quite the contrary is in fact true. "The principal destabilizing force has to do with the fact that the private rate of return on capital, r, can be significantly higher for long periods of time than the rate of growth of income and output, g … The inequality r > g implies that wealth accumulated in the past grows more rapidly than output and wages … The entrepreneur inevitably tends to become a rentier, more and more dominant over those who own nothing but their labour …" (p. 571).

Piketty identified two social groups that lead the wealth accumulation race: capital owners and managers, who appropriate unreasonable proportions of labour income and thus become capital owners themselves. "The share of wages going to the top centile (in France), which was less than 6 percent in the 1980s and 1990s, began to increase in the late 1990s and reached 7.5–8 percent of the total by the early 2010s. Thus, there was an increase of nearly 30 percent in a little over decade ... In the US the top decile income share rose from less than 35 percent of total income in the 1970s to almost 50 percent in the 2000s–2010s" (pp. 290–291). Piketty adds that data about firms' performance do not explain variations in managers' income (p. 334).

"The history of inequality is shaped by the way economic, social, and political actors view what is just and what is not, as well as by the relative power of those actors and the collective choices that result" (p. 20). In the first half of the 20th century, inequality was reduced by the two World Wars, the Soviet revolution, the Great Depression of 1929, and especially the intervention of the state by means of taxation and building up of the social state. When in the 1980s neo-liberal policies gained momentum, giving advantage to capital at the expense of the state, inequality started to grow again.

Piketty concludes his analysis by expressing concern about the increasing inequality of wealth distribution. He sees the main solution in "... a progressive annual tax on capital ...", which should be agreed upon on a global level. He also proposes other forms of state intervention, such as investment in education and training and other publicly funded services.

Milanovic's analysis complements that of Piketty with a stronger accent on inter-country wealth distribution comparisons in the last few decades. Analysing gains in real per capita incomes across the globe between 1988 and 2008, he identified three key groups. In the first group, there are people with "... the highest real income growth: some 80 percent during the twenty-years period ... In nine out of ten cases, they are people from the emerging Asian economies, predominantly China, but also India, Thailand, Vietnam and Indonesia ... They are the people around the middle of the distributions in their own countries, and ... in the world too" (pp. 18–19).

The second group contains people with the lowest or no income growth who "... generally belong to the lower half of their countries income distributions ... these people may be called the 'lower middle class of the rich world' ... In short: the great winners have been the Asian poor and middle classes; the great losers, the lower middle classes of the rich world" (p. 20). From the 1980s to 2010, the share of the middle class in the population dropped significantly in all developed countries (p. 194).

In the third group, there are the absolute winners, the top 1 percent, the 'global plutocrats'. They overwhelmingly come from the rich economies, half of them are Americans. "44 percent of the absolute gain has gone into the hands of the richest 5 percent of people globally, with almost one-fifth of the total increment received by the top 1 percent … the emerging global middle class has only received … between 2 and 4 percent of the increase of global pie …" (pp. 22–24).

One may conclude that the developed world is composed of "on the one hand, an increasingly wealthy, powerful and many would argue out-of-touch elite; on the other an angry, disillusioned and squeezed middle class, one pay cheque away from poverty" (World Economic Forum, 2017b).

On the basis of historical analysis, Milanovic arrives at more extreme conclusions than Piketty about the eventual consequences of increasing inequality. "A very high inequality eventually becomes unsustainable, but it does not go down by itself; rather it generates processes, like wars, social strife, and revolutions, that lower it" (p. 98). One of the observed consequences is a slide away from democracy, which in Milanovic's opinion goes in the direction of plutocracy in the USA, and in Europe in the direction of populism or nativism (p. 199). In addition to the measures for reducing inequality Piketty proposes, he makes an interesting proposal for the long-term equalisation of capital ownership (p. 221). If r > g, according to Piketty, it seems reasonable to make people 'capitalists' so as to enable their better participation in wealth distribution.

Both Piketty and Milanovic provide some promising data on the shrinking inequality gap among countries. Per capita GDP in Asia and Africa went from 37 percent of the world average in 1950 to 61 percent in 2012 (Piketty, 2014, p. 61). GDP per capita is growing much faster in China and India than in the USA (Milanovic, 2016, p. 131). However, if we leave BRIC and a few smaller countries aside, this is not necessarily true for all. A large number of countries in Africa, Asia and South America have been affected by climate change, wars, ideologically motivated internal conflicts and corrupt or incompetent leaders, which deprive the population of prosperity. Instead of economic growth, there are natural disasters, starvation and the destruction of production and infrastructure capacities. The migration of hundreds of thousands of people from Africa and Asia to Europe is only one of the visible consequences.

The situation does not seem promising even if all developing countries do manage to take off economically. Due to limited natural resources (World Resources Forum, 2017) and global population growth (UN Population Division, 2017), the pattern of development and lifestyles prevailing in developed countries, and to which all people on the planet have a human right to aspire to, is hardly feasible according to UN International Resource Panel Board member Potočnik (Guild, 2017). Potočnik does not believe this challenge can be successfully addressed solely by new technologies, such as those which will reduce energy and raw material consumption and pollution, and those that will increase productivity, including in terms of food supply. He thinks that radical changes are needed in individuals' lifestyles and in the organisation of all societies on Earth, especially those in developed countries. As an example, one could take the substitution of autonomous publicly shared e-cars for existing privately owned vehicles.

Without a global agreement on sustainable development and a shift in the development model, one can expect a decline in economic prosperity of developed countries, the blocked economic growth of the developing areas, regional wars over natural resources, as is already occurring, and overall hardship for the masses.

Social inequality and post-truth

In which respect can we consider social inequality as part of the post-truth reality? The first example would be if people in power ignore the lessons of both history and data, which show that the inequality in wealth distribution is at about the same level as at the start of the 20th century. What will be the result if they continue with policies that enable or even enhance inequality in wealth distribution?

Let me start with the concern of Piketty: "Can we imagine a twenty-first century in which capitalism will be transcended in a more peaceful and more lasting way, or must we simply await the next crisis or the next war (this time truly global)?" (2014, p. 471). Milanovic goes even further, saying that the First World War" ... was caused by imperialist competition, embedded in the domestic economic conditions of the time: very high income and wealth inequality, high savings of the upper classes, insufficient aggregate demand, and the need of capitalists to find profitable uses for surplus savings outside their own country" (2016, p. 95). Clearly the Russian proletariat and peasants had nothing to lose by joining the revolution against the tsar, landowners and later industrialists, who were squeezing them for the purpose of primary accumulation. Piketty claims (p. 297) there is absolutely no doubt that the increase in inequality in the USA contributed to the nation's financial instability in 2008 as inequality led to the stagnation of purchasing power of the lower and middle classes. If this is the case, the same argument could be used with respect to the Great Depression of 1929.

The lessons of history are quite clear. However, over the course of time social conditions change and today opposing views exist on the role of social inequality (Crossman, 2017). There is no consensus concerning at which point social inequality becomes dysfunctional and starts leading to crises and devastating social conflicts. If it contributed to social catastrophes in the first half of the 20th century, would the same level of wealth inequality be equally problematic a century later when the general standard of living is much higher and workers' organisations are weaker? We do not have exact scientific answers. Nonetheless, we can present some indicators that warn us against repeating the mistakes of the past.

First, let me mention a few positive cases. There is global agreement on sustainable development, which most countries have signed. Another promising indictor is increasing investment in education and new technologies in the majority of countries. As Piketty claims (2014, p. 71) "... historical experience suggests that the principal mechanism for convergence at the international as well as the domestic level is the diffusion of knowledge".

There are, however, quite some worrying indicators. One is the appearance of 'super managers' who appropriate increasing shares of income without reasonable justification in terms of their contribution to productivity growth, turning themselves into rentiers. "… when we collect data about individual firms, it is very difficult to explain the observed variations (in managers' income) in terms of firm performance" (Piketty, 2014, p. 334). It seems the greatest explanation for their enormous salaries is their power position. In addition, by officially referring to the importance of the human capital of their employees, in their leadership practices managers are increasingly using measures based on emotion and subterfuge to make the employees work harder.

There has not been any substantial reform of the financial system since the economic crisis of 2008, which was caused by the financial elite. The concentration of capital continues. The attempts of states to catch the capital escaping to tax havens seem quite ineffective, forcing journalists rather than financial authorities to reveal the corrupt practices of thousands who are avoiding paying taxes in their own countries. The proposal to impose taxes on bank transactions in Europe has not been realised. The idea to introduce a global progressive tax on capital (Piketty, 2014, p. 573) has yet to be seriously discussed. Although some public figures such as Christine Lagarde claim the world needs more redistribution of wealth and more inclusive growth, some gathered at the World Economic Forum in Davos state that growth should be given priority over redistribution (World Economic Forum, 2017).

Although research shows that higher social inequality is negatively related to economic growth (Ortiz and Cummings, 2011), attempts to increase workers' wages and strengthen public services have not been apparent. Based on neo-liberal beliefs, the dismantling of established welfare programmes continues in many countries. A good example is the stepping back from Obama Care in the US. In addition, the US is withdrawing from the international environment agreement and from UN institutions, bringing into question whether other international agreements have been achieved for the peaceful collaboration of countries.

It seems that, with its misperception and devaluation, social inequality is becoming part of the post-truth society. Moreover, it is increasingly contributing to strengthening the post-truth society in terms of people's perception of reality, and thus their support of post-truth politics. In which ways is this happening?

Let me focus on the perceived social position of the winners and losers mentioned by Milanovic. Although starting at quite a low level, the incomes and living standards of the new working and middle classes in developing countries are growing thanks to the increasing number of jobs and rising wages. Generally they believe that their living conditions are improving and that they have a bright future. However, this does not mean that social inequality is not an issue in developing countries (Awasthi and Shrivastav, 2017).

On the other hand, the losers are the working and middle classes in developed countries. It does not mean much if their standard of living is high above that of workers in developing countries. What matters to them is that in the last few decades their real incomes have not increased. The typical American worker earns less today than 45 years ago (Stiglitz, 2013). Workers are facing the loss of jobs and long-term unemployment. Jobs considered to be permanent have become precarious. The number of people in 'alternative work arrangements' rose faster than overall employment between 2005 and 2015. It is estimated that 540 million young people across 25 advanced economies face the prospect of growing up poorer than their parents (World Economic Forum, 2017a). At the same time, they are observing a tremendous increase in the wealth of the economic elite. The ratio of average worker to chief executive income in the US may reach as high as 1:500 (Stiglitz, 2013). At the World Economic Forum in Davos 2017, Winnie Byanyima, Executive Director of Oxfam International, said that the eight richest men in the world hold the same wealth as 3.6 billion of the world's poorest people. We are increasingly moving away from a situation in which the financial and managerial elite can justify the existing inequalities in terms of their contribution to society's functioning, which would contribute to social peace (Parsons, 1970).

One should not be surprised that feelings of frustration are overwhelming a great share of people living in developed countries. The values people once believed in and the principles that guided their behaviour are losing credibility. Living in line with their existing values no longer brings the expected results. People are seeking alternative ways to improve their social position. For instance, they were seeking quick gains by taking out loans and investing in real estate before the crisis of 2008. They have become prone to following the false promises offered by populists and nationalists. The support of voters for populist nationalist parties expressing racist, xenophobic, anti-migrant and similar views is rising, especially in Europe. Over the last 15 years, such politicians have won elections in Poland, Hungary and the Czech Republic, while gaining up to 20 per cent of the vote in Denmark, Austria, France and Finland. They are also on the rise in other countries (Milanović, 2016, p. 209). The situation to some extent resembles the 1930s when the 1929 crisis affected working and middle classes in Europe with lost jobs and income, and starvation, while pushing them into the hands of fascists and right-wing authoritarians who offered quick and lasting solutions based on nationalism, anti-Semitism, racism and xenophobia (Encyclopaedia Britannica, 2017).

With respect to such developments, social inequality has not only become an ingredient of the post-truth society in the sense that the power elite promotes it beyond a reasonable point as being a natural and necessary condition for social development. Social inequality generates post-truth. Because economic and political establishments do not react to social inequality, people support opposition politicians who promise radical and quick improvements to their social position, such as closing borders to immigrants who are supposedly taking the jobs and social benefits of local workers, the withdrawal from trade and environmental agreements to protect the domestic economy and jobs, the ban on genetic engineering so as to protect domestic food production companies and farmers from multinationals, etc. As found by Houle (2010), economic inequality increases the probability of backlash, encouraging a shift from democracy to dictatorship.

Some scholars believe that public support for post-truth politics is a consequence of weakening social values. However, the question of weak values and undesirable political developments in Europe and other developed countries is chiefly a question of increasing social inequality and low prosperity for a large proportion of the working and middle classes. It is true that social values are transferred from older to younger generations by families, schools, the church and other institutions as well as the media. Yet, the stability of values does not depend solely on preaching. It depends strongly on individual life experiences. The appeal to strengthen democratic values is in vain if the social position of the working and middle classes is not changed.

"It is long since past the time when we should have put the question of inequality back to the center of economic analysis and begun asking questions first raised in the nineteen century" (Piketty, 2014, p. 16). This question should not be underestimated due to the current level of overall economic prosperity, which in any case is subject to cyclical movements. The question is about long-term future developments, expanding prosperity to the middle and working classes of the developed countries, and preserving and improving upon democracy and other achievements of rationalism in the globalised world. We should step back from post-truth to and return to truth. This is a precondition for the effective implementation of measures to counter inequality and periodic instability, which Western civilisation is increasingly entering (Taylor, 2017).

References

Awasti, I.C. and Shrivastav, P.K. (2017), "Inequalities in economic and educational status among social groups in India: Evidence from village-based study in Uttar Pradesh", International Journal of Social Economics, Vol. 44 No 6, pp. 774–796.

Brown, D. (2009), "Scientists Speak out Against Federal Funds for Research on Alternative Medicine", available at: http://www.washintonpost.com/wp.dyn/content/article/2009/03/16/AR2009031602139.html (accessed 8 November 2017).

Crossman, A. (2017), "Sociology of social inequality", available at: http://www.thoughtcom/sociology-of-social-inequality-3026287 (accessed 17 November 2017).

Darwin, C. (1859), On the Origin of Species, John Murray, London.

Drezner, W. D. (2016), "Why the post-truth political era might be around for a while", available at: https://www.washingtonpost.com/posteverything/wp/2016/06/16/shy-the-post-truth-political-era-might-be-around-for-a-while/ (accessed 18 November 2017).

Encyclopaedia Britannica (2017), "National Socialism", available at: https://www.britannica.com/event/National-Socialism (accessed 20 November 2017).

Encyclopedia of Philosophy (1969), "Dewey John", auth., Bernstein, R., Vol. 2, p. 383, Mcmillan, New York.

Gay, P. (1995), The Enlightenment, The Rise of Modern Paganism, Knopf, New York.

Guild (2017), "Universities, Research and the Future of Europe", The Guild Forum, Solvay Library, June 1, Brussels.

Harsin, J. (2015), "Regimes of Posttruth, Postpolitics, and Attention Economies", Communication, Culture & Critique, Vol. 2 No. 8 pp. 327–333.

History (2017), "Enlightenment", available at: http://www.history.com/topics/enlightenment (accessed 12 December 2017).

Houle, C. (2010), Inequality, economic development and democracy, University of Rochester ProQuest Dissertation Publishing.

Jasanoff, S. and Hilton, R. S. (2017), "No Funeral Bells: Public reason in a post-truth age", Social Studies of Science, Vol. 47 No 5 pp. 751–770.

Kay, J. (2009), The long and the short of it. A guide to finance and investment for normally intelligent people who aren't in the industry, The Erasmus Press, London.

Laats, A. and Siegel, H. (2016), Teaching Evolution in a Creation Nation, University of Chicago Press, Chicago.

MacMillan, A. (2016), "Global Warming 101", available at: https://www.nrdc.org/stories/global-warming_101 (accessed 6 September 2017).

McLeod, S. (2015), "Unconscious Mind. Simply Psychology", available at: http://www.simplypsychology.org/unconscious-mind.htm (accessed 17 November 2017).

Merriam-Webster Dictionary (2017), "Truth", available at: https://www.merriam-webster.com/dictionary/truth?src=search-dict-hed (accessed 15 November 2017).

Milanovic, B. (2016), Global Inequality. A New Approach for the Age of Globalisation, The Belknap Press of Harvard University Press, Cambridge, Massachusetts, London.

NBC News (2009), "$34 billion spent yearly on alternative medicine", available at: www.nbcnews.com/id/32219873/ns/health-alternative_medicine/t/billion-spent-yearly-alternative-medicine/#.WliGvqinHct (accessed 12 January 2018).

Ortiz, I. and Cummins, M. (2011), Global Inequality: Beyond the Bottom Billion – A Rapid Review of Income Distribution in 141 Countries, UNICEF, New York.

Oxford dictionaries (2017), "Word of the Year", available at: https://www.en.oxforddictionaries.com/word-of-the-year/word-of-the-year-2016 (accessed 7 November 2017).

Paris Climate Deal: key points at a glance (2015), available at: web.archive.org/web/20151213005658/http://www.theguardian.com/environment/2015/dec/12/paris-climate-deal-key-points (accessed 10 November 2017).

Parsons, T. (1970), "Equality and Inequality in Modern Society, or Social Stratification Revisited", Sociological Inquiry Vol. 40 No. 2, pp. 13–72.

Piketty, T. (2014), Capital in the Twenty-First Century (translated by Arthur Goldhammer), The Belknap Press of Harvard University Press, Cambridge, Massachusetts, London.

Prior, N. A. (1969), "Correspondence Theory of Truth", in Encyclopedia of Philosophy, Vol. 2, p. 223, Macmillan.

Roberts, D. (2010), "Post-truth politics", available at: http://www.grist.org/article/2010-03-30-post-truth-politics/ (accessed 17 November 2017).

Roberts, J. R. (2015), "A Crime Against Humanity", unpublished manuscript, speech given on the occasion of the honorary PhD award by the University of Ljubljana, July 2015.

Sachs, J.D. (2015), The Age of Sustainable Development, Columbia University Press, New York.

Saint-Laurent, C. et al. (2017), "Collective memory and social sciences in the post-truth era", Culture and Psychology, Vol. 23 No 2, pp. 147–155.

Selin, H. (2017), "Global Warming", available at: https://www.britannica.com/print/article/235402 (accessed 6 September 2017).

Stiglitz, J. (2013), "Inequality Is a Choice", Opinionator, The New York Times, available at: http://opionator.blogs.nytimes.com/2013/10/13/inequality-is-a-choice/?_php=true&_type=blogs&_r=0 (accessed 20 November 2017).

Suiter, J. (20169, "Post-truth Politics", Political Insight, Vol. 7 No. 3, pp. 25–27.

Taylor, K.B. (2017), "Sunset of the American Dream", International Journal of Social Economics, Vol. 44 No 12, pp. 1639–1653.

Turner, H. J. (2009), "The Sociology of Emotions", Emotion Review, Vol. 1 No. 4, pp. 340–354, Sage.

United Nations Population Division (2017), "World Population Prospects: The 2017 Revision", available at: https://esa.un.org/unpd/wpp/Download/Standard/Population (accessed 18 November 2017).

Wikipedia (2017), "Post-truth", available at: http://www.en.wikipedia.org/wiki/Post-truth_politics (accessed 7 November 2017).

Wikipedia (2017a), "Global Warming", available at: http://www.en.wikipedia.org/wiki/Global_warming (accessed 10 November 2017).

Wikipedia (2018), "Truth", available at: http://en.wikipedia.org/wiki/Truth (accessed 31 July 2018).

World Economic Forum (2017), "Winnie Byanyima on wealth redistribution", available at: http://www.weforum.org/2017/01/davos-leaders-agree-we-should-share-more-of-the-worlds-wealth-or-face-the-populist-consequences/ (accessed 20 November 2017).

World Economic Forum (2017a), "Western Democracy in Crisis", available at: http://reports.weforum.org/global-risks-2017/part-2-social-and-political-challenges/2-1-western-democracy-in-crisis/ (accessed 20 November 2017).

World Economic Forum (2017b), "The myth of classless society", available at: http://www.weforum.org/agenda/2017/01/davos-populism-globalisation-social-divides/ (accessed 20 November 2017).

World Resources Forum (2017), "Natural Resources: what are they?", available at: http://www.wrforum.org/publications-2/publications/ (accessed 18 November 2017).

Zafirovski, M. (2010), The Enlightenment and its Effects on Modern Society, Springer, New York, Dordrecht, Heidelberg, London.

Lasse Skogvold Isaksen and Graham Clifford
(Norwegian University of Science and Technology)

Child Welfare Families and Schooling –
Disappointment and Misunderstanding

Abstract

In this article we present findings from a large representative survey of parents receiving child welfare (CW) support concerning their interactions with schools and their experiences in terms of their children's schooling. The main findings are that CW parents (contrary to prevailing stereotypes) are much more concerned about their children's challenges and difficulties in school. Their perspective, however, is informed by their emphasis on children's need for inclusion in school; parents are less concerned about the cognitive aspect and the emphasis on basic learning skills that is at the heart of modern schooling.

This article is based on material from our study entitles *The New Child Welfare*, based on a survey addressed to over 700 parents who were in contact with child welfare services, and a follow-up study in which 96 families were interviewed several times over a three-year period; 19 children were also interviewed (Clifford, Fauske, Lichtwarck, & Marthinsen, 2015). One aim of the study was to gain improved knowledge concerning parental perceptions of their children's difficulties. It emerged that schooling was an important issue for almost all parents. Unstructured qualitative interviews elicited a great deal of material concerning school, without specific prompting on the part of our interviewers. In our study we explore in what ways child welfare families experience and comprehend their interactions with the school system. Parents are clearly concerned about their children's schooling, and most often present a picture that is quite at odds with stereotypical notions of child welfare parents as being uninterested in or downright hostile to schooling.

We will emphasize four areas that emerged from the interviews; these might indicate how child welfare services should work to enhance their cooperation with CW families and schools, CW children's marginalized position in school, CW parents expressing concern about the situation for their children at school, parent isolation and lack of information and awareness of subject matter challenges, and parental attempts to help children in the school environment.

A core issue in the ongoing child welfare service policy discourse in Norway is the role of schooling. Our knowledge-based society has given schools a central role in modern socialization and integration dynamics. A national study showed that dropout rates in late secondary school among CWS children were around 80% (Clausen, Kristofersen, & Barnevern i Norge, 2008). The majority of CWS children do not receive an education that gives them reasonable access to the labor market. Secondary school is almost understood to be compulsory in the Norwegian context, and dropping out is often a direct route to the social welfare system. Dropping out later in secondary school in Norway is strongly connected to a lack of basic skills in reading, writing and mathematics (Markussen & Sandberg, 2004). Too many students do not receive an acceptable basic education that supports completion of upper-level secondary schooling. The unified school system sets out to provide equality in terms of opportunity, but it is now apparent that the traditional correlation between family socio-economic status and school achievement is becoming stronger (Bakken & Elstad, 2012). There is a clear shift toward a more accountability-based public policy, which pushes child welfare services to focus more on children's well-being, i.e. desired outcomes relate to social inclusion in later life (Isaksen, 2018).

Research has revealed some differences in how middle class (as defined in US terminology, described as "working class" in Europe) and low-income families interact with institutions such as schools. A case study conducted by Lareau and Cox showed that low-income families were able to predict and delay the occurrence of some problems; middle-class families had a more aggressive, directed approach and were better able to predict and actually prevent problems in relation to school (Lareau & Cox, 2011). Middle-class families guide and maneuver their children through the education system and can better ensure their social and academic development. Low-income families do not have the same capacity to interact with institutions such as schools.

There is very little research material that deals with the experience of child welfare parents and their perception of school. This is a serious deficiency when considering the importance of the parent-school partnership. A feature of the modern knowledge economy is the expectation that parents and schools will cooperate effectively on behalf of the child, and this is particularly important when children have difficulties and/or disadvantages that may affect learning or social integration in school. Many children in the child welfare system have difficulties in school. They often perform poorly and are not well integrated (Kristofersen & Clausen, 2008). In time this often leads to growing difficulties and effective marginalization at the lower secondary level, dropout at the upper secondary level and subsequent disadvantages in the labor market. Industrial society had a robust integration dynamic for young people that for some reason is no longer part of the education system (Frønes, 2007, 2010; Frønes & Strømme, 2010). In the knowledge-based society, the marginalization dynamic is linked to processes in the education system because the education system emerges as the central arena for social integration (OECD, 2001). Socialization before the shift to a more knowledge-based society emphasized the work ethic and discipline as qualifications for a labor market that needed strong-minded and disciplined young people. Social workers viewed school more or less as an arena which struggling children had to be protected from, i.e. as an arena in which working-class children were placed until they were old enough to join the workforce. The labor market was a gateway to social inclusion. In a knowledge-based society, a lack of success in school is a strong predictor of social exclusion as an adult, i.e. unemployment, low income, limited social participation and other deficits that contribute to marginalization (Isaksen, 2016). Output success related to well-being among children who receive assistance from welfare services seems to be particularly hard to attain so far as social inclusion is concerned (Frønes, 2007; Frønes & Strømme, 2010).

Family characteristics

The CW parents interviewed were mostly mothers and single parents. The majority were mothers without paid employment. About seven out of ten families were classified as multi-problem families in which health issues (especially mental health problems affecting parents or children, or both) were combined with poor material wealth, lack of social networks, and family relationships with a high level of conflict (Marthinsen & Lichtwarck, 2013). The remaining families included some in which teenagers had developed behavioral and or mental health difficulties at the onset of adolescence, or families which had to contend with long-term problems due to the chronic illness of a child, and a few families in which the parents had restabilised after earlier substance or alcohol abuse. In most cases, these were families in which children were exposed to considerable risk in terms of the quality of parental care provided. The sample did not include short-term CW client families. Norwegian research based on registration material has shown that children's level of achievement in school is poor among both short-term and long-term CW families, but worst among the latter as might well be expected. Household incomes are characteristically low – on average about a third lower compared with the general population of families. One in four of the families were categorised as middle-class using the European standard classification (EeSC) based on occupational status.

CW children's marginalized position in school

In interviews with younger children and teenagers from these CW families, we were struck by how often they gave accounts of their difficulties in school. Children under the age of 12 were often forthcoming about the problems they encountered in connection with specific school subjects, while teenagers often described their marginalized *positions*. They also had difficulties with school subjects (and often lacked basic skills), but at the same time they felt that what they were expected to learn and master was irrelevant and meaningless. Among these children, by far the most frequent and clearly articulated problems they shared with interviewers were problems encountered at school.

> "Its boring ... to stay there ... nothing is happening. I am sitting in the back row ... Nothing is happening at school, don't learn anything, so ... I don't know if I'll bother to go there ... I am playing and watching TV ... I learn more from TV than in school."

Children relate that they more or less are disconnected from ordinary instruction. A lack of basic skills as tools for learning and participation in the classroom seems to lead to anxiety about attending school.

> "I dread starting lower secondary ... do not understand English ... I do know some words ... some names of animals and colors and so on. However, I can barely read. The teacher never asks me to read out loud, because he knows that I can't read English."

Children we interviewed had developed different strategies to avoid negative attention, but at the same time they felt excluded.

> "I am like a chameleon, they don't notice me at all. I am good at hiding. I am sitting in the front row and he doesn't see me when I answer."

CW parents express great concern about the situation for their children at school

It would be quite wrong to assume that CW parents are not concerned about their children in the school environment. They are very concerned. They often think that teachers do not appreciate, or do not make the effort to grasp the real problems that their children encounter in school. Their focus is these issues of social integration rather than the cognitive developmental process that is the most important issue for schools and their teaching staffs. Of course a great number of these parents encountered considerable difficulties in school themselves, which they have told us about. They were often isolated or bullied, and many had to contend with severe difficulties at home that led to truancy and/or poor academic achievement. Many dropped out of school at the lower or upper secondary level. More than a few of them are bitter about the way in which school was unable to help them, or secure help for them from child welfare. Many have become determined that their own children should not suffer in this fashion, but they quickly realize that this is not easy to avoid. Today schools pay more attention to early signs of difficulty among pupils in the 6 to 8 age group, so most parents whose children have been attending school for a few years know all too well that their child is seen as having difficulties.

CW parents are most concerned about their children's social integration at school. Many of the children have learning difficulties as well as social or emotional problems (and in many cases behavioural and mental health problems) and parents are very concerned about this. They tend to judge school in terms of its success, as they perceive it, in integrating the child. For these parents, integration is considered to include both children's relationships with their peer group, and their experience in the learning environment, including both classroom management issues and the teacher's attitude to their children. CW parents do not articulate precise expectations relating to their children's academic progress in terms of cognitive and intellectual attainment. In open interviews, parents did not offer any views or concerns about performance.

A father presented his difficulty in relating to the educational system as follows. His teenage son had serious behavioral difficulties that the family felt unable to deal with:

> "We cannot see what could be done: we struggle and do as well as we can. One of the teachers provided ongoing support, and this was really useful. He had been recruited by child welfare. But when he left, got another job, the whole thing fell apart, we have asked the school to find another person, but nothing has happened. They say that they do not have the resources."

Here it was quite clear that the son's progress at school was not an issue for father. His expectation was that school should help his son, through a combination of encouragement and support, along with disciplining him for his unacceptable behavior.

Unclear expectation from CW families

Parents said that schools often failed to take account of the specific needs that their children had, and their own interaction with schools was often described as unsatisfactory. The impression is that communication between school and CW parents is poor. Many parents told us that their efforts to make teachers aware of the problems the children encountered lead to no improvement, and others said that some initial improvement after such efforts on their part was not followed up on. Few parents deny that their children do have real difficulties. It may well be that some have unrealistic expectations relating to how schools can deal with the challenge their children present. Nonetheless, the overall impression is that there is no real partnership between schools and CW parents. Parents often say that teachers do not really listen to what they have to say, or do not take them seriously. One can to some extent see parental dissatisfactions with schools as a reaction to situations where teachers fail to respond to the parents' own views about the difficulties their children encounter in school. More generally, however, there is a feeling on the part of parents that teachers do not support their child.

"The other kids learned how to provoke him fairly quickly, get him upset, and he got into trouble by trying to help other pupils and ending up on the wrong side of conflicts in the class; he got blamed. Later he did have some strategies to deal with quarrels, avoiding them and not getting involved, but when he cut school one afternoon he of course got blamed again, and at first he didn't tell us why. When we found out the whole story, his teacher was only interested in him having left school without permission, and not the reason for his absence."

These parents felt that a lack of understanding of their son's efforts to cope with his relationships with peers, on the part of the teacher, contributed to his difficulties

Parents are isolated

There are signs that parents are not integrated themselves, in the sense that they often feel disadvantaged and excluded in the parent group that is organized around parent-school meetings or (increasingly nowadays) organized informally by parents themselves.

"I find it hard to meet other parents. They all know that my daughter has dif-ficulties in school and I know that they see it as my fault. They don't need to say anything; I know this. But one or two of them have said hurtful things, and I have to admit that it takes me a long time to get over such things. So I try to find excuses not to go to meetings, though I know that is wrong too."

When children have obvious behavioural or mental health problems, we see that parents often feel stigmatized, or at the very least very apprehensive about contact with other parents. CW parents do not relate to the school as an organisation, their contact with school is restricted to their meetings with classroom teachers – for them the school is represented only by the teacher. They avoid other parents. Some-times a particular teacher does make a positive impression, but it is notable that par-ents on the whole seem to have better relationships with and more confidence in the social workers from child welfare than they have with school personnel.

Parents make attempts to help children in the school situation

Most CW parents make efforts to support their children in school, although they are often frustrated. On the one hand they have fairly clear ideas about risks their children are exposed to in school, as we have indicated a risk of social exclusion as well as the risk of association with peers who may exert a negative influence or be poor role models themselves. Almost all parents say that their children need help, and the most important and motivating factor in this connection is concern about the children's mental health or behavioural difficulties. A concern relating to teenagers is their prospects in relation to occupational training and employment, and the possibility (very real for many of these teenagers) that they will not complete secondary education or simply perform poorly. Put another way, CW parents have a realistic view of risks their children are exposed to. On the other hand the cognitive, intellectual and social project that is at the heart of modern schooling does not seem to engage them. Their focus is on the risk of exclusion and is not directed toward those areas of development and competence that qualify children for participation in the knowledge economy. The more marginalised the specific family by virtue of parents' poor social integration, the more likely it is that children are marginalised in school and in relation to peers. It is reasonable to assert that the path to social integration in the school setting nowadays is acquisition of basic cognitive, intellectual and social skills, and parents' focus on exclusion resulting from their children's mental health or behavioural problems does not take account of this.

> "He does have friends: but I want him to stop sitting in his room and spend more time with them. He had medication for his ADHD, but when this was taken away he spent more time on his computer and less with his friends. He suffers from something they call non-verbal learning difficulties and anxiety. I am not sure what his diagnosis really means. He is less anxious than he was, but there are quite a lot of situations he doesn't manage well. If I am to be honest, I would gave to say that he doesn't get much out of school and I am worried about how he will get on after school, in the future. I have done my best, but ..."

Discussion

Research in Norway has established that children in the child welfare system have significantly higher dropout rates at the upper secondary level. Though there has been a marked trend toward early intervention designed to help school children with learning difficulties and/or mental health problems, this does not seem to have led to significant improvements for child welfare children. Looked at broadly, this ought to lead to considerable concern. Failure in school for CW children and youth is a serious risk factor for negative outcomes later in life (Ferguson & Wolkow, 2012). The material reveals that CW children are placed in a marginalized position in school and are only partially able to participate in ordinary instruction. Schooling is one of the main areas when children's experience of inclusion and lack of success in school is reported as significant for their well-being (Phipps & Curtis, 2001). School failure is one of the most salient characteristics for CW children. Our findings correspond well with research on children in residential care (Ferguson & Wolkow, 2012). Child welfare services need to focus on a more systematic method concerning the dynamics of exclusion in a knowledge-based society.

Child welfare families encounter school in its modern form as a central institution within the knowledge economy. Whereas several decades ago child welfare dealt with children in part within institutional settings designed to foster self-discipline and diligence, modern schooling tends to assume that parents will encourage conformity and discipline as part of the self-regulatory project that a liberal society depends upon. In a sense, deprived children and families have not been enlisted in this project, and school may be at a loss as to how to deal with them, or inclined to see children's difficulties as part of a general social or cultural non-compliance with the entirely reasonable demands the schooling presupposes in its modern form.

In some ways, a model of schooling that includes seriously deprived children can be seen as a democratic, enlightened model in which no child is excluded. Still, there is an evident paradox if parents are unable to provide their child with the social and behavioral codes that afford real access to learning.

Child welfare does not seem to have any platform for intervention in school. Social workers seem to have an almost exaggerated respect for the school as a professional domain, and accept its policies and limitations as given. Coordination between child welfare services and schools seems to be restricted to exchanges of information, and an implicit acceptance of children's difficulties at school as a failure of individual adjustment. Whether or not school might find it acceptable to receive guidance from child welfare, the fact is that it is simply not offered. There is an underlying, perhaps naïve or uninformed tendency to see children's difficulties as individual traits, rather than being associated with the quality of their interactions. The idea that behavioral problems present in schools might have to do with the school setting is not part of the agenda. Child welfare workers do not reflect upon the quality of instruction, its content, or classroom leadership as major factors influencing children's behavior in school. This rigorously external position in relating to school deprives severely disadvantage children; they have no "advocate" in school. Basic skills – reading, writing, math – are the platform not only for academic achievement, *but also* social integration and interaction, so a sense of *belonging* in the modern school.

Parents' accounts are naturally focused on their child and his or her needs as they see them. Most often there are early signs that children might have difficulties, for example in relation to other children, not being accepted in the peer group or being subject to bullying. These may or may not be accompanied by other factors such as behavioral difficulties and/or a lack of concentration skills. Some children are described as anxious and vulnerable. Parents emphasize these difficulties, but much less often communicate concern about their children's cognitive level and basic competencies. During the primary school years, the general impression from parents' accounts is one of gradually escalating difficulties. Before or during puberty, there are often more dramatic and alarming changes, either in the form of behavioural problems or mental health issues, including depression, isolation and withdrawal.

Parents often attribute these difficulties to underlying mental health problems such as ADHD, anxiety and affective disorders. In truth, this is usually the culmination of a long process in which the children develop a gradually more and more marginalized position in relation to schoolwork and social integration in school as well as with peers more generally. This is a dispiriting, stressful and exhausting process for parents, whose optimism and energy are gradually eroded. Accounts of unsatisfactory encounters with school staff and failed negotiations are woven into this negative trajectory. Many parents are quite open about their own shortcomings, both in respect to providing consistent care and follow-up for their children, and in terms of managing the specific difficulties their children present. Nonetheless, the problems children present are a considerable challenge for parents, and strain their resources to the utmost.

The seriousness of these mental, social and emotional difficulties that affect children seems to divert attention from other concerns that parents might well have, for example relating to their children's acquisition of basic skills and general cognitive development. For parents and perhaps for schools too, the dominant narrative pertaining to these children is one of behavioural and social dysfunction. Communication between parents and schools about cognitive development and skills seems to break down. This ought to give rise to concern because school and other specialized agencies in many ways decide the agenda regarding what must be done to help the child, but concerns relating to behavior and mental health often take precedence.

In reading parents' accounts of their children's environment at school, it often emerges that parents have a clear idea of how the classroom situation does not meet their child's needs. This leads to frustration and in some cases resignation. It may well be that parent's expectations are often unrealistic. On the other hand, the Norwegian unitary school model, based on an explicit normalizing ideological framework, does make it difficult to address many of these special needs.

Child welfare parents often feel excluded from the parent group. This might be thought to be a consequence of social discrimination, but it is clear that the platform for cooperation and reflection among parents who represent their own "normal" children in a parent group, or in interactions with teaching staff or school leaders, may not support efforts to integrate children with special (and often multifaceted) need profiles. An integrative school policy is hard to realize, and real conflicts of interest may well arise. The dynamics involved are complex since CW parents often avoid what they perceive as discrimination and hesitate to involve themselves with other parents. They are in any case likely to experience the kinds of isolation that have been described in research that deals with families of children with mental health and behavioural problems. These findings relating to parents' sense of exclusion are conneted to the forms of help that can compensate for or mitigate isolation. These are not seen as being part of conventional social support, but rather viewed in unsentimental terms, as a prerequisite for better parental functioning in support of the child at school.

Child welfare parents are not part of the parental network. In interviews, such parents never referred to school policy or the schools' institutional structure and its impact on their child. In an important sense, they are disconnected from the "polit-ical" environment that school is situated within. They do not feel that they have influence or leverage when it comes to schooling, and many moreover feel excluded. Another important issue, actually the most important issue, is that parents who receive child welfare assistance do not have a grasp of the implicit contract between schools and parent that underpins the modern cognitive developmental project that school has assumed. They have a perception of the school as an arena of acute risk for their child, but it is the risk of social exclusion that they are concerned with. They want to see their child accepted by peers, and they are alarmed when teachers do not seem to appreciate the extent of the social and behavioral difficulties that their child has; seen from their vantage point, the teachers in fact treat their child unfairly or insensitively. In an important sense, children from these marginalized families are without social capital in school. Parents do not always have the resources to invest in their children, or may not see that such investment is a part of the contract that schools expect nowadays. In addition, their perception of school issues is restricted to specific individual needs and problems that relate to their own child. They do not see the school as an institution, and their concern may even contribute to or rein-force a tendency on the part of school staff to see the child concerned as a "problem child" or as a deviant.

In about a third of the families in our study, parents themselves had a history of difficulty at school, and they gave descriptions of this. Some felt that school had ignored signs that they suffered deprivation and maltreatment; others said that schoolteachers made little effort on their behalf when they had difficulties at home. Some parents had an extensive history of truancy during their own schooling and had effectively dropped out before the age of sixteen. Even more common was a per-ception that they had been different from other pupils and more or less excluded both by teachers and by fellow students. These negative experiences with their own schooling played an important part in parents' perception of school as an environ-ment in which their own children would risk being disadvantaged. It was evident that social exclusion was much more of a threat when looked at from a CW parents' perspective, specifically moreso than any risk attached to their children's poor aca-demic performance.

Many children in our research had mental health difficulties. Parents of chil-dren living at home did not perceive that the child welfare system, child mental healthcare and school coordinated their efforts on behalf of children. Their experi-ence was that help offered was fragmentary with too little contact and poor follow-up. Parents saw that diagnoses could help, in that a child with a diagnosis would be entitled to help and more assitance at school, but in practice it seemed that this most often did not occur. Parents actively disliked meetings in which they met represen-tatives of child welfare services, schools and health services. They often felt unable to represent themselves or their child in such settings, and sometimes felt that the agencies represented at these meetings had a common agenda – one that they did not share.

Parents quite clearly had the most confidence in the child welfare system. Their perception was that their children needed help and that child welfare services could help. No such confidence was expressed toward child psychiatry or schools. Even though parents were often disappointed in relation to decisions made in terms of child protection, they would still repeatedly make efforts to maintain a dialogue. This seems to be related to parents' perception of child welfare as empowered to make decisions about the child, and their view of social workers and their immediate superiors as those who had real discretion to make decisions. Placement of children outside the home, in foster homes or in group care, was by no means always contested by parents, and most parents with children placed outside the family home saw placement as beneficial in the sense that they saw that children made progress after placement. A general finding in the study was that parents whose children were placed elsewhere had much lower levels of stress compared with those whose children were at home. Another important finding was that children of parents who were not socially integrated were very often themselves poorly integrated in respect to peers and fellow pupils. Parents' general appreciation of risks their children were exposed to were prevalent, included the risk of poor social integration, the risk of mental illness and behavioral difficulties, and the risks posed by peer groups involved in drug and alcohol use as well as antisocial behavior.

References

Bakken, A., & Elstad, J. I. (2012). *For store forventninger?: kunnskapsløftet og ulikhetene i grunnskolekarakterer* (Vol. no. 7/12). Oslo: Norsk institutt for forskning om oppvekst, velferd og aldring.

Clausen, S.-E., Kristofersen, L. B., & Barnevern i Norge. (2008). *Barnevernsklienter i Norge 1990–2005: en longitudinell studie*. Oslo: Norsk institutt for forskning om oppvekst, velferd og aldring.

Clifford, G., Fauske, H., Lichtwarck, W., & Marthinsen, E. (2015). *Minst hjelp til dem som trenger det mest?* (Nordlandsforskning Ed.). Bodø: Nordlandsforskning.

Ferguson, H. B., & Wolkow, K. (2012). Educating children and youth in care: A review of barriers to school progress and strategies for change. *Children and Youth Services Review, 34*(6), 1143–1149. doi: http://dx.doi.org/10.1016/j.childyouth.2012.01.034.

Frønes, I. (2007). Theorizing indicators. *Social Indicators Research, 83*(1), 5–23. doi:10.1007/s11205-006-9061-7.

Frønes, I. (2010). *Kunnskapssamfunn, sosialisering og sårbarhet.*

Frønes, I., & Strømme, H. (2010). *Risiko og marginalisering: norske barns levekår i kunnskapssamfunnet*. Oslo: Gyldendal akademisk.

Isaksen, L. S. (2016). Better Schooling for Children in Residential Care. In *The Welfare Society – an Aim for Social Development* (pp. 127–137): LIT Verlag.

Isaksen, L. S. (2018). *Educational accountability reform in Norway: education policy as imitation*. New York: Peter Lang.

Kristofersen, L. B., & Clausen, S.-E. (2008). *Barnevern og sosialhjelp*. Oslo: Norsk institutt for forskning om oppvekst, velferd og aldring.

Lareau, A., & Cox, A. (2011). Social Class and the Transition to Adulthood: Differences in Parents' Interactions with Institutions. In M. Carlson & P. England (Eds.), *Social Class and Changing Families in an Unequal America* (pp. 134–164). Stanford: Stanford University Press.

Markussen, E., & Sandberg, N. (2004). *Bortvalg og prestasjoner: om 9798 ungdommer på Østlandet, deres vei gjennom, ut av, eller ut og inn av videregående opplæring, om deres prestasjoner et år etter avsluttet grunnskole*. Oslo: Norwegian Institute for Studies in Research and Higher Education.

Marthinsen, E., & Lichtwarck, W. (2013). *Det nye barnevernet: fase I – en antologi*. Oslo: Universitetsforl.

OECD. (2001). *The well-being of nations: the role of human and social capital*: OECD.

Phipps, S., & Curtis, L. (2001). *The Social Exclusion of Children in North America*. Retrieved from Halifax, Nova Scotia.

Hans Kolstad

The Paradigm of Economic Growth – A Challenge to Welfare Society?

Abstract

This paper questions the ideology of economic growth as an effective foundation for the welfare society.

"Growth" is a relatively unexplored concept in economic philosophy. Its roots, however, go back to early Greek philosophy, where growth originally was related to the cyclic processes of nature and the biological life of man. This way of thinking about growth was later transmitted to the field of economics, leading to a cyclic understanding of the economy, based on nature both as a model and as a guide.

In modern times, this conception has been replaced by a linear concept of growth, where the economy is considered to be open-ended. From this perspective it may be formulated in a mathematical and exponential manner.

Here I suggest a new conceptual framework for economic growth based upon a circular understanding of the economy. I do not describe only an economy that promotes greater resource productivity while aiming to reduce waste and avoid pollution. It will above all be argued that the concept of circular economy has to been enlarged to include social and ethical values, as well as whether it should lay the foundations of a sustainable welfare society.

Introduction

We live in a society with a dominating ideology of economic growth. Yet the notion of economic growth itself is relatively new. A short retrospective of economic history shows that in humanity's early history, there was no concept of any kind of economic growth in the modern sense. Man produced and traded within the framework of a stable economy. The global economy grew extremely modestly. According to a report prepared for the OECD, in the period from year 0 to 1820, the economy grew at between 0 and 0.22 percent a year. Until year 1000, European growth remained stable at around zero. From 1000 until 1820, growth in Europe and then the United States increased at an average rate of 0.34% per year. In reality it was only Europe and the United States that experienced anything resembling growth. Only with the industrial revolution did the Western world began to bring economic growth up to the 2 to 3 percent level, which is almost considered as a normal state by today's conventional economists (Maddison, 2001).

Only in a fairly short period, in light of mankind's 50,000 year-old history, did the Western world experience a period of high growth. In the 1960s, the growth in high-income economies was at 5.4%, coinciding with an almost explosive rise in prosperity. However, in the years following this period, growth has steadily fallen. In the 1970s, growth fell to 3.8%, in the 1980s it fell to 3.1% and in the 1990s to 2.5%. In the first decade of the 2000s, economic growth went down to 1.4% (World Bank, 2005).

It is today acknowledged that growth is currently on a temporary hold in our part of the world. This means that we most likely will not be able to experience another period of 5% growth. At best, there will be a rise in growth that is slightly above zero.

In other words, the potential for increasing growth is far from certain. On the contrary, several indications reveal that high economic growth will be nothing more than a parenthesis in human history. The promoters of growth, which primarily includes cheap and easily accessible energy and raw material resources, are no longer present. All indications show that we should prepare for the time after consistent growth.

What does this prospect mean for the future of the welfare society? This is the question that this paper raises.

Normally, one would think that the lack of economic growth is the main cause of the turmoil that the welfare society is experiencing today. However, in this paper I shall be making an attempt to think the other way around and ask if, by continuing the pursuit of growth and the constant striving for increase in material wealth, we do not risk the possibility of putting the prosperity and welfare into an even greater state of turmoil than the one we are witnessing today.

These are the crucial questions:

1. Is the paradigm of economic growth compatible with or even necessary for the upholding of the welfare society in the long run?
2. If not, is there another economic paradigm that would be more consistent with the welfare society?
3. This, of course, leaves us with perhaps the most difficult question: What values do we understand as being essential to social welfare?

The discussion of these questions constitutes the three parts of this paper. In the first part, I shall be describing two different but classical economic models of growth and their implications for the welfare state.

In the second part, I will be presenting a different model that radically breaks with the classical conceptions of economic growth.

In the third and last part, I will be discussing the impact of this new model on the values that are implied by the modern concept of the welfare society.

Cyclic versus linear growth

The distinction between cyclic and linear growth corresponds to the difference between the understanding of economics in the early periods of European history (antiquity and the Middle Ages) and that of today.

Let us take a quick glance at the concept of growth in antiquity. Originally, it is derived from nature or the biological and zoological realm, where in a general way it means the process by which a thing's nature is attained. Thus, "growth" is an expression of the transformation of a living being from one form to another, such as how a plant grows from seed to flower or how a caterpillar transforms in a pupa and finally becomes a butterfly.

Nature's growth can be given four characteristics: The first is that growth is understood on the basis of an organic structure, secondly, that it is cyclic, thirdly, that it has a final, internal goal, which is inherent to the thing's own nature, and the fourth that it is triggered by external factors (such as fertilization, nutrition and geographical and climate conditions).

The Greek philosopher Aristotle (384–322 BC) transferred the principles of nature to the economic sphere. The result was an understanding of economic growth built on the same principles that characterize all natural growth (Aristotle, ed. 1999).

According to Aristotle, the state can be compared to a living organism whose engine is the economy, much as the heart can be said to be powering the human body. In each case, the fundamental principles of the development of the organism are contained within the motor.

This means that the economy was conceived by Aristotle using the model of an organic unity, and hence as an organic system of exchanges and interactions. The better the economy served as a unified organic whole, the more perfect the state would be.

Secondly, Aristotle's idea of economy was founded on the fundamental principle that all natural change is cyclic. Like in nature, economic growth was the expression of a process by which the nature of a given economic system was realized. Beyond this, the economy will collapse before giving birth to a new economic system of exchange and interactions.

Hence, Aristotle perceived economic growth as growth with one ultimate objective, which was nothing other than the manifestation of the economic system's own nature. The economy had its own inner impetus and evolved toward its final form. Economic growth was latent from the beginning, similar to the idea that all change resulted from an inherent possibility. Consequently, growth was possible, but only as a natural kind of growth with one final objective. Beyond this objective, there were no other goals related to the economy. In short, the goal was simply for the economy to have a natural growth rather than an artificially created one. Natural growth meant growth in natural conditions, and not a generated growth, which one gets when steering the economy by seeking the greatest possible profit for the individual.

If growth has one final objective, then the notion of unlimited growth is made impossible. The concept of growth reaching a final goal was part of the basis for Aristotle's rejection of interest income as a legitimate source of income: earning money from money was not natural, but artificial, as it went against the natural exchange of money.

Economic growth on other principles was not part of the Aristotelian concept of economics. Hence, accumulation of material wealth and riches or economic speculation was artificial and a threat to the nature of economy. Earning money was permitted, but only within an economy perceived to be a natural, organic cycle.

The fourth factor that characterized ancient economics was the fact that it was caused by external and not internal factors. The first characterized natural growth, the second artificial growth (as it leads to an "inflation" of the economy). Economic growth as natural growth was understood in relation to external circumstances, such as wars or conquests (and not as an internal creation in the economic system, i.e. as the result of an inherent universal expanding force, which drives the economy beyond its natural limits).

Aristotle based his economic views on the economy, as it was understood at his time among the Athenians, where the same cyclic understanding of economics was behind the development of the first known welfare state in history. The Athenian welfare state was characterized by various kinds of social and economic security, comprising a codified law system that predictably redistributed wealth to provide economic and social security, which ultimately benefited not only the elite but ordinary Athenians as well. Among these provisions were economic help to orphans of men who fell in battle (the boys were raised by the state, daughters were given dowries), handicapped citizens were provided with a basic daily stipend, older citizens, no longer able to do hard manual labor, were employed in various forms of paid government service, and the laws governing the import of grain were designed to ensure an adequate supply of food to the populace at affordable prices. All of this was possible only because the government returned a substantial part of its revenues to society in the form of basic social insurance. Athenians were, if only to a degree, buffered against certain forms of hardship and catastrophe that remain all too familiar even in the contemporary world, and as a result the entire community did better over time (Ober, 2008, pp. 256–257).

The general point is that social and economic security in classical and democratic Athens was recognized as something valuable and an essential part of the cyclic concept of economic growth. The latter did not favor only rich people, but included the whole population as well. Assistance was not provided as a gift of mercy from the state, but as an integral part of a fully developed cyclic economy. The collected taxes were redistributed among the needy, thus creating a smaller cyclic economy within the bigger one.

In the Middle Ages, economic growth was predominantly characterized by the same cyclic notion of economy as that of Aristotle. Here too, the economy was based on the model of nature.

In line with this perception, accumulation of wealth was considered evil, created by the devil. However, it became acceptable for another reason, specifically when the accumulation of money could serve as a marker of social recognition or contribute to society's common good through donations and sponsorships.

Hence, accumulation of wealth should be understood in a moral or theological perspective. The discussions about the acquisition of wealth, usury and greed, were about moral deliberations, and defenses for wealth meant its utility in a social context.

If we now turn our attention to the idea of economic growth in modern times, we are confronted with a quite a different concept.

In the 17th century the cyclic and moral/theological worldview was replaced by a new understanding, which meant a new idea of the world.

Between the 1600s and the 1700s, the entirety of ancient knowledge surrounding morality and natural philosophy was reevaluated and reinterpreted, and new knowledge was added that was based on experiences and experiments. Discoveries of new material resources along with novel inventions and crafting techniques completed and improved the existing theoretical knowledge. The result was the assumption that production could be improved in order to provide a higher yield.

This caused a new understanding of the world, where progress and development was the main focus. Time and history were understood as linear processes moving forward. This idea was later systematized and shaped by the Enlightenment historians (and in parallel, the understanding of nature in the theory of evolution). Simultaneously, this thought made the idea of an indefinite, exponential economic growth a possibility.

The new understanding of growth was built on the following four principles:

Firstly, growth was no longer understood in a cyclic way but linearly, i.e. as being synonymous with forward movement.

Secondly, the idea of linear growth made it possible to imagine infinitely developing growth or an endless accumulation of wealth. Hence, the economy was no longer understood as a closed, organic system of exchange and interactions with an inner goal, but as an open system susceptible to mathematical exponential growth.

Thirdly, the new understanding of economics implied an economic system that is ruled by its internal mechanisms rather than outside influences. The British/Scottish economist and moral philosopher Adam Smith (1723–1790) was the first who used the notion of interior, triggering factors to drive the economy rather than external factors. Adam Smith believed that growth was an elementary effect of the most basic economic principle: saving is normal, and those who save, invest. With investment, an accumulation of capital arises, which in turn can be reinvested and create new, increased capital, and so on (Smith, 1776/1922).

Fourthly, the linear understanding of the economy was built on a mechanical world-view, meaning a quantifiable or measurable mechanistic depiction of the world.

During the Scientific Revolution in the 1600s, a mechanical worldview was gradually introduced. The result was a concept of experience consisting of identifying the objects in a quantitative way through measuring, weighing and counting. The result could be transferred to and calculated through mathematical formulas. Consequently, nature was mathematized: through mathematics, nature could be formalized in an abstract manner and broadly organized into recognizable and reproducible formulas, charts and tables. In short, mathematics became the language of nature as well of the study of man and society, along with economics.

The problem with the mechanical understanding of the world was that all abstract logical concepts, including both ideas and numbers, hence the mathematical-mechanistic frames of understanding, presuppose an inner, mental space, where the logical and mathematical variables are mentally expressed. The logical and mathematical magnitudes are visualized in this inner "room": they denote all mental spatial relationships. However, there is nothing in the mental space that shows that a real outer space also exists that accurately matches the interior one. In this sense, spatialization and mechanization of the outer world can be called an abstraction.

The conception of a linear mathematical growth is only possible within the mental space. When we treat the economy as endless, exponential growth, we do the same thing with economics that the physical sciences do to nature, the human being and the society: we are breaking the tie that unites economics with real life and thus we are living with an abstract image of the world.

The divide between an inner mental space, where mathematical objects so to say are "lodged", and an outer world that is something different, leaves us with many paradoxes. This is particularly the case with the linear growth concept of economics, which forms a glaring contrast to the concept of nature. Nature is cyclical, while the new economic frame of understanding is linear. Briefly said, the latter implies that a linear framework of understanding is applied to the cyclic processes of nature, thus creating a gap between the human understanding of an economy and the outer nature or external reality, which inevitably will cause problems.

Growth in the modern sense is dependent on several factors, such as labor, technology and capital, as well as the organization of production, markets and resources (raw materials). In terms of the topic of this paper, the question of natural resources is central. It is here that the distance between linear economic growth and a natural cyclic economy manifests itself in the most dramatic way. At some point, scarcity of resources will become dire. Other negative aspects of the same economic understanding are pollution, due to technology being applied to the industrial processing of natural resources and to consumption, which may cause the economy to collapse or at best it may lead to a stationary or "stagnant" economy, with little or no growth. It is this situation that some economists already predicted in the early history of the linear economy,[1] and that we today are seeing the consequences of.

Secondly, the fact that economy is conceived as an inner, mental system of spatial relationships between mere quantitative entities makes the economy become an abstract concept that has nothing to do with the *practical* activities of *daily life*. This is most apparent in the fact that the economy is no longer an agent of exchange or a facilitator of interactions. Rather it becomes an end in itself. And when we make an agent become a goal in itself, we get an abstraction at an even higher level, or if you will, to the second power, which is nothing other than what the speculative economy is about. Moreover, when you turn a means into a goal in and of itself, you will sooner or later create economic bubbles, which necessarily will provoke financial crisis. In my opinion, many aspects of today's economic crisis in the Western world can be explained by this mechanism of turning means into ends.

Thirdly, a linear economy focused exclusively on speculation or on the turning of means into ends, also involves manipulation, i.e. abuse of power and exploitation. The linear economy is ultimately an expression of manipulative power-utilization where money no longer fulfills its primordial purpose, which is to be a social tool. By becoming an instrument for an exploitative elite, the economy is alienating itself from man and society.

The abstract linear and mathematical conception of economics has several consequences for the welfare society.

Firstly, in the linear economy welfare becomes merely a question of costs and benefits for the society.

Secondly, welfare as a pure mathematical concept loses its ties to human values. Welfare becomes something granted from the state to the individual, depending on the politicians' good will, and not part of the individual's own rights.

Thirdly, welfare within an increasingly expanding economy risks becoming very expensive. The result is the danger of an increasingly limited welfare system, which necessarily will create social inequality and underclasses of people, resulting in the opposite of what welfare is meant to be about.

---

1   For instance Adam Smith (1776/1922), John Stuart Mill (1848) and John Maynard Keynes (1932).

Fourthly, welfare itself risks being an object of speculation in the sense that its main purpose is to assure the possibility for certain people's careers. In short, the important thing ends up being the administration of welfare and not its outputs. Hence there will be a gap between the wages of the administrators and the individual payments that it offers to the most needy in the population. This will again increase the inequality in the society in addition to creating an ethical and political problem.

Lastly, economic crises also risk causing a welfare crisis, thus becoming a threat to the whole welfare system.

In summary, the critical question is this: Is a linear and exponential understanding of economic growth able to preserve the welfare society in the long run, or are we running the risk of it falling apart altogether?

This question takes me to my next point.

A new concept of growth

The challenge is to determine how to change the modern paradigm of economic linear growth into something more sustainable with regard to the welfare society?

The following is an attempt to think about the economy in a new way that avoids the pitfalls of the linear concept of growth.

Briefly, the idea is to replace linear growth with a circular concept of growth. This does not mean a return to the cyclic understanding of economies based on nature, as it was in antiquity. It means a circulation economy based upon certain fundamental human and societal values.

We can get a first idea of what I mean by a circular economy by thinking of the economy as a big wheel. So that it can revolve properly around its axis, it is necessary that each element of the wheel move with the all the other elements. No part can be excluded from the wheel's movement.

Now, let us imagine a wheel moving forward. The entire wheel must roll. If only parts of it move, while the rest of the wheel is stationary or even is moving backwards, movement is impeded.

An economy that is understood as a wheel must include everybody in the society. Noone can be left out. A circular economy is inclusive and not exclusive.

That everybody must be included means that everyone must have the opportunity to *actively take part* in the circular economy. This requires an open society based on each individual's participation, in contrast to one that is closed and favors an elite that controls the economy from the top down. In other words, a circular economy encourages participatory democracy.

Therefore, a circular economy requires a new redistribution of the material and economic resources within the society, and it also implies a just distribution of gains.

A way of meeting this condition could be to introduce a basic income guarantee for everybody, by which all citizens or residents of a country receive a regular, unconditional sum of money, either from a government or some other public institution, independent of any other income.

In a certain sense, a circular economy permits economic growth. However, "growth" in this case is not equivalent to abstract, linear growth, which favors the wealthy or powerful elements in the society. "Growth" means the movement of the whole wheel as such, and not only parts of it. It is this growth that makes the whole wheel move forwards with all its parts.

This means that circular economy in the sense that I am using the word is not only inclusive; in a social sense, it is also organic and dynamic.

A circular economy based upon these ideas limits speculation. The problem with speculation is that it causes a gap or break in the circulating of the economy. It takes profits out of the system, considered as a unified whole, and creates smaller systems within the wheel. Thus it creates inequality, which in the long run risks causing civil unrest.

Another consequence of a circular economy is a new way of measuring a country's prosperity. The idea is to expand the gross domestic product by not only including material wealth but also the economic value of an economically active population instead of a passive population who are simply recipients of social goods.

A circular economy is also friendly to nature as a lack of natural resources would stop the wheel from turning or cause gaps within the wheel. Circulation in the economy takes care of nature because it presumes that business relies on natural renewable resources. This is true today and will even be more pressing tomorrow. Hence, a circular economy is inclusive by also including future generations.

Finally, a circular economy is compatible with an economy based upon recycling. Such an economy is not only based on human and societal values. It also applies to the production of materials included in industrial production as well as to contamination and waste. This means that one should attempt to avoid pollution and excessive waste through recycling goods for use in further economic production. Examples of this are the modern recycling economy and the so-called "cradle to cradle" economy. The "cradle to cradle" economy is a new production theory, which includes a cyclic economy in which the product is reused when its lifecycle has ended. Furthermore, everything that is left over from the production process is also somehow used.[2]

---

2   The main idea of the "cradle to cradle" economy is simple to describe: Everything produced ought to cause as little environmental waste as possible at each lifecycle stage. Residual products of a production will be reused, since it is viewed as a component of the original production material. Thus, it can be reused to create new products. There is a continuous attempt to optimize the number of ways in which a product's material can be reused. The ideal is that we will design and produce our goods without loss, waste and pollution by using the excess production materials and also old products to create new ones.

The main difference between a circular economy and the cyclic economy of antiquity and the modern linear economy concerning the conception of growth can be summed up as follows:

In antiquity, growth was seen as a result of a natural development towards an inherent final goal, trigged by external factors.

Traditional modern economies, in general, regard growth as an endless, exponential function based upon internal factors.

A circular economy implies a theory of growth that is based upon the idea of the economic circulation within the society.

Like the concept of growth in antiquity, growth in circular economies becomes the result of a natural development that is characterized by its organic and dynamic character. However, in contrast to the economy of antiquity, a circular economy has no final or inherent goal. The central point of a circular economy is embedded within society and is a means to its development.

In a circular economy, endlessly expanding growth is not necessary for the economy to function. In this case we get a wheel revolving around its own axis, depending upon external factors such as new technologies for the exploitation of natural renewable resources. However, in order for the wheel to move forwards, there must be some growth or expansion in the modern sense of the word. Therefore, a circular economy allows growth and expansion based upon internal factors, on the condition that they make the wheel advance as a unified, organic whole instead of supporting only a part of it.

This leaves us with the final and fundamental question: In what sense is growth necessary for the welfare society?

Economic growth and the welfare society

The essential thing is that the wheel turns around as a whole, not that it actually moves forward. An organic growing economy might even be better than an exponential expanding one, as it more constructively can focus upon the fundamental values of the welfare society instead of narrowing the scope to the growth itself.

In order to examine this point further, I shall briefly return to the main characteristics of the new economy that I previously have propounded.

Firstly, a circular economy is to be understood by its overall inclusive character, which means equality among all participants. This again entails equal material resources for everyone in order to participate in the economic wheel and social equality so that nobody is left out.

Secondly, a circular economy is characterized by its organic character, i.e. a feeling of everyone being part of a whole.

And thirdly, a circular economy is based on the idea of social justice and a feeling of legitimacy. It is a just economy.

These three characteristics are essential conditions for the economic wheel to revolve, or even to move forwards. At the same time they constitute a self-perpetuating process by being further reinforced through their application to economic and social questions. They are both conditions and results thereof.

These characteristics furthermore point to certain fundamental values that are incorporated in this economy:

1. *Collective values:* A community is built on a collective bond that binds people together. The economy must promote this bond, often called the social contract.

2. *An ethical understanding of the individual:* Each individual has intrinsic value. In an ethical sense, a human being can never be treated as a resource. He or she must be treated as a goal in itself. Moreover, the fact that each individual has intrinsic value is synonymous with respecting the dignity of the individual. These values, together with each person's own dignity, are also a goal of the economy.

3. *Human rights:* Human rights cannot be understood as rights that the society grants to the citizens without being framed as a contradiction. On the contrary, human rights are inherent rights that people have in virtue of their fundamental nature, and by such, limiting the power of political authorities. The circular economy's aim is to lay a material foundation for the unfolding of these rights without the direct involvement of the state. This will in turn strengthen current political ideas like participatory democracy, local democracy, fighting poverty, the rule of objective law and distributive as well as redistributive justice.

4. *Nature's intrinsic value:* Nature's intrinsic value means that the nature is characterized by a vibrant life that has its own assumptions and objectives, independent of human interests. The economy's aim is to strengthen the understanding of nature's intrinsic value rather than the opposite. It does so by adapting to nature's cyclic and organic growth so that this also becomes the growth of the economy.

The greater the distance between the economic system and nature, the more dramatic the measures must be to reduce it this disparity. The ideal for a new environmental policy is to decrease the gap, preferably until the two coincide. Here, ancient economic understanding can be of help.

Thus, circular economy means an economy in which money is primarily what it was meant to be from the very beginning: a medium of exchange. What is new is that money must serve some qualitative goals. The essential aspect about this type of economy is that it is self-perpetuating in its own qualitative characteristics. At the same time, these premises also constitute the society's higher qualitative values, while they simultaneously entail respect for nature's intrinsic value.

The result is a new society based on the four values mentioned above: collective values, an ethical understanding of the individual, human rights and nature's intrinsic value.

Another name for these values is welfare.

Traditionally, welfare is understood as being synonymous with a socially just allocation of common goods in a society.

What I propose is a deeper understanding of the welfare concept. It will then be apparent that true welfare does not consist of quantitative amounts being allocated to the people, but primarily in terms of certain qualitative values or criteria that determine how the total amount should be shared among the people. These qualities are those that are mentioned above. Without these values we cannot speak of any true welfare society.

A circular economy, as I have presented it here, is an attempt to determine such general qualitative values that are aimed at the best interests of the fundamental values of the welfare society and not at maximizing personal profit. It also supports an ethical understanding of the individual, it is related to the notion of basic human rights as a foundation for society, and it respects the intrinsic value of nature.

It is now possible to determine what I mean by a new conception of economic growth. Growth is another name for the reinforcement of the qualitative values defining the welfare society. As the economy presupposes these values and reinforce them through their application to the economy, the economy in this sense must be understood as the motor upholding the welfare society.

The essential thing here is that economic growth itself is not necessary for the welfare system to function. As long as the economy serves its purpose, that is as long as it reinforces the social values within the welfare society, then the economy is serving its purpose without the risks and pitfalls of the current linear economy.

Conclusion

In this paper I have not covered how a circular economy, in the social sense of the word, best can be put into practice. What I have concentrated on is the conceptualization of such an economy, i.e. the fundamental principles behind it. Moreover, I have stressed that this principle is to be found in certain qualitative values, which a circular economy attempts to reinforce.

These values are the same as those that explain the welfare society. Hence, the idea is that a circular economy is to be regarded as a vehicle for common welfare.

In examining a circular economy in more detail, I have compared it with the economic paradigms of antiquity and the modern linear economy.

In pointing out that circular economy has its intrinsic goal in a theory of qualities essential to the welfare society, I have referred to the resemblance with the economy in antiquity.

In claiming that internal factors to stimulate growth also to a certain extent can be accepted in a circular economy, I have pointed out the resemblance with modern economy.

However, a circular economy is different from a cyclical economy in that its goal is not the perpetuation of the economy as a naturally given organism, the potential of which it is supposed to develop, but certain social values that it is meant to bring about. Likewise, it differs from modern economics in that its growth is more of an internal character than an exponentially expanding one. It does not exclude a quantitative expansion like some kind of linear movement into the future. However, this is not the goal and it must in any case be controlled by certain qualitative values, which remain the only absolute goal.

Understood in this sense, a circular economy is something quite new that might give hope for the society of the future.

In which way can it solve or remediate actual problems concerning the world's financial situation? This has not been the topic of this paper as it concerns the more formal and technical aspects of a circular economy. I think it can solve these problems, at least in a better way than the linear economy that has created them. I will end by presenting this hope, and leave the challenge here as a still open question.

References

Aristotle (ed. 1999). *Politics* (book I, chapters 8–12). Translated by Benjamin Jowett. Kitchener, Ontario: Batoche Books.

Keynes, J. M. (1932). Economic Possibilities for our Grandchildren. In J. M. Keynes, *Essays in Persuasion* (pp. 358-373). New York: Harcourt Brace.

Maddison, A. (2001). *The Worlds Economy: A Millenial Perspective*, OECD.

Mill, J. S. (1848). *Principles of Political Economy*. London: John W. Parker.

Ober J. (2008). *Democracy and Knowledge. Innovation and Learning in Classical Athens.* Princeton/Oxford: Princeton University Press.

Smith, A. (1776/1922). *An Inquiry into the Nature and Causes of the Wealth of Nations*, London: Methuen.

World Bank (2005). *Economic Growth in the 1990s: Learning from a Decade of Reform.* Washington, DC.

Gordana Berc (University of Zagreb)

The Role of Social Services and Psychosocial Support in Times of Migrant Crisis

Abstract

Migration is a global phenomenon that in some cases is reaching the point of crises. European countries are still facing the last migrant crisis of 2015 in which more than 2 million migrants and refugees arrived from Africa, Syria and elsewhere in the Middle East. The majority of the migrants were men, women, children, and elderly people who were exhausted after their long and dangerous journeys from their home countries to Europe. The target destinations were Germany, Austria, and Scandinavian countries, but the route used was the so-called Balkan route, made up of countries where they stopped briefly or stayed and applied for asylum.

In order to provide social services and psychosocial support for the migrants and refugees, cooperation between social, judicial, health and school systems in the receiving countries was needed. A systematic interdisciplinary, individual and holistic approach in order to meet the basic needs of migrants is important, as well as competent professionals who are able to provide services in these very specific circumstances. Croatia is one of the Balkan countries through which more than 650,000 migrants have been transferred through 2016, when the Balkan route was closed. Social services and psychosocial support in Croatia were provided in cooperation with the state and non-governmental sectors.

Introduction

Migration is a global phenomenon that has been common in human history for centuries in the context of trade relations, the expansion of empires, economic or religious wars, as well as a variety of others reasons (Global Crisis Centre, 2017). Migration is also a movement that is usually initiated as an outcome of connections between sending and receiving countries on a historical, political, or economic basis. In this context, is important to highlight well-known push and pull factors, since they are form the motivation of the people when making the decision to move, and also because such factors could shape migration patterns. Pull factors are related to perceived economic advantages, better opportunities and quality of life, as well as to higher incomes and better social services for individuals and families, and the establishment of stronger social ties in the destination country. Push factors include negative factors or risks connected with the home country such as political or economic insecurity, fear for personal safety as well as discrimination based on race, nationality or religion, which could include oppression and persecution during times of war (Roestenburg, 2013).

In 2015 the European Union was faced with a large number of migrants and refugees from Africa, as well as from Syria, Afghanistan and some Asian countries, who were escaping from the devastation of war, oppression and discrimination. They made the long and dangerous journey in order to enter western European Union countries, such as Germany and Austria, motivated by their wish for better opportunities for their families and themselves in those countries. In that year, member states registered 1.3 million asylum seekers, which was the biggest number of registered refugees in last 60 years, and the largest movement of refugees on the European continent since World War II (Lalić Novak, 2015; Rogelj 2017).

Authorities in European Union countries received more than 2.5 million asylum applications in 2015 and 2016, and 61% of them resulted in a positive decision (European Parliament, 2017). Based on this data, it is clear that European Union was faced with a migrant crises provoked by push factors in home countries. A migrant crisis occurs when the number of migrant arrivals increases significantly in a short period of time; this is usually a combination of refugees and economic migrants.

The Convention on the Status of Refugees, adopted in Geneva in 1951 (UNHCR 1951) defines a refugee as a person who left his or her home country based on a fear of persecution because of nationality, race, religion, group affiliation or political convictions, and moreover has no plans to return to the home country and is seeking protection in the host country (Pezerović & Milić Babić, 2016). Data shows that the majority of migrants and refugees (almost 90% of them) have paid organized criminals in order to get across borders. In 2015 more than 34,900 people arrived by land and 1,011,700 migrants arrived by sea (International Organization for Migration, Global Crisis Centre, 2017). Stokholm (2015) claims that the Mediterranean Sea 'is considered as the world's most hazardous route in use by migrants and refugees', most of them from Africa, as more than 3,500 people lost their lives (Stokholm, 2015:1). The majority of migrants who took the land route traveled from Turkey to Bulgaria through Hungary, Croatia and Slovenia, creating the so-called Balkan route, which was the one of the most important routes from Syria and neighboring countries to the countries of Western Europe. Countries in the Balkan region, for most of refugees and migrants, have been defined as transit countries, which required different resources and services in terms of their registration and temporary settlement.

Such transitory settlement includes basic criteria like providing shelter, food, and health support for exhausted men, women, children and elderly people who made a very long and dangerous journey. For many European Union countries, this has presented a big challenge on different levels (Guerra & Brindle, 2018). One of these was financial support. In order to provide needed services for registering over two million asylum applications since January 2015 to 2016, financial support was established (Carballo, Hargreaves, Gudumac & Maclean, 2017).

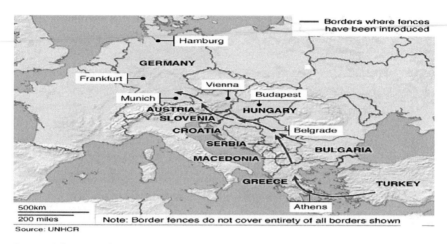

Figure 1: Balkan route during the migrant crisis in 2015 (Source: UNHCR)

For example, in 2015 the budget of 174 million Euros for emergency cases was fully utilized in that year as well as the budget of 161 million Euros for 2016, of which 146 million Euros was transferred to Greece (European Commission, 2017). UNI-CEF had US$34 million available as of October 2017, and from 2015 on has provided 261,000 refugee and migrant children with a range of services (UNICEF, 2018).

In order to regulate such a complex mechanism of providing needed services for migrants and refugees, there are a few important international documents that regulate migrant status in the European Union in order to protect their human rights. One is the Human Rights Recommendations and Guidelines based on the Universal Declaration of Human Rights, adopted by the United Nations in 1948. Article 14 of the named declaration states that every person has the right to seek and obtain asylum in cases of flight from persecution (Lalić Novak & Kraljević, 2014). Also, the United Nations Convention on the Rights of the Child from 1989 aims to protect the best interests of the child, and each EU member state should make this a primary consideration when receiving children of migrants and refugees.

The Dublin III Regulation is a document from the European Parliament and European Council from 2013 that was adopted on 23 June 2013. This document regulates standards for the acceptance of applicants for international protection, obligations of receiving EU states, criteria for determining the member state responsible for visa and asylum applications, administrative cooperation, detentions procedures, conditions based on linking family members, personal interview procedures, and other important criteria in order to protect migrants' human rights in receiving countries which are members of the EU (European Council and Parliament, 2013).

Besides the above mentioned general regulations based on human rights protection, the Dublin III Regulation in Chapter II Article 4 and 5 regulates the criteria that should be met in face-to-face meeting with those seeking asylum, such as personal interviews with the asylum applicants. In Article 5 of this regulation (EU), no. 604/2013, it is defined that:

> *In order to facilitate the process of determining the Member State responsible, the determining Member State shall conduct a personal interview with the applicant. The interview shall also allow the proper understanding of the information supplied to the applicant. The personal interview shall be conducted in a language that the applicant understands or is reasonably supposed to understand and in which he or she is able to communicate. The personal interview shall take place under conditions which ensure appropriate confidentiality. It shall be conducted by a qualified person under national law. (Regulation (EU) no 604/2013 of the European Parliament and of the Council of 26 June 2013)*

In addition to this content, D'Angelo, Blitz, Kofman and Montagna (2017) described the *main reception conditions criteria* for the receiving countries:

1. *Protection* criteria, which includes providing a safe place for children, the sick and elderly people, as well as restoring family link services and legal counseling. It is also important to invest efforts in preparing host communities for migrant reception in order to prevent tension and xenophobia.

2. *Washing* includes criteria focused on providing separate toilet and shower areas for women, children and men, as well as water taps, wash facilities, and places for garbage disposal.

3. *Food provision* includes access to meals and types of food like hot and dry food. This condition includes providing special facilities for breastfeeding.

4. *Health provision* is focused on providing healthcare in local health institution as well as ensuring access to needed psychosocial programs.

5. *Communications* including access to the Internet and charging for mobile phones, thus guaranteeing two-way communications.

6. *Information* criteria includes providing information about health services, asylum procedures, food distribution, shelter allocation, restoring family links, UNHCR services and local NGO services.

According to the current migrant crisis experience, these authors reported that the process of profiling migrants on a country-by-country basis is limited in order to meet the migrant rights to asylum (d'Angelo, Blitz, Kofman & Montagna, 2017). They also highlighted that in these situations the Reception Conditions Directive,

Charter of Fundamental Rights, the Refugee Convention and UNHCR's guidelines on refugee protection should be respected.

Although regulations on migrants and refugees status are clear, there are many challenges that some countries are facing in providing social services and psychosocial support in conditions of crisis.

Social services in migrant crisis conditions

Providing social services for numerous migrants and refugees in different groups (men, women, children, unaccompanied children and youth, elderly) who escaped from war and torture is a significant challenge for receiving countries. The challenges could be recognized on both the macro, mezzo and micro levels in the context of access to services in the receiving country. Some of the macro-level challenges are limited resources in terms of the national welfare state services. Mezzo-level challenges include the lack of cooperation mechanisms between the public and the civil sector. Micro-level challenges refer to the capacities of the local sectors to meet the needs of individuals (Eurodiaconia, 2011). Roestenburg (2013) also explains that migration initiates the activations of services and resources in a receiving country on a macro level, including providing state services, mezzo-level action such as intermediate mechanisms involving non-governmental organizations and agencies, and micro-level activities like the creation of individual social networks and related support. Some of these levels of providing services will be described next; the focus is on providing social services to migrants and refugees.

Due to the high number of migrants and refugees (around 2.5 million) from Syria, Afghanistan and some other Asian countries, migrants who crossed the European continent in 2015 and 2016 are today one of the most vulnerable and socially excluded groups (European Parliament, 2017). In receiving countries, migrants are usually faced with limited access to the education and employment system as well as to health and social services. Therefore, access to basic social services that the state provides (macro level) like accommodations, healthcare and employment were needed for their everyday lives as well as food, clothing, psychological support, cash benefits, and legal advice (Eurodiaconia, 2011). Guerra and Brindle (2018) claim that social services have strong institutional responsibilities since their purpose is to ensure healthcare and educational support, language skills training, career counseling and support as well as resources for social integration. Also, effective coordination between service sectors like child protection services, education and help in finding employment was important in order to ensure the successful integration of migrant children and youth. However, many European countries have been experiencing limited capacity when it comes to ensuring basic social services like housing, so their social service systems have provided alternative accommodation solutions for refugee families like private rentals (Guerra & Brindle, 2018). In many countries, for example in Serbia, which was one of transit countries on the Balkan route, new centres were established to accommodate the refugees. Also, social welfare centres in Serbia became the most affected public social services on the local level along with civil organisations that have ensured significant additional support to migrants – representing providing access to resources on mezzo level (Čekerevac, Perišić & Tanasijević, 2018).

The family system (micro-level) is a significant supporting resource, even in conditions of migration, because families have their own internal strengths, emotional bonds and coping mechanisms as well as their own faith and sense of purpose. These families are usually faced with risk factors that are related to discrimination, poverty and unemployment (Roestenburg, 2013). Therefore social services should provide a living situation for them to minimize these social risks by finding job possibilities for parents that would ensure the economic and social stability of their families. In addition, day centres that are provided by social services also support refugee families by providing meals for children, help with maintaining personal hygiene, homework assistance, and parenting support (Eurodiaconia, 2011).

Here it is worth highlighting that undocumented migrants are also a group of people who have limited access or no access to the social welfare system, including housing, healthcare, education, and employment (Eurodiaconia, 2011). Example of undocumented migrants are unaccompanied children for whom social services are key in terms of safety as well as in the process of ensuring access to the healthcare system, language training programs, educational system, and other programs that could enhance their long-term social inclusion (Guerra & Brindle, 2018).

In 2017 UNICEF used professional teams to provide various social services and psychosocial assistance for more than 15,300 migrants and refugees children. It is interesting to note that countries on the European Union borders received the greatest number of refugee children (Greece, Italy); moreover, the number of children included in social services and psychosocial support activities was over what was planned for and predicted (see Table 1). Around 9,800 children have benefitted from community-based child protection programs and psychosocial support activities. This could not be realized without the help of over 4,600 well-trained, frontline professionals, who provided care facilities for unaccompanied and separated children in asylum centres and reception points across the region (UNICEF, 2018).

In order to meet migrants and refugees needs, it is important to plan and coordinate the services of active psychosocial stakeholders that are focused on this target groups and can provide a high quality response. One of the approaches that is often in use is a holistic and integrated approach (International Federation Reference Centre for Psychosocial Support and Red Crescent Societies Reference Centre for Psychosocial Support, 2009).

Table 1. Child protection data (UNICEF, 2018)

CHILD PROTECTION	UNICEF 2017 targets	UNICEF 2017 results
Children (boys and girls) receiving psychosocial and other community-based child protection support in family support hubs, child-friendly spaces and mother-baby centers		
Greece	6,000	6,783
Serbia	4,800	3,073
Front-line workers trained for child protection standards/child protection in emergencies		
Austria	500	120
Bulgaria	300	132
Croatia	50	43
Germany	775	1,375
Greece	500	476
Italy	1,000	1,472
Serbia	300	272
Slovenia	200	468
The former Yugoslav Republic of Macedonia	150	164
Turkey	200	104
At-risk children, including unaccompanied and separated children, identified through screening by outreach teams and child protection support centres		
Greece	2,000	1,982
Italy	4,700	6,515
Serbia	1,000	3,950
The former Yugoslav Republic of Macedonia	150	254
Turkey	2,500	2,627
Children provided with legal aid and/or counselling		
Bulgaria	2,000	200

Holistic and integrated approach in providing services in a community

A holistic approach is a useful approach in providing community services. It brings a lot of benefits in terms of community development, and it can increase social cohesion and networking and community resilience as well as improving the quality of life for community members on an individual basis. Based on this approach, planned and coordinated interventions should provide participation of community members at different levels – individuals, households, different subgroups, and the whole community (if possible) in order to realize psychosocial well-being for all. Psychosocial well-being is mostly shaped by the specifics of the community context and it has an impact on the personal and social level.

There are three core domains that the psychosocial working group highlight in order to define the psychosocial well-being of individuals and communities (International Federation Reference Centre for Psychosocial Support and Red Crescent Societies Reference Centre for Psychosocial Support, 2009:27):

a) *Human capacity* refers to physical and mental health potential, and specifically considers individuals' knowledge, capacity and skills. Personal strengths and values are very important components of personal capacity.

b) *Social ecology* refers to social connections and support such as relationships, social networks, and support systems directed at the individuals and community.

c) *Culture and values* influence the individual and social aspects of community functioning, and thereby play an important role in determining psychosocial wellbeing. They are correlated with cultural norms and behavior shaped by the value systems in each society, as well as with individual and social expectations.

For migrants, psychosocial well-being could be significantly determined by external factors, such as livelihood, shelter and physical health (International Federation of Red Cross and Red Crescent Societies Reference Centre for Psychosocial Support, 2009, p. 25). For example, if planned intervention activities are focused on programs for children then their parents, teachers, peers and other important actors in the community who are involved in the development of their wellbeing should also be included in intervention activities.

Psychosocial support activities are part of the intervention activities spectrum that can provide resources for the needy in order to increase their coping mechanisms and to encourage recovery as quickly as possible. These interventions are specifically for the individuals and groups with trauma experience, which also includes migrants and refugees.

Challenges of providing psychosocial support for migrants and refugees

Experts define psychosocial support as "a process of facilitating resilience within individuals, families and communities in order to enable families to bounce back from the impact of crises." (International Federation Reference Centre for Psychosocial Support and Red Crescent Societies Reference Centre for Psychosocial Support, 2009, p. 25). Psychosocial support is an essential segment in the process of improving mental and physical health and recovering the coping mechanisms of people with recent crisis experience (ICRC, 2017).

Providing psychosocial support services is an important part of professional support for the needy in response to their crisis experience in order to reduce the development of mental health problems and social exclusion. Crisis situations are defined as sudden catastrophic events that result in various forms of reactions, especially emotionally related trauma affecting family members and friends, who experienced fear for their existence and loss of control over their own life (International Federation of Red Cross and Red Crescent Societies Reference Centre for Psychosocial Support, 2009).

Psychosocial support is usually practiced in the treatment programs of vulnerable groups, facilitating social adjustment to new circumstances, structuring expectations or accepting the reality of the situation, and rebuilding self-confidence (Lalić, 2015). Standard professional support services and interventions involve organised and professional psychosocial support activities, including children's counselling, family counselling, psychosocial support for teachers, support for professionals working with refugees, and finally, recreational activities for children and adolescents (UNHCR, 2014).

Psychosocial interventions are made up of numerous social activities designed to foster psychological improvement, social support, and education in psychosocial functioning. There are also a few specific types of psychosocial support interventions (ICRC, 2017):

1) *Basic psychological support* is targeted at individuals and group in order to improve their immediate functioning.

2) *Psychotherapeutic support* for individuals and groups includes reducing the impact of the distressing symptoms and the improvement of people's capacities and coping mechanisms for daily functioning. These interventions are provided by local professionals such as psychologists and other mental health practitioners (e.g. counsellors, social workers, psychiatrists, community actors who are trained to provide psychotherapeutic support).

3) *Psychosocial group activities* are aimed at the peer support groups or social activities, with the main goal being connecting people who have been through similar experiences so they have the possibility to build a social support network, develop trusting relationships, and exchange problem-solving experiences. These interventions are provided by community actors trained by mental health practitioners.

4) *Information and sensitization activities* are focused on raising awareness of mental health and psychosocial issues with the purpose of providing general information on mental health and psychosocial issues (MHPSS), such as the impact of violence and accessibility to services. These activities are referred to the group of people with community influence or who work with people with MHPSS needs.

5) The same resource defines the hierarchy for mental health and psychosocial support activities in crisis and describes four levels of emergency interventions starting with the forth level, which usually covers the majority of people in this kind of need such as migrants and refugees (Ajduković, Bakić & Ajduković, 2016; ICRC 2017).

IV

Basic interventions and services include activities surrounding providing for basics needs (food, shelter, medicine, clean water, etc.), humanitarian aid and safety zones which helps in creating conditions for mental health and psychosocial well-being improvement processes. Also, activities to support social interaction and community empower mechanisms are included in order to create a secure environment.

III

On the third level, provision of psychosocial support is necessary in order to improve people's psychological and social functioning as well as their well-being through social activities. The role of schools in the community in these circumstances is often very significant in providing shelter and other places to feel safe.

II

On the second level, the provision of activities for individuals, families and social groups is necessary in order to improve everyday psychosocial functioning and coping strategies. At this level, crises intervention needs to provide assistance to people who, after a few weeks of experiencing stress, are struggle with strong difficulties in their daily functioning (psychological first aid, empowerment by helping to solve existential problems and accessibility of psycho education).

I

On the first level (at the peak of the pyramid) are specialized services that provide mental health and psychiatric care for the people who experience serious difficulties in everyday functioning (see Figure 2 and Table 2).

The basic approach that is applied in the cases of crisis and catastrophes such as persecution and refugee flight is the psychosocial approach. The purpose of the psychosocial approach is to ensure to that the victims of disasters can meet their basic needs and reduce the consequences of repressed stress. This approach also includes activities to develop the resiliance and coping mechanisms of individuals, families and communities in order to recover from the impact of crisis situations, over both the short and long term (International Federation Reference Centre for Psychosocial Support and Red Crescent Societies Reference Centre for Psychosocial Support, 2009)

Figure 2: Pyramid for mental health and psychosocial support in crisis situations (according to IASC Guidelines, 2007; ICRC, 2017)

Table 2: Mental health and psychosocial support services in crisis situations (according to IASC Guidelines, 2007)

Responses suggested to ...	INTERVENTION HIERARCHY	Impacts on population due to crises
Individuals or families	1. SPECIALIZED SERVICES	Severe psychological disorders
Individuals, families or group interventions	2. FOCUSED, NON SPECIALIZED SUPPORT	Mild to moderate mental health disorders
Psychological support activities	3. COMMUNITY AND FAMILY SUPPORTS	Mild psychological distress (natural reactions to crisis)
Fulfilling basic needs, providing security	4. BASIC SERVICES AND SECURITY	General population affected by crisis

In applying this approach, experts rely on the personal strengths and skills of individuals and families to recover from a crisis situation. To this end, it is important to stick to the five basic objectives during the implementation of a particular psychosocial intervention (Hobfoll et al., 2007, according to Ajduković, Bakić & Ajduković, 2009):

1. *Encouraging a psychological sense of security* aims to reduce the effects of post-traumatic stress responses and the belief that the world is dangerous (Friedman & McEwen, 2004, Smith, Kerrie & Bryant, 2000, Ward & Bryant, 1998, according to Ajduković, Bakić & Ajduković, 2009).

2. *Soothing* has the purpose to stabilize and calm people who are emotionally overwhelmed and disoriented after a long period of exposure to crises. In these cases panic attacks, dissociation, post-traumatic stress disorder, depression and somatic disorders might develop.

3. *Encouraging feelings of self-efficacy and collective effectiveness* has the purpose of fostering the capacity for successful coping with the consequences of a traumatic event and to create potential for the victims in terms of controlling their own emotions and solving a number of problems related to relocation or the refugee experience in general.

4. *Affiliation and integration* have the goal of providing opportunities for various forms of social support in order to develop feelings of acceptance and understanding for socially isolated people. It is necessary to identify people with good social support and networks, and those who are socially isolated, in order to create conditions for social networking for those who are more socially isolated.

5. *Encouraging feelings of hope* is intended to help people not to fall into despair, feeling of abandonment, and that "everything is lost". Encouraging every hope and optimism is also important in empowering people's proactive potential for achieving positive future outcomes for themselves and for their family members (e.g. finding a job, seeking accommodations).

Therefore, according to the International Organization for Migration (2018), psychosocial support is focused on the migrants' well-being protection in connection with their migration trauma experience. This support includes activities that reduce psychosocial vulnerabilities and issues based on cultural differences.

Since working with refugees and asylum seekers requires additional knowledge and skills, professionals who work directly with this population should be additionally trained in order to be prepared to interact with them, to assist them and to provide the services they need.

The role of professionals and their competence in the process of providing psychosocial support for refugees and migrants in conditions of migrant crisis

Traumatic experience that migrant and refugees went through in their countries of origin and the long and dangerous journey to the receiving county are usually incredibly stressful. As was explained previously, there are levels of psychosocial support that should be provided in order to reduce the effects of trauma. Even when basic needs are met, after a longer period time it is necessary to recognize specific physical and mental conditions in the people who might develop depression, anxiety, or mental health issues such as PTSD. Professionals who provide services for the migrants and refugees who experienced forced migration and who need long-term recovery treatment usually work in the field of mental health interventions for groups and individuals, providing family counselling, cognitive behavioural therapy, and instruction in relaxation techniques (Diaconu, Racovita-Szilagyi & Bryan, 2016).

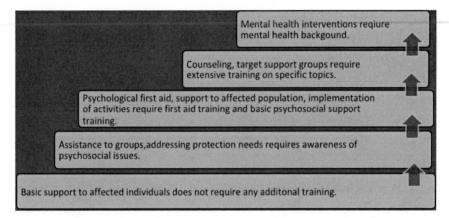

Figure 3: The need for professional training in relation to the level of psychosocial intervention (according to the International Federation of Red Cross and Red Crescent Societies Reference Centre for Psychosocial Support, 2009:131)

According to the International Federation Reference Centre for Psychosocial Support, there are various levels of specialized training that volunteers and professionals should attend in order to provide the best quality services possible (International Federation Reference Centre for Psychosocial Support and Red Crescent Societies Reference Centre for Psychosocial Support, 2009). The levels of complexity of affected people's needs require more specific and specialized education and training in order to provide an effective response (see figure 3).

On the first level are basic needs, and for this level training is not required. On the second level addressing safety needs is necessary, which require the ability to highlight awareness of psychosocial issues. On the next level, psychological first aid and support for the needy is the basic function, and that requires applicable first aid training and basic psychosocial support training. The forth level is focused on providing counselling for the traumatized and distressed, so extensive training is required along with specific knowledge and skills. Finally, on the fifth level, affected people need mental health interventions that require specific knowledge, skills and practices from the fields of psychiatry, psychology and mental health care.

Beside these skills and knowledge, and other that were mentioned previously in this chapter, it is important to highlight the program administration service area that includes assessment skills, planning and program development, monitoring and evaluation, data collection, observational skills, communication skills, and report writing skills.

Professionals who do therapeutic work with refugee families have a double role and responsibility – they must simultaneously consider recovery treatment for the parents and also monitor the children's socialization, education, and recovery process. Together with other professionals, social workers often provide shorter psychosocial interventions for refugee families. Diaconu, Racovita-Szilagyi and Bryan

(2016) claim that social workers play key roles in addressing the mental health issues of forced migrants in a variety of settings. Usually a social worker is the first person who makes professional contact with refugees in the receiving country, facilitating social services support and psychosocial assistance as well as addressing mental health issues and providing information on the legal system and documentation process. There are experiences that describe situations in which school counsellors did have a lack of basic knowledge and skills in working with refugee children who attended the school or were newly settled in the area with their families. Experience showed that social workers were called to educate teachers and counsellors, in order to introduce them to the best practices in working with this population and addressing their specific needs (Mioara, Racovita-Szilagyi & Brittni, 2016). On the other hand, Hidar (2018) says that social workers are particularly limited in terms of systemic possibilities when serving immigrant and refugees, and they are also sometimes called on to balance security issues and human rights within current immigrant and refugee policies.

Carballo, Hargreaves, Gudumac and Maclean (2017) claim that experience with the recent migrant crisis in the area of forced migrations require new thinking, increased resources, and better training for healthcare staff and other professionals, among them social system personnel. Experience suggests that most migrants and refugees are young and relatively healthy, but they come from countries where the healthcare system functions at a substandard level, and people thus had a limited access to vaccinations and medicine. For some host countries, this population could be a good source of labor force but on the other hand they could experience social isolation because of their health issues. Therefore, in these conditions healthcare staff is more required to provide the first humanitarian aid, and collaboration with social system staff is also needed in organizing coordination to provide help and social services for the migrants and refugees.

Overview of the Croatian experience with the migrant crisis – one example

Croatia is one of the several transit countries that is situated on the Balkan route that was the most commonly used in the period including 2015 and 2016 (see Figure 1). In that period of time, Croatia received approximately 650,000 refugees who escaped from war and disasters in Syria; their final destination was the western countries in the EU. In order to respond to refugees needs and to provide humanitarian aid, Croatia organized transit and reception centres in the following cities: Slavonski Brod, Opatovac, Tovarnik, Zagreb (Hotel Porin), Kutina, and Ježevo.

This refugee crisis has some similarities and differences with the one in the 1990s. In the 1990s during the war for independence (1991–1994), Croatia had a population of around 4.2 million people, and received about 1 million refugees from devastated parts of the country, as well as from Bosnia and Herzegovina. Similarities with the new crisis are found in the high level of humanitarian-related response (Esterajher, 2015). There were no language or cultural barriers in the Croatian case, which made the process of providing social services and psychosocial assistance less demanding and challenging than in 2015–2016.

In providing psychosocial assistance during the recent migrant crisis, professionals were faced with a significant difference in understanding the stress and the illness of the migrants who were from a different culture. Namely, according to Muslim culture, the soul and body are inseparably linked and represent a great unity. For this reason, people who come from this culture use metaphors and comparisons to describe their concerns and illness (Ajduković, Bakić & Ajduković, 2016). In addition, in order to provide accurate registration system for asylum seekers, Croatia had to adjust its policies to the EU standards. Also, in that period of time the EU border regime was changed and a few neighboring countries closed their borders, which increased the number of asylum applications from 226 to 2,225 in one year alone. One of the most important challenges in this situation was the efficient coordination between the public service sector and non-governmental organizations. For example, the Croatian Red Cross provided psycho-social support services for unaccompanied refugee children that were organized and contextualized in order to meet their specific needs. In this case, professionals from CRC were in charge of coordination and in daily contact with police, social services organizations such as centers for social welfare and the UNHCR (Orišković & Diklić, 2016).

Conclusion

Providing access to social services and psychosocial support for the migrants and refugees i represents a challenge for the receiving countries on the macro, mezzo and micro levels. Resources of the state welfare services, as well as cooperation mechanisms between the public and the civil sector, and linking local service capacities is crucial in terms of providing social services. Social services include providing accommodations, healthcare, food, clothing, psychological support, cash assistance, legal advice, and assistance in asylum application procedures (Eurodiaconia, 2011). Psychosocial support is focused on empowerment of peoples' recovery capacities and copping strategies to promote constructive everyday functioning (Lalić Novak & Kraljević, 2014). Traumas associated with migration and refugee experiences require the systematic, holistic and individual approach that is provided by trained volunteers and professionals. Experiences from 2015 until today have shown that the European Union is faced with a major challenge in providing social services for the individual member states. In 2015 and 2016, European Union countries received more than 2.5 million asylum applications from the continent of Africa, the Middle East and some Asian countries (European Parliament, 2017). Around 1.3 million of the refugees and migrants who migrated using the land path in 2015 created the so-called Balkan route, and 800,000 people passed through the western Balkan countries of Macedonia, Serbia, Slovenia, and Croatia. Experience with receiving forced migrants in these countries, along with some EU member states (i.e. Greece and Italy), showed that there are some challenges in meeting the basic needs of refugees (e.g. limited capacities in cooperation with state and non-government sector) (Šelo Šabić, 2017).

Nowadays, we are experiencing a new Balkan route through Albania because of new migrant movement; this likewise requires member state collaboration on many levels (political, security, financial, etc.). It also requires efficient, stabile and cooperative social services and psychosocial support systems in each receiving country in order to provide timely humanitarian response to ensure the human rights of the needy.

References

Ajduković, D., Bakić, H., & Ajduković, M. (2016). Psychosocial support in large-scale crisis. Zagreb, Croatia: Croatian Red Cross.

Alencar, A. (2017). Refugee integration and social media: a local and experiential perspective, Information, Communication & Society. DOI: 10.1080/1369118X.2017.1340500

Carballo, M., Hargreaves, S., Gudumac, I., Maclean, E.C. (2017). Evolving migrant crisis in Europe: implications for health systems. *The Lancet: Global Health*, 5(3), 252–253. Retrieved from https://www.thelancet.com/journals/langlo/article/PIIS2214-109X(17)30040-2/fulltext

Čekerevac, A., Perišić, N., & Tanasijević, J. (2018). Social Services for Migrants: The Case of Serbia. HKJU-CCPA, 18(1), 101–125.

d'Angelo, A., Blitz, B., Kofman, E., Montagna, N. (2017). Mapping Refugee Reception In the Mediterranean: First Report of the Evi-Med Project. Retrieved from https://www.mdx.ac.uk/__data/assets/pdf_file/0023/409055/EVI-MED-first-report-final-15-June-2017.pdf?bustCache=885776

Diaconu, M., Racovita-Szilagyi, L. & Bryan, B. A. (2016). The Social Worker's Role in the Context of Forced Migration: A Global Perspective, *Interdisciplinary Journal of Best Practices in Global Development*: 2(2), Article 1. Retrieved from: http://knowledge.e.southern.edu/ijbpgd/vol2/iss2/1.

European Commission (2017). The EU and migration crisis. Retrieved from http://publications.europa.eu/webpub/com/factsheets/migration-crisis/en/.

Eurodiaconia (2011). Policy paper: Social Services and Migration. Retrieved from https://eurodiaconia.org/wordpress/wpcontent/uploads/2015/09/Policy_Paper_Social_services_and_migration.pdf.

European Parliament (2017). EU migrant crisis: facts and figures. Retrieved from http://www.europarl.europa.eu/news/en/headlines/society/20170629STO78630/eu-migrant-crisis-facts-and-figures.

European Parliament and European Council (2013) Regulation (EU) No 604/2013 of the European Parliament and of the Council of 26 June 2013. Official Journal of the European Union, L 180/31. Retrieved from https://eur-lex.europa.eu/LexUriServ/LexUriServ.do?uri=OJ:L:2013:180:0031:0059:EN:PDF.Esterajher, J. (2015). Experiences of Displaced Persons and Refugees and the Contemporary Refugee-Migrant Crisis in Croatia. *Političke analize*, 6(23), 15–22.

Global Crisis Centre (2017). Managing the refugee and migrant crisis: The role of governments, private sector and technology. Retrieved from www.pwc.com/crisis.

Guerra, V., & Brindle, D. (2018). Promoting the social inclusion of the duty of social services. Retrieved from http://www.esn-eu.org/news/1014/index.html.

Haidar, A. (2018). Social Workers and the Protection of Immigrant and Refugee Rights. Retrieved from http://www.ssa.uchicago.edu/social-workers-and-protection-immigrant-and-refugee-rights.

International Committee of the Red Cross (ICRC) (2017) Guidelines on Mental Health and Psychosocial Support. Retrieved from https://www.icrc.org/en/publication/4311-guidelines-mental-health-and-psychosocial-support.

Inter-Agency Standing Committee (IASC) (2007). IASC Guidelines on Mental Health and Psychosocial Support in Emergency Settings. Geneva, Switzerland: IASC.

International Federation Reference Centre for Psychosocial Support and Red Crescent Societies Reference Centre for Psychosocial Support (2009). Psychosocial interventions: A handbook. Copenhagen, Denmark: International Federation Reference Centre for Psychosocial Support. Retrieved from http://pscentre.org/wp-content/uploads/PSI-Handbook_EN_July10.pdf.

International Organization for Migration (2018). Emergency manual: Psychosocial support. Retrieved from https://emergencymanual.iom.int/entry/24089/psychosocial-support.

Lalić Novak, G. (2015). Principle of Restitution and Access to Asylum System: Two faces of the same coin. *Migracijske i etničke teme*, 31(3), 365–385.

Lalić Novak, G., & Kraljević, R. (2014). Protecting refugees and vulnerable migrant groups. Zagreb, Croatia: Hrvatski Crveni Križ.

Mirdal, M., Ryding, E., & Essendrop S. (2012). Traumatized refugees, their therapists, and their interpreters: Three perspectives on psychological treatment. Psychology and psychotherapy: Theory, research and practice, 85(4), 436–455.

Pezerović, A., & Milić Babić, M. (2016). The importance of counselling work with refugee children. *Ljetopis socijalnog rada*, 23(3), 363–380.

Roestenburg, W. (2013). A social work practice perspective on migration. *Social Work/Maatskaplike Werk*, 49(1), 1–21. Retrieved from http://socialwork.journals.ac.za/pub/article/view/72.

Rogelj, B. (2017). The Changing Spatiality of the "European Refugee/Migrant Crisis", *Migracijske i etničke teme*, 33(2), 191–219.

Stokholm, T. (2015). *The Mediterranean Migrant Crisis: A Critical Challenge to Global Nation-States*. London: University of East London, Centre for Social Justice and Change. Working Paper Series No. 3. doi:10.15123/PUB.4783.

Šelo Šabić, S. (2017). The Impact of the Refugee Crisis in the Balkans: A Drift Towards Security. *Journal of Regional Security*, 12(1), 51–74.

UNICEF (2018). Refugee and migrant crisis in Europe. Retrieved from (6.6.2018.) https://www.unicef.org/appeals/refugee_migrant_europe.html.

UNHCR (2014). Syria regional response plan: Strategic overview. Retrieved from http://www.unhcr.org/partners/donors/52b170e49/2014-syria-regional-response-plan-rrp6-january-december-2014.html.

Danijel Baturina, Gojko Bežovan
and Jelena Matančević (University of Zagreb)

Challenges of Third Sector Development in Croatia

Abstract

In Croatia, the third sector is characterized by path dependency, which emphasizes the history in which the freedom of association was limited, combined with the turbulent development of the sector in the 1990s. Today, the impacts of the third sector are perceived in many areas, but there are the challenges in terms of its further development. Challenges for the development of the third sector in Croatia were investigated through quantitative and qualitative research. The results show that challenges can be divided into three broader groups: institutional framework, work of organizations and the general values and modernisation capacities in society. In the conclusion, by integrating the results of research, some specific recommendations to policy makers and practitioners in the third sector are given that could stimulate the sector's further development.

Introduction

Currently there is a significant need for the third sector[1] to have an impact. Demographics, labour market trends and increasing social tensions due to the emergence of new social risk factors are just some of the biggest social challenges that Croatia, and Europe in general, must face now and in the coming decades.

It is becoming increasingly clear that governments and the institutionalised welfare state can't deal with all the problems that society faces. The third sector regularly fills the gap between the market (first sector) and state institutions (second sector), promoting values such as justice and solidarity while at the same time making concrete progress in the area of social inclusion and integration (European Com-

---

[1]   The third sector as a concept is connected with the idea that the basic social institutions are state and market, so civil society, in this case, makes up the third sector (Corry, 2010). The third sector is seen as an alternative to the state and the market, moreover it is the most important alternative that will supplement and balance their important roles. The main advantages of the third sector are seen in its combination of entrepreneurial orientation and organisational efficiency of the private sector with the public good of public sector (Etzioni, 1973). More details on the definition of the institutional components of the third sector can be found in Salamon and Sokolowski, 2014. In the Croatian context, the third sector includes legal entities like associations, foundations, private institutions and some non-profit cooperatives (Bežovan, 1996). What we consider to be the third sector are the social enterprises that are formed in Croatia as well as savings and credit cooperatives (Baturina, 2016.b).

mission, 2012). As such, it becomes an increasingly important element of the institutional mix in Europe, but on the other hand organisations adapting some characteristics of more market-compatible structures (Zimmer and Pahl, 2016). Nevertheless, the third sector is taking on a greater role as a response to growing challenges and new social risks, thus it is becoming a major partner of welfare states in various capacities.

In Croatia, the third sector is characterized by path dependency, which emphasizes the history in which the freedom of association was limited along with the turbulent development of the sector in the 1990s (Bežovan, 2008). Today, the impacts of the third sector are perceptible in many areas (Baturina, 2016.b), but there is a question surrounding the challenges of strengthening this impact, which in turn are shaping the future of third sector development.

This chapter focuses on the results of empirical research, with the goal being to analyse the challenges for the development of the third sector in Croatia. First, current research and literature on the challenges faced by the third sector in Croatia will be presented. In next section, a short description of the methodology of the research will be followed by a presentation of empirical research challenges related to third sector development. The results will be discussed in light of the current trends of the development of the third sector in the context of policies and areas where the third sector is of the greatest importance. In the conclusion, the results of the research will be integrated. Also, specific recommendations to policy makers and practitioners in the third sector that could stimulate its further development will be highlighted.

Trends in third sector development in Croatia

The specific historical legacy and path dependency marked the development of the third sector. Civil society in Croatia, as a narrower section of the third sector, was rediscovered in the early 1990s, when civil society organizations (CSOs) were most notably active as humanitarian organisations, with financial and technical support from international organisations, and in the circumstances of the war and the specific social problems and needs of war victims. In the period that followed, up until the late 1990s, the relationship between civil society and the undemocratic government was rather conflict-ridden, which led to the negative public image of CSOs, which are largely referred to as NGOs (non-governmental organisations)[2]. From the early 2000s onwards, the institutional framework, the policy environment and the general socio-political environment of the civil society have been improved under the coalition government (Bežovan 2005).

---

2   NGO was a more used term for the sector in the 90s, influenced by foreign donors from Anglo-Saxon countries and their tradition of using that label. Afterwards, civil society organisation was adopted, as the term is more used in the continental European context.

Several trends can be observed as challenges to development. In last fifteen years, there has been a significant improvement in the legal and policy framework. However, state paternalism (which is weakening) and a condescending attitude towards the third sector (Matančević and Bežovan, 2013) are still dominating. The centralised state overregulates the development of services and social programs, and the development of local social programs is not well coordinated and planned (Stubbs and Zrinščak, 2012). Clientelism is still playing a role in shaping the sector. This is especially the case in the social welfare domain.

The impact of citizens on public policy remains small (Bežovan and Zrinščak, 2007; Bežovan and Matančević, 2017). There are a small number of organizations with the necessary capacity to promote alternative public attitudes (TASCO, 2011). Local authorities and the government do not regularly invite third sector organisations to participate in public policy. Still, the impact of the third sector is evident in some important areas, such as social policy, environmental protection and human rights issues.

Poor networking and poor cohesion within the sector is an additional obstacle to the establishment of effective advisory mechanisms. In general, the third sector in Croatia lacks horizontal information exchange and cooperation (Vidačak, 2007). The process of Croatian accession to the European Union resulted in the partial Europeanisation[3] of certain public policies, including policies towards the third sector. Some policy standards from the EU level were accepted in Croatia. Recently, more space for participation has opened up, mostly due to new online methods of dialogue.

Distribution of civil society organisations is proving to be problematic (Bežovan, 2003). Civil society organisations are mainly concentrated in large cities and towns, which are usually located in the county centres. Earlier studies have described problems in terms of networking among Croatian third sector organisations. Organisations which use membership for protecting and promoting the interests of the members are more likely to network well (Bežovan and Zrinščak, 2007). Also, the organisations demonstrate low levels of networking on an international level. (Matančević and Bežovan, 2013; Bežovan and Zrinščak, 2007). It can be argued that organisations do not have enough support for that kind of activity. Organisations still show a reluctance and lack of skills for effective networking (Bežovan, et al., 2106.b), apart from coalitions of more prominent organisations in the sector having some specific worldview or idea of public good.

---

3   Defined in Radaelli (2004) as consisting of processes of a) construction, b) diffusion and c) institutionalisation of formal and informal rules, procedures, policy paradigms, styles, 'ways of doing things' and shared beliefs and norms which are first defined and consolidated in the EU policy process and then incorporated into the logic of domestic (national and subnational) discourse, political structures and public policies.

In terms of welfare mix development and the role of the third sector, Bežovan and Matančević (2017) argue that the non-profit sector in Croatia was not part of the concept of social policy reform and the development of a new social system. Social institutions, and especially the private sector, are less cooperative with other stakeholders and less helpful when it comes to the creation of a combined social policy, although they do practice social contracting.[4] Earlier studies on the welfare mix have shown that mistrust and a lack of cooperation exist between the various stakeholders in the social field (Bežovan and Matančević, 2017). Results of further research note that in Croatia, nonetheless, the method for the development of the welfare mix has been established (Bežovan, 2009; Bežovan and Matančević, 2017). A need to increase the impact of stakeholders in the preparation, adoption and implementation of social programs as well as open space for debate on relevant challenges for the development of the welfare mix is apparent. In addition, it appears that some of the personnel working in social institutions and state administration have reservations about the competence of employees in third sector social services organisations (Bežovan and Zrinščak, 2007).

Regarding social entrepreneurship, as part of the third sector in our context, there is insufficient information and a lack of understanding of the term. Due to the fact that their status is not recognisable or established, social entrepreneurship faces numerous obstacles. Socio-cultural factors have an important role in limiting the development, related to the collective experiences of the past that have created animosity towards certain aspects of social entrepreneurship. Problems related to financing, which is a limiting factor connected to ensuring the autonomy of action, the lack of human resource capacity and expertise needed to set up a social enterprise are identified (Vidović, 2012; Vincetić, et al., 2013; Baturina, 2016.a). The entire cooperative sector in Croatia, as well as the social economy sector, is lagging behind the trends and developments in these sectors when compared in European countries. In doing so, the general problems of the development of small businesses, including a lack of knowledge and technology, inadequate financial resources, and problems in the policy frame are affecting cooperatives in particular (Babić and Račić, 2011).

Discussing the Croatian experience and the understanding of the development of social innovation (Bežovan, et al., 2014a, 2014.b), it can be seen that social innovation is a neglected topic, and the concept is unknown in the creation and implementation of public policy. Also, it is important to say that the concept of best practices is not recognised as an instrument of policy, which significantly limits innovative work. However, civil society is still recognized as a space for the discussion of social innovation and a new perspective to address social risks in innovative ways. Volun-

---

4   The research (Matančević, 2014) shows that social institutions operate within a financial framework with features of non-transparency, discrimination toward private service users and social welfare clientelism.

teer work, trust, and commitment to co-operation are the factors affecting Croatian social innovations (Bežovan, Matančević & Baturina, 2014a; Bežovan, Matančević & Baturina 2014.b; Bežovan, Matančević & Baturina, 2016a).

Croatia is a society with low levels of trust (Šalaj, 2011; Rimac, 2014; Nikodem and Črpić, 2014), and this contributes to the low level of active citizenship (Matančević and Bežovan, 2013; Bežovan and Zrinščak, 2007). Given these circumstances, the stability of the sector is possibly more dependent on the development impulses "from above", and less on the initiative and aspirations of citizens within the different communities in which they operate (Matančević and Bežovan, 2013). In addition, several studies have warned of the negative attitude of citizens to civil society organisations. The media, especially national television, often are not interested in showing the positive activities that they have carried out, but more interested in scandals and negative stories (Bežovan and Zrinšak, 2007). It is shown (Vozab, 2012) that organisational representatives perceive that the media are not on their side. Problems encountered in terms of co-operation are lack of media interest, lack of investigative journalism and high advertising prices (National Foundation for Civil Society Development, 2011).

Overall, previous research shows that human resources and sources of funding are also sources of instability for most organisations. In 2015, 1.7 billion HRK (around 220 million EUR)[5] was allocated for programs and projects of civil society organisations[6] from all of the public sources at the national and local levels. On average, the relative largest share of the organisation's revenues is made up of funds from the government, i.e. various ministries and the National Foundation for Civil Society Development. There is a very small proportion of citizens who use the tax benefits for donations (Institute for Public Finances, 2009). Foreign donors, especially the EU, are a very important source of income for organisations from pre-accession processes to date. Entrepreneurs are not actively involved in philanthropic programs for supporting third sector organisations (Bežovan and Zrinšak, 2007). Civil society organisations (or, more precisely, non-profit organisations – NPOs) in Croatia enjoy certain tax benefits. An enabling fiscal framework for CSOs was created rather late, after the 2000s.

The share of organisations with stable human resources is relatively small. Low financial sustainably of the third sector as a whole makes it difficult to hire and retain experts and educated young people. The weak personnel structure of human resources is an obstacle to strengthening the professional development of third sec-

---

5   Report on financing projects and programs of civil society organizations from public sources in 2015.

6   The number of registered associations as of 31 December 2014 was 52,450 – most of them in sports (33.45% of total) and culture (15.32% of total). Other prominent categories were technical, economic and social organisations. (Government Office for Cooperation with NGOs, 2015).

tor organisations (Bežovan and Matančević, 2011; Matančević and Bežovan, 2013; Bežovan et al., 2016.b.) Recruiting of new staff is most often carried out depending on the projects at hand, without a clear system. Third sector organisations often point to problems related to an inadequate number of employees and negative attitudes in the working environment (Juretić and Jakovčić, 2014). As the most significant obstacles to a career in organisations in the sector, respondents of a survey indicate poor working conditions and stress (Škrbić and Stražnik, 2008).

The growth of the sector, not only in scope and funding but also importance, is not resulting in the introduction of the programs and topics on the third sector in university education. For this field, education through the formal education system is still seriously limited (Bežovan, Ledić; Zrinščak, 2011). However, research has shown that, as far as the specific education for the acquisition of competence in the sector, there is a growing number of courses in higher education institutions that deal with the area of civil society (Bežovan, et al., 2011).

The level of volunteering has proven to be low. So far, a lot of research on volunteering has been conducted in Croatia (Forčić, 2007; Črpić and Zrinščak, 2005) that points to this fact. Civicus Civil Society Index 2008–2010 (Bežovan and Matančević, 2011) research has shown that 8.85% of citizens volunteer in social civil society organisations.[7] Citizens usually participate in some humanitarian actions or civil initiatives as opposed to sustainable activism and supporting the work of CSOs. Advocacy organisations rarely engage in activities to increase its membership. Recently, there is more attention being paid to the civic virtue of volunteering and working for the public good. However, it is important to note the limitation factor in the impossibility of involvement of volunteers in social, health, educational and cultural institutions. The problems of the capacity of third sector organisations for the development of quality and sustainable programs of inclusion of volunteers are also present (Bežovan and Matančević, 2011). The USAID sustainability index of civil society organisations in Croatia in 2013 (CERANEO, 2014) states that associations are still not able to mobilize citizens and get strong support from the public.

Methodological note

The analysis will be based on the results of two researchers (Bežovan et al., 2016b, Baturina, 2016), one quantitative and one qualitative. The first research (online survey) (Bežovan et al., 2016b) was carried out as part of the FP7 project Third Sector Impact (TSI). The initial sample included 903 third sector organisations[8] but after

---

7   Assessment of volunteering varies significantly depending on the sources and the different concepts of volunteer engagement.

8   Organisations were selected from the state registry of non-profit organizations and other public body registries. Only organizations in fields of social services, culture, and sports and recreation were sampled. However, due to the structure and purpose of the survey as well as the

the process of removing organisations with inactive e-mail addresses, 799 organisations remained. An online survey was answered by 170 organisations, which was a return rate of 21.7%. Among those who answered, 48.24% organisations were from the social services area, arts and culture were represented by 22.94% of organisations, and sports and recreation by 10.59%. There were 18.24% respondents that did not fit any of these categories. Regarding the position in the organisation, there were 60 (35.29%) executive directors, 33 (19.41%) board members, 34 (20.00%) project leaders, and 43 (25.29%) "other". The first part was focused on assessing the major or minor problems faced by respondents' organisations in areas of finance, human resources, governance, image, space and equipment, inter-organisational relationships, the legal environment, and sector infrastructure. In the second part, opinions were explored in terms of several possible trends in the development of the third sector.

A second part of the results is from research conducted in the framework of a doctoral dissertation, "The impact of the third sector on the socio-economic development of Croatia" (Baturina, 2016)[9]. A main part of the results will refer to qualitative research, which looked into perceptions of key stakeholders in terms of the barriers to the socio-economic development of Croatia and barriers to their development. This involved qualitative research with semi-structured interviews with key stakeholders in the sector (16). The sampling strategy for interview participants was based on a deliberate stakeholders sample according to the "best informant" criterion. They are selected on the basis of having as much insight into the impacts and barriers third sector organisations have to working and to contacting a wide circle of organisations, and many of them as implementing bodies are continuously involved in evaluating and monitoring a large number of organisations' projects and programs. The data obtained from interviews were analysed using framework analysis. The framework analysis has been developed in the context of research of publicly (social, health and other) applied policies to gain specific information that will enable specific insights and recommendations in a shorter period of time (Ritchie and Spencer, 1994). The primary goal is to describe and interpret specific social issues in specific environments.

As stated above, secondary data sources including prior research and reports, legislative and official documents and relevant sector strategies were used.

---

process of changing information about associations in the official association register (because the associations had to harmonise their statutes with the new law) the sample was not representative.

9   The specific impact of the third sector on the dimensions of impact on the welfare and quality of life, social innovation, civic engagement, empowerment, advocacy, community building, economic impacts and the impact on human resources were explored.

Research results

Challenges to the greater impact of the third sector will be looked at through two types of empirical results. The first concerns a survey conducted as part of the Third Sector Impact project. The second, through qualitative research, investigates the perceptions of key stakeholders in the sector.

In the area of financing, several organizations consider the lack of financing as a significant problem. Coupled with that, there were issues with low employee pay. In terms of governance, no serious issues were highlighted. Equipment was cited as the obstacle preventing organisations from getting work done. Barriers were also found regarding image and limited public awareness. The operating context showed issues with government control, but also of competition with other organisations. The legal environment seems to be the biggest barrier. In all facets, most of the organisations had significant difficulties.

Table 1: Assessment of major or minor problems confronting organizations (Bežovan et al., 2016b)

Potential barrier[*]	% of respondents that perceive it as a serious or very serious problem for their organizations
Lack of government funding	84.70%
Lack of sponsoring by private companies	68.83%
Lack of private individual contribution	60.59%
Low pay of employees	49.41%
Difficulties recruiting volunteers	45.29%
Inability to pay salaries due to lack of funds	42.35%
Bad condition of TSO facilities	62.35%
Out-dated technology	59.41%
Limited public awareness of organisations	52.94%
Strong governmental control	48.24%,
Competition with other TSOs	42.94%
Legal restrictions	66.47%
Lack of favourable tax treatment	57.65%
Lack of clear legal status	56.47%
Increasing bureaucracy	88.24%
Lack of support organisations	80.00%

* Barriers to third sector organisations were explored in eight overall dimensions: financing, personnel, governance, image, equipment, operating context, legal environment and sub-sector infrastructure.

In the comments section, some new developments towards the professionalisation of third sector organisations are seen. At the same time, organisations are also becoming more responsible towards stakeholders.

Table 2: Survey statements (more in Bežovan et al., 2016b)

Survey statements (most relevant)	% of respondents that agree or strongly agree
My organisation devotes more resources to fundraising now than it did ten years ago	68.24%
It is important for executives to have a business background in my organisation	70.00%
The need to raise revenue from business activities is keeping us from serving our real purpose	47.06%
EU financing is an important financial resource for my organisation	40.59%
We are increasingly implementing measures to improve the participation of stakeholders	60.59%

The results of qualitative research deepen and expand upon the limited survey insights. By analysing data, the following categories and codes are utilised[10], of which most relate to the character of the relationship between the state and the third sector. This is important for functioning in a welfare dimension.

As a category, there are **legal framework and administrative requirements** within which the following codes are found: *legislation, the understanding of the sector by legal and institutional actors, statistical monitoring of the sector, and increasing of the bureaucracy.*[11] Most of the obstacles encountered by participants in the qualitative research can be labelled structural obstacles. They relate to the lack of acknowledgment of the sector's contribution by the state, the lack of cooperation in general and the inclusion of support in terms of the institutional framework for the development of the third sector. New areas of third sector activity are not recognised, so the sector is faced with some misunderstanding and also the disadvantages of basic factors such as recording statistical data on the role of the third sector. This is compounded by the growth of administrative requirements that exhaust organisational resources, and in part pull them away from their strategic goals and towards bureaucratisation of action. Third sector organisations spend significant resources to address these demands. One part is seen as the effect of EU funding. "Projectisation" that generates duplication of bureaucratic processes becomes the "everyday life" of the work of such organisations, which they must comply with, but they still resist such a mode of functioning.

---

10   Due to limited space, we have only shown research results in a general form with some characteristic quotes in the footnotes. Interviews in quotations are signified by order of interviewing from KS1 – which represent key stakeholder 1, to KS16, which represents key stakeholders 16. For more detailed analysis and quotations illustrating categories and codes, see Baturina, 2016.b.

11   Some characteristics defining quotations from this category: KS13: "*The other thing is what the sparrows on the trees are already talking about, that the laws change at tremendous speed and are often very contradictory. And they are followed by the implementation measures and mechanisms that are often not sufficiently clear and sufficiently elaborated upon to be applicable in practice*" and KS7: "*Unfortunately, there is a potentially negative effect of European funding, with all these positive effects, which is over-bureaucratization of project management procedures that state is often implementing, but authorities do not have time to deal with impact measurement because they are so concerned with other stages that are burdening them, like preparing documentation, receiving reports, processing, and collecting a lot of other paperwork.*"

A further category is **political support and understanding of the sector** with the codes: *recognition of the role of the sector, and political support and sustainability.*[12] This highlights the role of political actors that can greatly shape the relationship with the third sector, which is not yet sufficiently developed. Political support is perceived by stakeholders as the key to further strengthening the sector's impact. It has been shown that the political actors and the state administration do not recognise the importance of the sector. This is supported by the changing nature of political options emerging from democratic processes. It is reflected not only in terms of power but also in the relationship and infrastructure of joint action and potential co-operation that develops over time. The lack of support for the work of the third sector is recognised in terms of sustaining the continuity of high quality projects. In this sense, the sector is condemned to projectisation rather than developing a common partnership in relation to issues that would be of mutual interest in improving the socio-economic position of citizens.

The next category is **social norms and values**, within which the following codes are found: *trust, personal responsibility and prevailing attitudes.*[13] In this respect, respondents note a lack of trust in the society that increases the costs of co-operation, and there is moreover inadequate promotion of cooperative work. Likewise, respondents find that there is a certain lack of sense of personal responsibility that would stimulate more active engagement in terms of influencing personal and general social well-being. There are still some values that reflect the scepticism towards private initiatives, both in the third sector and in the wider community. Citizens still rely on the state as a source of solutions for all of their problems, according to the perception of a part of a research.

Furthermore, the category **public image of the sector** encompassed the codes: *public perception, the relation of the media to the sector, the local media and the capacities of organisations for media engagement.*[14] The sector still faces difficulties

---

12 Some quotations from this category: KS9: "*Stepmother relationship, I really mean the state has a stepmother relationship, I hope that, I think we have this, all of us working in this civil society have this problem of misunderstanding of the governing parties about what the third sector is.*" From KS9: "*Because no one recognizes that part, because everything is painted in a way that everyone is doing something to meet some of their basic needs and to have some benefit. Then we still have the problem of starting every four years from scratch, talking to the new government.*"

13 Some illustrative quotations from this category: KS4: "*First, there was no trust, so we have worked on trust. Now, again, there is a policy of distrust. It depends on the political context, right-oriented political options definitely do not accept civil society as an equal partner.*" and KD9: "*We've got some sort of unnatural system of thinking. Nothing in Croatia is done without some personal benefit. And that is a big problem in Croatia. And everyone in Croatia must begin to change consciousness when a non-profit organization is established. For now, who will benefit is primarily considered. That certainly is not for me.*"

14 Some illustrative quotations from this category: KD2: "*When you go to such research then it appears that 50% of people think that associations are needed, that they are useful, you know it, that they need to be financed, and all together. Then you have these public attacks in which you think that nobody understands anything.*" From KS5: "*... and then again on the other hand, like*

with building a positive image with the public as well as gaining citizen recognition. It seems that organisations cannot find ways to access the media, and also the features of the media content displayed today do not support the placement of what the sector offers in an appealing manner. It is noteworthy that there is a perception among the respondents that there has been an adversarial atmosphere recently for third sector organisations.[15]

Discussion

Challenges to the development of the third sector in Croatia that were investigated through quantitative and qualitative research can be divided into three broader groups that will be discussed next.

The first concerns the **institutional framework** in which laws and strategies, the economic activity of the sector and the tax framework can be categorised. In last fifteen years, there has been significant progress and improvement in the legal and policy framework. Nevertheless, partial state paternalism and a condescending attitude towards civil society organisations are still dominant. Significant problems with legal restrictions and the lack of a clear legal status are perceived as being problematic by the majority of project survey respondents. In addition, the recent Act on Associations from 2014 is in a sense limiting freedom of association. Strategies in relevant areas of the third sector such as cooperatives are non-existent, or in the case of social enterprises are developed but face many challenges when it comes to implementation. The lack of recognition of and support for the economic activity of third sector organisations by the tax system is a significant obstacle. Currently, the tax framework is unclear in regard to the economic activity in the sector, and this is a disincentive for its development. In addition, a new act covering financial operations and accounting (2015) limits the work done, especially for smaller organisations. Other aspects of the third sector, such as social entrepreneurship and social economy or private welfare organisations, do not even have that privilege. Their area is still accompanied by lacking legal and regulatory clarity as well as a lack of recognition.

The second group of challenges and obstacles is mainly related to the **work of organisations.** It highlights several aspects. These are the possibilities for secur-

---

everywhere in society, you have organizations that work well and those who hustle and those who darken the image of all the good work the organizations have done."

15 In addition, more related to third sector characteristics, we have the category of **human resources of the third sector** within which we find the codes related to *skills and education*. The last category is the **characteristics of work of organisations**, within which we find the codes: *networking capacity and strategic planning of organisations*. According to the perception of different research participants, the limited capacities of organisations and sectors are seen as obstacles to the greater impact of the sector. Participants see the need for sector educators to track current trends in knowledge development.

ing funding, human resources, volunteers and the "bureaucratisation" of the organ-isation's work. In the area of funding, many organizations see the lack of financial resources as a significant problem, which is causing related problems such as pay-ing salaries. Research has shown that some organisations have problems with their sustainability, which was possibly affected by the turbulence of 2016 and the reduc-tion of some funds for the development of civil society. Diversification of funding sources is therefore a trend. More organisations are developing economic activity and are "producing" a greater number of project applications. They rely on "gen-erous" EU funding, which they are relatively successful in acquiring. Although financing is a significant obstacle, innovative financial instruments such as micro-credit, ethical financing, social impact investment, and special credit lines for social entrepreneurship[16] are still under development (Kadunc, Singer & Petričević, 2014; Baturina, 2016). Resistance towards the establishment of ethical banking in Croatia, which would be step towards sustainable investment in social development, is show-ing the limitations of the socio-cultural environment. Philanthropy in our context has certain potential, but it is underdeveloped, partly due to lacking capacity for the mobilisation of resources. The financial crises that struck Croatia more than other countries between 2008 and 2014 put pressure on public finances and negatively impacted resources for the third sector and social development in general.

The share of organisations with stable human resources is small. The unsustain-ability of human resources is a barrier to the stronger professional development of third sector organisations as well as their sustainability, which was also recognised in previous studies. Recruitment of new staff is usually carried out depending on current projects, without a strategically developed system. Moreover, work in the third sector is becoming increasingly stressful. The growth of the sector, not only in scope and funding but also in terms of importance, was not accompanied by the introduction of educational programs, which would further strengthen the human resources of organisations. The level of volunteering is generally low, as shown by various studies. More recently, the civic virtue of volunteering gained a little more attention. When compared to a decade ago, it is noteworthy that volunteering is better acknowledged and some infrastructure is being developed. Volunteering is usually sporadic, for instance in relation to humanitarian actions in the community. The problem is also the lacking capacity of civil society organisations for the devel-opment of quality and sustainable programs for the involvement of volunteers. In our research, organisations have also reported difficulties in recruiting volunteers.

· The increase in bureaucratic demands is a significant barrier that almost all the organisations in the study have noticed. In addition, the vast majority of them

---

16   Also, relatively generous resources anticipated in strategy for development of social entrepre-neurship (2015–2020), due to the questionable nature of the capacity of the administration but also of the sector and its potential for absorption, are in danger of not being purposefully used for development of that sector (Baturina, 2016.b, Baturina, 2018).

acknowledge the lack of support for organisations. Organisations use a variety of strategies to adapt in order to survive in precarious times. They apply to the increasing number of funding sources, which brings additional administration tasks. Projectisation is the trend in the sector. With this, professionalisation occurs, especially in relation to project preparation and management skills. It distracts organisations from their primary missions, and they increasingly resemble private companies.

The third aspects of the challenges are the **general values and modernisation capacities in society**. Public image and a level of trust in society, openness to new concepts such as social entrepreneurship and social innovation, potential for good governance and welfare, and capacity to measure impacts are included in this aspect.

Several research projects have shown that Croatia is a society with a low level of trust. Coupled with low level of active citizenship and negative attitudes towards civil society organisations, the stability of the sector is more dependent on the development impulses "from above", and less on the initiative and aspirations of the citizens within the different communities in which they operate. The culture of social dialogue (Stubbs and Zrinščak, 2005; Stubbs and Zrinščak 2012) in Croatia is still not developed. At the local level, where interaction can be closer, relationships also often depend on political support or political favour for the sector. The relationship between the third sector and the state in the Croatian context is particularly defined by a different kind of political pressure on the third sector.

There is insufficient information about social entrepreneurship in the Croatian context and a lack of understanding surrounding the concept. Important factors limiting greater development are socio-cultural and related to the collective experiences of the past. Problems related to financing and lack of human resource capacity and expertise to launch social enterprises were identified. Civil commitment was shown to be capable of growing into social entrepreneurship initiatives, for examples as studied in the case of RODA (Bežovan, Matančević, Baturina, 2016.c) or the cultural hybrid organisation Lauba (Bežovan, Matančević, Baturina, 2016.b) The cooperative sector is ignored and there is no recognition at a policy level. It lags behind the development trends of other European countries. It is burdened by problems such as lack of knowledge and technology, inadequate sources of funding and problems in the functioning of the rule of law.

The concept of best practices is not recognised as an instrument of policy, which significantly limits innovative activity. Social innovation as a concept is not recognised by the stakeholders. The third sector is recognised as a space for debate on social innovation as well as new perspectives for solving social risks in innovative ways. Volunteer work, trust and commitment to co-operate are sources of Croatian social innovation. Croatia is far from the level where they would be recognised as a factor of employment, quality of life, social inclusion, and the development of new relationships in the state and society. Hence, the greater focus is on the governance that would stimulate innovation (Brandsen, Cattacin, Evers &Zimmer 2016). Good governance is a new concept in the Croatian environment. It was partially imported by the Europeanisation of public policy, but it is often misunderstood as public administration.

Europeanisation also brought some legitimacy to the third sector in their inclusion in preparation and implementations of public policies. EU financing represents developmental potential, which the third sector is using more effectively than other sectors, but there are certain limitations in terms of knowledge and examples of good practices from which lessons can be learned. There is limited capacity in public administration and government to create real and effective partnerships, involve stakeholders or encourage innovation.

The third sector in Croatia was not part of the concept of social policy reform and the building of a new social regime. Nonetheless, more recent studies show that the way was partially paved for the development of welfare mix, but the principles of co-governance and co-production are not yet part of the discourse and practice of public policy. A monopoly of the state in the provision of social, health, educational and cultural services and the disregard for private initiatives is one of the key obstacles; these are difficult to overcome.

Impact measurement is an important issue. Creating a clear link between the results of programs and projects and their specific contribution would reduce the "doubts" and increase confidence in third sector organizations, so it is necessary to encourage this area further. It turns out that, although the key stakeholders in the sector and organisations recognize the need for measuring the impacts, capacities in this area are lacking. Organisations and implementation bodies do not apply the practice of measuring the impact nor have they developed the tools. Policies based on evidence are not yet part of our public policy.

Conclusion

When Croatian third sector development is analysed in a specific relational context, it must be noted that strengthening the positive impacts of the third sector is a trend in Western countries. Civil initiatives there occupy significant public space; the third sector is seen as space for entrepreneurial initiatives to foster public good and societal development. They follow their path of development imposed by local culture, but the third sector plays an increasingly important role[17] in responding to the challenges of the social state and society in general, although there are certain adjustments to be made due to the economic crisis (Pape et al., 2016). Barriers to further third sector development in Europe include changes in volunteer management, scarce resources, bureaucratisation of poorly paid and insecure jobs, and lack of infrastructure (Zimmer and Pahl, 2016). Many of the challenges, as presented in

---

17 Its development partly corresponds to the degree of development of society, as demonstrated by the experiences of the research countries in the FP7 project Third Sector Impact.

the results and discussion here, are analogous challenges of the Croatian context of the sector.

In the context of transition countries, it is also the case in Croatia that there is a certain domination of the social sphere by the Croatian public and political sectors. This also shapes modernisation capacities because often the criterion of political affiliation and nepotism is put ahead of the criteria of competence. In addition, the public sector is too bureaucratised and has not shown itself as a place of entrepreneurship in terms of innovating solutions or making changes. On the other hand, the third sector does not seem capable enough to give a stronger incentive to self-development[18]. Despite the modest capacity of organisations and the sector overall (Baturina, 2016.b), impact measurement can strengthen such organisation's work, increase sector impact, and drive public policy through project piloting and evidence-based policy. Good governance would encourage all stakeholders to revitalize cooperation spaces that include the third sector and the state. This would also trigger greater investment in specific organisational capacities, make possible new financing mechanisms, and positively impact the currently limited trust and negative picture of the sector. In addition, recommendations surrounding the opening up of space for social innovations, as well as greater legislative and tax leniency related to the sector's specificity would enhance its development.[19]

References

Babić, Z., & Račić, D. (2011). Zadrugarstvo u Hrvatskoj: trendovi, pokazatelji i perspektiva u europskom kontekstu. *Sociologija i Prostor*, 49, 191(3), 287–311.

Baturina, D. (2016.a). *Wind in a back" or "bite of more than we can chew" First Strategy and institutional trajectories of development of social entrepreneurship in Croatia.* Paper presented at: Solidarity in Transition? Researching Social Enterprise in Post- Communist Societies": An International Scientific Colloquium. Tirana, 21 April 2016.

Baturina, D. (2016.b). Utjecaj trećeg sektora na socio-ekonomski razvoj Republike Hrvatske. (docotral dissertation). Zagreb: Pravni fakultet Zagreb.

Baturina, D. (2018). First Strategy for the development of Social Entrepreneurship in the Republic of Croatia and potentials for the development of the sector. *Croatian and Comparative Public Administration* (Accepted for publishing).

Bežovan, G. (2005). Rizici izgradnje civilnog društva bez građana. In: Horvat, V. (ed.) Kakvu Europsku uniju želimo? U potrazi za razlozima demokratskog deficita (EU i RH). Zagreb: Fondacija Heinrich Böll.

---

18 An example of the current Strategy for Creating an Enabling Environment for Civil Society Development 2018–2022 shows modest civil sector capacity for the development of the vision of the sector's future.

19 More recommendations that can contribute to the development of the sector in Bežovan et al., 2016.b.

Bežovan, G. (2008.). *Civilno društvo i kombinirana socijalna politika.* In: Puljiz, V. Bežovan, G., Matković, T., Šućur, Z., Zrinščak, S. (eds.) Socijalna politika Hrvatske. Zagreb: Pravni fakultet Sveučilišta u Zagrebu.

Bežovan, G. (2009). Civilno društvo i javna uprava kao dionici razvoja kombinirane socijalne politike u Hrvatskoj. *Hrvatska Javna i Komparativna Uprava*, 9(2), 355–391.

Bežovan, G., & Zrinščak, S. (2007). *Civilno društvo u Hrvatskoj.* Zagreb: Hrvatsko sociološko društvo.

Bežovan, G., & Matančević, J. (2011). *Izgradnja identiteta: izazovi profesionalizacije organizacija civilnog društva. Civicus-ov Indeks civilnog društva u Hrvatskoj* (istraživački izvještaj). Zagreb: CERANEO.

Bežovan, G., & Matančević, J. (2017). *Civilno društvo i pozitivna promjena.* Zagreb: Školska knjiga.

Bežovan, G., Ledić, J., & Zrinščak, S. (2011). Civilno društvo u sveučilišnoj nastavi. *Hrvatska i komparativna javna uprava*, 11(1), 173–202.

Bežovan, G., Matančević, J., Baturina, D. (2014.a). *Varaždin.* In: Evers, A., Ewert, B. i Brandsen, T. (eds.) Social innovations for social cohesion: transnational patterns and approaches from 20 European cities. Liege: EMES.

Bežovan, G., Matančević, J., & Baturina, D. (2014.b). *Zagreb.* In: Evers, A., Ewert, B. i Brandsen, T. (eds.) Social innovations for social cohesion: transnational patterns and approaches from 20 European cities. Liege: EMES.

Bežovan, G., Matančević, J., & Baturina, D. (2016.a). Socijalne inovacije kao doprinos jačanju socijalne kohezije i ublažavanju socijalne krize u europskim urbanim socijalnim programima. *Revija za Socijalnu Politiku. 23* (1), 61–80.

Bežovan, G., Matančević, J., & Baturina, D. (2016.b). *External and Internal barriers to Third Sector Development-Croatia.* Working paper. Part of work package 5 "External and Internal barriers to Third Sector Development" of the research project entitled "Third Sector Impact.

Bežovan, G., Matančević, J., & Baturina, D. (2016.c). Zagreb: Parents in Action – Innovative Ways of Support and Policies for Children, Women and Families. In: Brandsen, T., Cattacin, S., Evers, A., Zimmer, A. (eds.) (2016). *Social Innovations in the Urban Context.* ChamHeidelberg, New York, Dordrecht, London: Springer.

Brandsen, T., Cattacin, S., Evers, A., Zimmer, A. (eds.) (2016). *Social Innovations in the Urban Context.* ChamHeidelberg, New York, Dordrecht, London: Springer.

CERANEO (2014). *Indeks održivosti OCD-a u Hrvatskoj za 2013. godinu.* Zagreb: CERANEO.

Corry, O. (2010). Defining and Theorizing the Third Sector. U: Taylor, R. (eds.) *Third Sector Research.* New York, Dordrecht, Heidelberg, London: Springer.

Črpić, G., & Zrinščak, S. (2005). Civilno društvo u nastajanju. Slobodno vrijeme i dobrovoljne organizacije u Hrvatskoj. In: J. Baloban (ed.) *U potrazi za identitetom. Komparativna studija vrednota: Hrvatska i Europa.* Zagreb: Golden marketing – Tehnička knjiga.

European Commission (2012). *Work Programme 2013 (Revision) Cooperation Theme 8 Socio-Economic Sciences and Humanities.* European Commission C(2012) 9371 of 14 December 2012.

Etizioni, A. (1973). The third sector and domestic missions. *Public Administration Review,* 33(4), 314–323.

Forčić, G. (2007). *Volonterstvo i razvoj zajednice. Sudjelovanje građana u inicijativama u zajednici. Istraživanje uključenosti građana u civilne inicijative u zajednici kroz volonterski rad.* Rijeka: SMART – Udruga za razvoj civilnog društva.

Government Office for Cooperation with NGOs (2015). *Associations in the Republic of Croatia.* Zagreb: Government Office for Cooperation with NGOs.

Institut za javne financije (2009). *Mogućnosti stvaranja poticajnog poreznog sustava za razvoj i djelovanje organizacija civilnoga društva i organizacija koje djeluju za opće dobro u Republici Hrvatskoj s usporednom analizom stanja u zemljama članicama Europske Unije.* Zagreb: Nacionalna zaklada za razvoj civilnog društva.

Juretić, J. & Jakovičić, I. (2014). *Rodna ravnopravnost u vrednovanju rada i zadovoljstva radom u organizacijama civilnoga društva.* Zagreb: Prostor rodne i medijske kulture "K-zona".

Kadunc M., Singer, S., & Petričević, T. (2014). *A Map of Social Enterprises and their Eco-System in Europe, Country Report: Croatia.* Brussels: European Commission.

Matančević, J. (2014). *Obilježja modela kombinirane socijalne politike u pružanju socijalnih usluga u Hrvatskoj. (doktorski rad)* Zagreb: Pravni fakultet, Sveučilište u Zagrebu.

Matančević, J., & Bežovan, G. (2013). Dometi i ključni čimbenici razvoja civilnog društva u Hrvatskoj temeljem tri vala istraživanja. *Revija za Socijalnu Politiku,* 20(1), 21–41.

National foundation for Civil Society Development društva (2011). *Procjena stanja razvoja organizacija civilnoga društva u Republici Hrvatskoj. Izvještaj istraživanja u 2011. godini.* Nacionalna zaklada za razvoj civilnog društva.

Pape, U., Chaves-Ávila, R., Benedikt Pahl, J., Petrella, F., Pieliński, B., & Savall-Morera, T. (2016). Working under pressure: economic recession and third sector development in Europe. *International Journal of Sociology and Social Policy,* 36(7/8), 547–566.

Radaelli, C. (2004). Europeanisation: Solution or problem? *European Integration online Papers.* 8, (16) http://eiop.or.at/eiop/texte/2004-016a.htm.

Rimac, I. (2014). Komparativni pregled odgovora u anketi Europska studija vrijednosti 1999. i 2008. In: Baloban, J., Nikodem, K., Zrinščak, S. (eds.) *Vrednote u Hrvatskoj i u Europi: Komparativna analiza.* Zagreb. Kršćanska sadašnjost. Katoličko bogoslovni fakultet Sveučilišta u Zagrebu.

Ritchie, J., & Spencer, L. (1994). Qualitative data analysis for applied policy research. In: Bryman, A. & Burgess, R. (eds.), *Analyzing Qualitative Data.* London: Routledge, 173–194.

Salamon, L. M., & Sokolowski, S., W. (2014). *The Third Sector in Europe: Towards Consensus Conceptualization, TSI Working Paper Series No. 2.* Seventh Framework Programme (grant agreement 613034), European Union. Brussels: Third Sector Impact.

Stubbs, P., & Zrinščak, S. (2005). Proširena socijalna Europa? Socijalna politika, socijalna uključenost i socijalni dijalog u Hrvatskoj i Europskoj uniji. In: Ott, K. (Ed.) *Pridruživanje Hrvatske Europskoj uniji: Ususret izazovima pregovora.* Zagreb: Institut za javne financije: Zaklada Fiedrich Ebert.

Stubbs, P., & Zrinščak, S. (2012). Europeizacija i socijalna politika: između retorike i stvarnosti. In: Puljiz, V., Ravlić, S., Visković, V. (eds.) *Hrvatska u Europskoj uniji: kako dalje?* Zagreb: Centar za demokraciju i pravo Miko Tripalo.

Škrbić, N., & Stažnik, M. (2008). *Odgovornost i predanost pod stresom" – Analiza stanja zaposlenosti mladih i planiranja dugoročne profesionalne karijere u organizacijama civilnog društva u RH.* Zagreb: *DIM* – Udruga za građansko obrazovanje i društveni razvoj

Šalaj B. (2011). Civilno društvo i demokracija: što bi Tocqueville i Putnam vidjeli u Hrvatskoj? *Anali Hrvatskog Politološkog Društva*, 8 (1), 49–71.

TASCO (Technical Assistance for Civil Society Organisations in the IPA Countries). (2011). *Needs Assessment Report – Croatia.* Zagreb: TACSO.

Ured za udruge Vlade Republike Hrvatske, (2017) *Izvješće o financiranju projekata i programa organizacija civilnoga društva iz javnih izvora u 2015. godini.* Zagreb: Ured za udruge Vlade Republike Hrvatske.

Vidačak, I. (2007). *Lobiranje – Interesne skupine i kanali utjecaja u Europskoj uniji.* Zagreb: Planetopija.

Vidović D. (2012). *Socijalno poduzetništvo u Hrvatskoj. Doktorska disertacija.* Zagreb: Filozofski fakultet, Sveučilište u Zagrebu.

Vincetić, V., Babić, Z., & Baturina, D. (2013). Definiranje područja i potencijal razvoja socijalnog poduzetništva hrvatske u komparativnom kontekstu, *Ekonomski Pregled: Mjesečnik Hrvatskog Društva Ekonomista Zagreb.* 64 (3): 256–278.

Vozab, D. (2012). Communication models of civil society organizations in Croatia. *Observatorio, special issue "Networked Belonging and Networks of Belonging"* http://obs.obercom.pt/index.php/obs/article/view/578

Zakon o financijskom poslovanju i računovodstvu neprofitnih organizacija, *Narodne novine*, 121/2014.

Zimmer, A. & Pahl, B. (2016) *Learning from Europe: Report on third sector enabling and disabling factors.* TSI Comparative Report No. 1, Seventh Framework Programme (grant agreement 613034), European Union. Brussels: Third Sector Impact.

Vjollca Krasniqi (University of Prishtina)

Domestic Violence: Gendered State Rationality and Women's Activism in Kosovo

Abstract

As an expression of power, domestic violence is a means through which people seek control over the personhood and sexuality of less powerful individuals; those predominantly affected are women. Domestic violence is thus a profoundly gendered practice. In Kosovo, having too long been considered a private issue, domestic violence has been moved into the realm of that which is both forbidden and punishable by law. Yet, implementation of legislative measures to combat domestic violence has been slow to materialize, resulting in increasing vulnerability and insecurity for women in the home. This article explores the construction of intimate violence as a criminal offence in the legal framework of Kosovo, developed as a cooperative effort between the state and civil society, in particular the women's movement. It shows how the legislation is just one more institutional rationality that enables the gendered hegemony of the state. This analysis draws on the women's movement response to the limits of the law in practice to combat domestic violence and the collective struggle to disrupt the social, economic, political and interpersonal power that continues to be in the hands of men. The article concludes that prospects for combatting domestic violence rest on the interplay between formal state interventions and civic activism that seeks to transform entrenched patriarchal norms in state relations, institutions and practices, as well as in the private sphere.

Introduction

As a key actor in regulating social, economic and political life, the state exerts overarching control over gender and sexuality through mechanisms such as marriage laws, legal provisions against gender-based violence, and reproductive rights. The state also defines gender ideologies, conceptions of femininity and masculinity, and the role of women (Moore, 1998). Against this backdrop, the purpose of this article is to examine how gender has shaped legal reform, and more broadly Kosovo's social and political institutions. By focusing on domestic violence, it asks how law as a form of state power works in Kosovo, and moreover how the law effects gender power relations across public and private domains. It will show that gender has been a medium and a means of neoliberal legalism, constituting the rationality of governance of the international post-war protectorate of the United Nations Mission in Kosovo (UNMIK) as well as upon independence of the Kosovo state. The article draws on women's movement responses to the limits of the law in combating domestic violence and the struggle to transform gender relations of power. It argues that prospects for combatting domestic violence rest on the interplay between formal state interventions and women's civic activism that seek to undo entrenched patriarchal norms in state relations, institutions and everyday life.

The topic of domestic violence in Kosovo, while having stimulated legal reform, institution building, and social policy, has gained little attention in academic scholarship. This article seeks to fill that gap. The relevance of this study lies in its engagement with a set of concepts on gender and state formation, laws related to gender and domestic violence, as well as women's agency against violence in Kosovo. In this article, the legislation on domestic violence is considered for the gendered hegemony of the state's leadership; needless to say, the state is a gendered institution. The state consistently reinforces gender hierarchies instead of challenging them through its various control and regulatory practices.

At the foreground of the issue of domestic violence in the domain of state rationality, the article devotes attention to ideological shifts and dramatic events that have occurred in the recent history of Kosovo. While focusing on the contemporary events in Kosovo and state formation, the article looks at the legacy of socialism, war and post-war reconstruction, international protectorate status and peacekeeping, as well as post-independence institution-building. The analysis provided in this article, therefore, takes advantage of the concept of "the history of the present time", from Michael Foucault, to map out the context and its multiple series of events in an ongoing historical process (Foucault, 1970, p. 320). It is thus a multi-layered analysis of the interaction between the state and the women's movement in Kosovo. Through the prism of the law on domestic violence, the article examines the state as a historical entity, uncertain, and evolving. It also engages women's activism in combating domestic violence. It will show that the laws on domestic violence, just as the totality of policies on gender equality, are doomed to be short-lived unless they are premised on demands of the women's movement for accountability and matched by concomitant cultural changes that undo patriarchal norms, gender stereotyping and tokenism in political representation.

The Gender Agenda in State Systems in Kosovo – Past and Present

While scholarship on the welfare state draws distinctions between West European and former socialist East European states and their regulation of welfare regimes, Susan Gal and Gail Kligman have pointed out similarities between the two:

> "[...] In their ideals at least, the socialist states of East Central Europe were a
> form of welfare state/heavily subsidized foods and rents, full employment, rela-
> tively high wages for workers [...] and the provision of nominally free cheap
> health, education, childcare, maternity benefits, and cultural services would
> have warranted classifying them as welfare state, if these services had in fact

been adequate in quality and quantity, and generally available. The structural
similarities to Western welfare states are striking" (Gal & Kligman, 2000, p. 63).

This applies to socialist Yugoslavia, whose social policy was viewed as egalitarian and emancipatory for women as it promoted gender equality and enabled women to participate in the labour market. Women were given legal rights in terms of marriage and divorce, and the state sought to socialize childcare and domestic tasks to lessen women's double burden. Nonetheless, at the same time the state fostered gender ideologies and resisted any significant changes in the notions of femininity that posited women as being secondary and subordinate to men. Occupational segregation and the sexual division of labour persisted in spite of an ideological commitment to gender equality. Women were expected to perform the dual roles of wage earner and mother. Thus, the trope of motherhood was left untouched as a social and national duty (Iveković & Mostov, 2002).

The wars in the 1990s in the former Yugoslavia and the conflict of 1998–1999 in Kosovo together altered both societal structures and state apparatuses. For a decade Kosovo Albanians organised themselves politically in parallel institutions, establishing a system of political representation, education, health and welfare, and taxation (Clark, 2000). These conditions provided a complex ground for gender inequalities as women were faced with multiple patriarchies and structures of oppression and domination.

The international administration in Kosovo pursued neo-liberal policies of economic restructuring in the post-war period that, upon its independence, were extended by the Kosovo state. The UNMIK protectorate and its neo-liberal policies impacted gender differences on all levels of community and society, as well as in the practices of everyday life. As a political pattern, the neo-liberal rationale fosters the ideology that for each and every problem there ought to be a technological fix (Harvey, 2005, p. 68). In the Kosovo context, these "fixes" have placed emphasis on privatization and minimal state intervention in the market and economy, limited welfare and health protection, a lacking pension system, and neglect of gender issues. Indeed, when UNMIK was set up, the gender question was never seen as important. As early as 2000, this was starkly revealed by a gender audit commissioned by two women's groups, the Urgent Action Fund and the Women's Commission for Refugee Women and Children. The aim of the audit was to identify actors and decision-makers of the "international community" and to enable women's groups and international representatives to devise strategies for gender mainstreaming. As Chris Corrin, the report's author stressed, the "international community" had no intention of mainstreaming gender issues within political policy-making processes (Corrin, 2000).

However, the discourses on gender and gender mainstreaming have been a rhetorical device of the international peacekeeping establishment and Kosovar political elites. Yet, concerns related to gender equality have remained marginal in Kosovo state institutions as sovereignty and territorial integrity dominated the political agenda. Gender has been deployed as a tactic of state-formation. It has also been part of the Kosovo's political discourse on democracy and modernization, in line with Western liberal values. Clare Hemmings has noted the following:

> *"The use of gender equality as a marker of an economic and regulatory modernity marks the subject of gender equality as Western, capitalist, and democratic, and the West capitalism, and democracy themselves as sites to create the possibility of, and reproduce, rather than hinder, gender equality. Critically, they position the objects of gender equality as non-Western or postsocialist, and such contexts, and particularly cultures or economies, as creating and perpetuating traditional gender inequalities not part of the modern world"* (Hemmings, 2011, p. 9).

This applies to Kosovo too, where the enactment of gender policies at the state level serves the modernist and liberal state-building ideologies in Kosovo that require a political identity oriented towards Western values of democracy.

To be sure, there have been some improvements in gender equality. Several laws and state entities have been developed which aim at gender mainstreaming. For example, the Kosovo Constitution, which was ratified on April 9, 2008, guarantees gender equality as a fundamental right (Constitution of the Republic of Kosovo, Article 7.2). In addition, the Convention on the Elimination of all Forms of Discrimination Against Women (CEDAW), the European Constitution on Human Rights, and other international treaties including the Universal Declaration of Human Rights, Convention on the Elimination of All Forms of Racial Discrimination and the Convention on the Rights of the Child, which safeguard equality, are applicable in the constitution and laws in Kosovo (ibid. Article 22). The Kosovo Criminal Code sanctions any form of discrimination and violence on the grounds of one's gender or sexual orientation (Kosovo Criminal Code, 2012).

Moreover, in 2004, the Kosovo Assembly adopted the Law on Gender Equality, which was amended in 2015; it aims to prohibit gender inequality and promotes equality between women and men (Law on Gender Equality 2004; 2015), and the Anti-Discrimination Law to combat all forms of discrimination (Anti-Discrimination Law 2004). In 2010, the law against domestic violence, which criminalizes any form of violence occurring within the domain of the domestic sphere and family relations, was adopted (Law on Protection against Domestic Violence 2010). In 2013 the law against trafficking was passed to combat and prevent human trafficking (Law on Protection and Combatting of Trafficking with Persons and Protection of Victims of Trafficking 2013). Moreover, the electoral laws for national and municipal elections (Electoral Law 2008), require each political party to have to have a gender quota of at least 30% female and at least 30% male candidates on the list. As a result of this rule, women currently occupy more than 30 percent of the seats in the Assembly of Kosovo (Kosovo Agency of Statistics, 2016, p. 4).

Following the adoption of the gender equality law in 2004, a set of state entities were created to promote implementation and monitoring of gender equality laws in Kosovo, commonly referred to as gender equality mechanisms. These mechanisms have included: the Agency for Gender Equality in the Office of the Prime Minister; officers for gender equality within ministries and municipalities; the Parliamentary Committee on Human Rights, Gender Equality, Missing Persons, and Petitions; and the Women's Caucus at the Kosovo Assembly.

Gender-mainstreaming, an issue so current in feminist thinking, raises the question of whether women should work with the state and utilize such mechanisms to improve their conditions or whether they should resist its male-dominated ideology to avoid being co-opted by it. As Shirin Rai has pointed out, the state is an ambiguous terrain, requiring complex negotiation and bargaining by those working within its boundaries, as well as those working from the outside. Gender mechanisms can be effective in advancing women's interests, but only under certain conditions. In most cases, they must include clear access to state resources as well as strong democratic movements to hold state bodies accountable (Rai, 2003, p. 19). This is also salient for the Kosovo context. Despite the gender laws and state institutions to safeguard equality between women and men, many legal challenges and limitations exist that hinder their implementation. This may be partly due to structural constraints in budget allocation, but more often it is due to lack of political will to enact the gender policy as a serious matter. This has resulted, at best, in ad hoc inclusion of gender in policy-making and weak implementation of laws in general. A closer examination of the issue of domestic violence more clearly illuminates the gendered state's performance and the limits of gender mainstreaming in practice.

Domestic Violence: An Expression of Unequal Power Relations

It is, of course, nothing new to say that domestic violence is a fact and that it is regularly occurring. It is closer to every one of us than we may want to acknowledge (Buzawa & Buzawa, 2017, p. 1–3). Violence in relationships between men and women is connected with power. In Kosovo, just as in most societies, social, economic, political and interpersonal power rests in the hands of men. Domestic violence is an expression of power and it disproportionally affects women. It is a means through which people seek control over women, their personhood and sexuality. It is thus a profoundly gendered practice.

Domestic violence can take different forms: physical, sexual, psychological, economic and emotional. It undercuts all societies and cultures. The meaning of domestic violence lies in the context as its various forms are expressed differently in different contexts. To explain domestic violence, one has to relate it to social, cultural or ideological factors, class, gender and sexuality, family dynamics and structures of power, including patriarchy and the state. Attempts to conceptualize gender-based violence should scrutinize not only the social and cultural constructions of gender, of masculinity and femininity, but also the state itself and its gender policies (Moore, 1988; MacKinnon, 1989; Gal & Kligman, 2000).

There is always a risk that stems from the prevailing understanding of domestic violence as a private issue and not worthy of attention. This is especially true in Kosovo; a society caught in major structural deficiencies such as slow economic development and poverty. The societal risks such as lack of employment, job insecurity, and fewer opportunities for upward social mobility may all contribute to violent social exchanges and interactions in the private domain. But as Purma Sen has pointed out, it is wrong simply to portray gender-based violence as an aspect of underdevelopment and of poor societies (Sen, 1999, pp. 65–86). It is rather based on unequal power relations.

In Kosovo, domestic violence is a fact of life. Yet systematic data collection on domestic violence is absent and there are no longitudinal studies on the prevalence of gender-based violence in general, and domestic violence in particular. This renders unknown the real scale of domestic violence. However, two research projects conducted in 2008 and 2015, with a Kosovo representative sample, have archived the incidence, patterns and public perceptions of domestic violence in Kosovo. The data indicate that domestic violence affects more than half of the population in Kosovo (62%) (KWN, 2015, p. 5). Yet an overwhelming majority of those affected by domestic violence are women. Domestic violence, however, is not confined only to women. It is also directed towards children, people with disabilities, the elderly, and non-heteronormative people. The majority of the perpetrators of domestic violence are men (as fathers, husbands or partners) and victims are their wives, partners, and children (ibid., p. 35).

Domestic Violence Law in Kosovo: *De Jure vs. De Facto Gap*

The introduction of domestic violence as a criminal offence in Kosovo legislation was initiated by UNMIK as the ultimate law-making authority in post-war times, and until the first Assembly of Kosovo was established following elections, portrayed as "landmark elections", for self-government in November 2001 (International Crises Group, 2001). The UNMIK Regulation on Protection Against Domestic Violence (UNMIK Regulation No.2003/12) constituted the very first legislation in Kosovo that criminalized acts of domestic violence, addressing the prosecution and punishment of the perpetrators of violence in the family; specifically, it dealt with protection from domestic violence. This regulation was made into law and adopted by the Kosovo Assembly in 2010.

The law against domestic violence not only criminalizes domestic violence, it enlists a number of measures and institutions responsible to act in cases of domestic violence, such as the Kosovo police and Centers for Social Work (CSW). As set out in the law, the following acts conducted in a domestic or family relationship are considered domestic violence: causing bodily injuries; forcing another person into performing a non-consensual sexual act or sexual exploitation; causing the other person to fear for her or his physical, emotional or economic well-being; kidnapping; causing property damage; unlawfully limiting the freedom of movement of another person; forcibly entering the property of the other person; forcibly removing the other person from a common residence; prohibiting the other person from entering or leaving a common residence or engaging in a pattern of conduct with intent to degrade the other person (Law on Against Domestic Violence, 2010, Article 2, 1.2). The law stipulates the issuance of protective orders depending on the acts of domestic violence that have occurred. The violation of a protective order constitutes a criminal offence, the penalty for which is a fine ranging from €200 to €2000, or imprisonment for up to six months (ibid., Article 25).

In addition to the law against domestic violence, there is a program and an action plan to address domestic violence that deals with prevention, protection, rehabilitation, reintegration, and coordination on domestic violence cases (National Strategy on Protection against Domestic Violence and Action Plan 2016–2020). A national coordinator oversees the implementation, monitoring and reporting on the implementation of policies, activities and actions related to the Kosovo strategy to counter domestic violence.

The law and the strategy against domestic violence in Kosovo exist *de jure*, but are far from being *de facto*. The shortage of putting the law into practice have included 'delays in the issuance of protection orders; lenient sentences, poor reasoning of judgments and limited attention to enforcement of protection orders" (KWN, 2009, p. 23–31). This has had grave consequences for many persons and families. Several women have been killed in their own homes, and justice for the families of women victims of domestic violence is yet to be achieved. Moreover, survivors of domestic violence lack social integration, so they also undergo secondary victimization and stigmatization, loss of custody of children, and often have to return to living with the violent partner or spouse. They therefore continue to live with fear, pain and humiliation.

Women who are abused feel ashamed of what happened; this oftentimes can result in a loss of social status and a lack of respect in the family and community. Kosovo continues to value traditional gender roles – for both women and men. As in many other contexts, the culture in Kosovo fosters gender stereotypes. A typology of gender stereotypes in Kosovo is related to *paternalism*, such as the following: women need men to protect them; women are physically weak; girls are weak; boys are strong; women are fragile and need protection. The second relates to prejudices about *competence* – women are for the home; women have less competence and capabilities. The third is *sexist/misogynist*. In the context of violence, the popular myth in Kosovo is that women provoke violence: by not conforming to the family rules or by the way they dress or look, especially in those cases where sexual violence is involved. Hence, in cases of intimate partner domestic violence where women are abused by male perpetrators, it is women who are blamed for the actions of their abusive partner. Effects of victim-blaming are negative and manifold, affecting not only the survivors of domestic violence but also the society at large. Victim-blaming operates as a silencing and policing tool that prevents survivors from seeking justice as it portrays them to be at fault for the violence that has been committed against them (Meyer, 2015).

Moreover, it has been widely documented that existing social services for survivors of domestic violence are less than adequate; including poor coordination of actors and institutions, lack of resources, and a lack of gender awareness among the judges, prosecutors, and social workers (KWN, 2009; 2015). Indeed, social workers and women's non-governmental organizations (NGOs) that run shelters for survivors of domestic violence in Kosovo are crucial actors. Yet the strategies they deploy are not necessarily the same. They stand in opposition because they foster different ideological concepts of gender and equality between women and men, and within the family.

Indeed, the approach social workers in Kosovo adopt with respect to domestic violence is grounded on the family law (Kosovo Family Law, 2004). To be sure, the family law gives power to the social workers and CSW to mediate in divorce cases prior to court proceedings. The evidence from examining practices in social work has indicated that social workers often perceive that their role is to preserve the family through mediation. Hence, social workers tend to overlook violence in family relationships as they strive to maintain the family at any cost. Moreover, social workers tend to miss the link between gender and power, and they are moreover trapped in the ideological construct that does not perceive the family as loci of unequal power relations. This practice contributes to reinforcing the ideal of the traditional family and gender relations that do not impact the patriarchy in the home, society, culture, and law. This clearly constitutes a point of conflict with the approach of the women's shelters that focus, in contrast, on women's agency and autonomy. This departure is partly related to education, but it signifies ideological positions between paternalism on the one hand, and on the other freedom of choice and self-determination that encourage women's autonomy and agency. Yet these two approaches point to the existing social ordering and shifting gender arrangements in Kosovo.

The landscape of domestic violence in practice has remained a field of non-state actors, primarily of women's NGOs. Indeed, it is the women's NGOs that run shelters for survivors of domestic violence in Kosovo. Most shelters were established immediately after the war with the financial support of international donors. They are the only organizations aiding survivors of gender-based violence. Shelters are located in the capital, Prishtina, and other cities: Prizren, Peja, Gjakova, Ferizaj, Gjilan, Mitrovica, and there is a recently opened shelter in the municipality of Novo Brdo. Additionally, there is one shelter run by the Ministry of Labor and Social Welfare for survivors of human trafficking and one run by a woman's NGO, both located in Prishtina. Shelters provide free and safe accomodations, food, basic health care, advice on legal rights and legal representation in court, some education and training tailored to individual needs, as well as individual and group counselling.

The Ministry of Labor and Social Affairs supports the shelters of survivors of domestic violence with up to 50% of the running costs, and the municipalities provide the remaining 50%. Shelters are also expected to fundraise to collect additional funding to provide long-term support and address the reintegration issues of survivors of domestic violence. Yet the funding is far from adequate, and shelters find it difficult to address the needs of survivors of domestic violence and their integration in society. Since their establishment, shelters have been supported by international donors and organizations such as the International Organization for Migration, the United Nations Development Fund, the Swedish Women's organization Kvinna till Kvinna, the United States Embassy, the Norwegian Embassy, the Dutch Embassy, the Finnish Embassy, the Austrian Development Cooperation, the Community Development Fund and Caritas (KWN 2012, p. 53).

Let us now explore women's activism against domestic violence in Kosovo. Women's activism is important in the reinterpretation of women's relationship to the state and the approaches of the state to counter domestic violence.

The Women's Movement in Kosovo and the Issue of Domestic Violence

Today, Kosovo has a dynamic women's movement. It can be defined similarly to other social movements "where women are the major actors and leaders, who make gendered identity claims as the basis for the movement, and who organize explicitly as women" (Knappe & Lange, 2014, p. 364). The Kosovo Women's Network (KWN) is an umbrella organization and driving force of the women's movement in Kosovo. It includes more than one hundred women's organizations and groups across Kosovo, representing women from various ethnic backgrounds. It focuses on the capacity building of women's organizations, politics and decision-making, health, domestic violence and trafficking, and women's economic empowerment (see KWN at http://www.womensnetwork.org).

The history of the development of the women's movement in Kosovo, as in any society, is complex and multi-faceted. In Kosovo, the women's movement emerged in response to the political violence in the 1990s and it expanded rapidly in the post-war period, with many women's groups and organizations, mostly NGOs, responding to the problems and needs of families and communities. As grass roots initiatives operating through *face-to-face* interactions with women and communities, these organizations had first-hand experience with gender issues and inequality. The women's movement adopted "consciousness rising as a method of analysis, mode of organizing, form of practice, and technique of intervention" (MacKinnon,

1989, p. 84) that enabled an increasing self-organization of women. Catherine A. MacKinnon has argued that

> "*Consciousness raising [...] inquiries into an intrinsically social situation, into that mixture of thought and materiality which comprises gender in the broadest sense. It approaches its world through a process that shares its determinations: women's consciousness, not as individual or subjective ideas, but as collective social being.*" *(ibid., pp. 83–84)*

Such a methodology created various forms of mobilization, politics and practices that sought to transform unequal power relations. It has generated an activist culture that stimulates organizing practices ranging from consciousness raising groups, public campaigns and advocacy, protest marches, art, and advocacy in gender equality at the community level. Moreover, this methodology has made possible advocacy for women's rights and gender equality both at the state level and civil society.

As Hank Johnston pointed out, in a general sense, the reason for the increase in the number of advocacy groups is the extension into areas where the state role had been minimal or absent (Johnston, 2011, p. 69). The applicability of Johnston's argument is supported by the Kosovo context, wherein women's agency is to be seen in relation to post-war reconstruction and the lack of state interventions. Women's movement projects have included: psychosocial support and trauma recovery, education, leadership training, support for start-up businesses, and the access to justice. Women's agency has decentralized politics by expanding the notion of democratization to pertain to the domain of gender, intimacy and family. It has challenged the absence of the state and the constraints to make the law work, and also more generally to politics that falls short in terms of "translating coercive power into egalitarian communication" (Giddens, 1992, p. 185).

As an agent that pursues politics by means other than those that are usual and customary, and hence part of contentious politics (Johnston, 2011, p. 1), the Kosovo women's movement has shaped the Kosovo state. The women's movement has pushed for inclusion of gender as an integral part of law, politics and decision-making. Similarly to women's movements globally, the Kosovo women's movement has invested considerably in engaging and state-building politics and practices, such as legal reform and institution building.

Collective Mobilization: The Kosovo Women's Movement Demands to End Violence

The women's movement has been at the forefront of all actions against domestic violence through providing shelters, psycho-social counselling and legal support. It is the KWN that initiated research on domestic violence to contribute to the development of the national strategy and the law against domestic violence. It developed a three-year strategy on gender equality that includes provisions for the prevention of gender-based violence and support for female survivors of violence, women's access to healthcare services, women's political participation and economic empowerment, and the capacity building of networks addressing these issues (Kosovo Women's Strategy 2015–2018).

Thus, the Kosovo women's movement gained insight regarding the prevailing public opinion and beliefs about domestic violence from the research they conducted, as discussed earlier in the text. They took on the task of addressing the needs of those individual women affected by domestic violence in Kosovo. The KWN continued with conducting gender assessments, revealing the shortcomings of the state institutional mechanisms for gender equality. They pushed for changes in that policy and enhanced strategies to support battered women that are not relegated solely to paper but instead active implementation. The Kosovo women's movement was confronted with the limitations of the state on the one hand, along with the prevailing public opinion that supports the view of a home free from state intervention, and where domestic violence, in many respects, is considered a private issue.

Cognizant of the fact that the law as part of state rationality is not achieving the desired socio-cultural transformation, the movement resorted to street protests as a strategy for countering the gendering of the state. On the International Day for the Elimination of Violence against Women and the 16 days of activism against violence against women (see http://www.un.org/en/events/endviolenceday), when the local and global meet to raise public awareness and mobilize for gender justice and social change, the KWN organized a protest march in Prishtina (see Image 1). The protest capitalized on the slogan "say enough to violence against women". The

Image 1: Kosovo Women's Network Marching: Say Enough to Violence Against Women, Source: KWN. Photo used with permission.

Image 2: Staging Protest Against Violence Against Women: No More Excuses, Source: KWN. Photo used with permission.

KWN protest addressed both the state and Kosovo society at large, calling on them to raise their voices against violence against women. Aiming to give voice to the survivors of domestic violence, protestors on another occasion, in a symbolic gesture, placed quotations from women survivors of domestic violence on the fence of the Parliament and other government building (see Image 2).

The protests can be seen as a demand for a freedom of intimacy without physical, emotional or economic fear and coercive power as the basis for a new politics of intimacy and democracy. Thus, women's activism challenges the dynamics of a gendered state in Kosovo. Enhanced women's activism in Kosovo and their focus on violence point to the fact that the advancement of "self-autonomy in the context of pure relationships is rich with implications for democratic practice in the larger community" (Giddens, 1992, p. 195). Women's activism has made it clear that the law, while promising positive changes, requires an active citizenship to question the culture of impunity blurred in the gendered state rationality.

Conclusions

Domestic violence is a fact of life in Kosovo. The rather low level of reporting means that the real scale and forms of violence in the home are unknown and hidden. Having been considered too long a private issue, domestic violence is now punishable by law. Legislation in Kosovo has debunked the myth of the family as an egalitarian site of domestic relationships. Its relevance relies on the fact that it criminalizes any form of violence in intimate or family relationships and for the first time, legally, the abusive person is denied any form of power.

However, domestic violence is far from being recognized as a major social problem in Kosovo. This is telling when looking at the state approaches to domestic violence. The law against domestic violence lacks implementation; the action plan, as well as the state gender equality mechanisms have continuously remained underfunded. This has rendered the state interventions against domestic violence as tactical, strategic and symbolic, which has left women survivors of domestic violence without meaningful support and reintegration into society, education and the labor market.

The women's movement in Kosovo has brought new perspectives on gender relations, politics, governance, and everyday life. To be sure, the movement recognizes the limitations on transforming laws and policies in Kosovo and moreover, translating them into practice. Women's mobilization to resist violence has demonstrated that the law has neither been translated into practice nor has it ended gendered ideologies and stereotypes that stigmatize and devalue women survivors of domestic violence. Moreover, women's activism has confirmed that the law is slow in changing traditional gender regimes. The Kosovo women's movement has insisted on the political character of domestic, familial, and sexual practices departing from traditional accounts that dismiss such questions as non-political and call for egalitarian gender regimes to be realized.

The law against domestic violence has altered the boundary between the private and public as well as politics and intimacy. Nonetheless, for the law to translate into practice it also requires activism that seeks to rearrange both democracy at the state level and in the domain of the family. Taking note of the protests, one can conclude that combating domestic violence is not a utopian project. Its success, however, is contingent upon the interplay between formal state interventions and women's civic activism that addresses structural inequalities and gendered symbolic systems simultaneously. All in all, the vibrant women's movement offers a hopeful glimpse of the future without violence as a precondition for social development and gender justice in Kosovo.

References

Buzawa, S.E. & Buzawa, G.C. (2017). Introduction: The Evolution of Efforts to Combat Domestic Violence. In Buzawa, S.E. and Buzawa, G.C. (eds.) *Global Responses to Domestic Violence* (1–21). Switzerland: Springer International Publishing AG.

Clark, H. (2000). *Civil Resistance in Kosovo*. London and Sterling, Virginia: Pluto Press. Corrin, C. (2000). Gender Audit of Reconstruction Programmes in South Eastern Europe. New York: The Urgent Action Fund and Women's Commission for Refugee Women and Children.1–35.

Foucault, M. (1970). *The Order of Things: An Archaeology of the Human Sciences*. New York: Pantheon Books.

Gal, S. & Kligman, G. (2000). *The Politics of Gender After Socialism*. Princeton, New Jersey: Princeton University Press.

Giddens, A. (1992). *The Transformation of Intimacy: Sexuality, Love & Eroticism in Modern Societies*. Stanford, CA: Stanford University Press.

Harvey, D. (2005). *A brief history of neoliberalism*. Oxford, New York: Oxford University Press.

Hemmings, C. (2011). *Why Stories Matter: The Political Grammar of Feminist Theory*. Durham and London: Duke University Press.

International Crises Group (2001). Kosovo: Landmark Elections. Retrieved from https://www.essex.ac.uk/armedcon/world/europe/south_east_europe/kosovo/KosovoLandmarkElection.pdf.

Iveković, R. & Mostov, J. (2002). *From gender to nation*. Ravenna: Longo.

Johnston, H. (2011). *States and Social Movements*. Cambridge, United Kingdom: Polity Press.

Knappe, H. & Lange, S. (2014). Between whisper and voice: Online women's movement outreach in the UK and Germany. *European Journal of Women's Studies,* 21 (4), 361–381.

Kosovo Agency of Statistics. (2016). Gratë dhe Burrat në Kosovë' [Women and Men in Kosovo]. Retrieved from https://ask.rks-gov.net/media/1705/grate-dhe-burrat-ne-kosove-2011.pdf.

Kosovo Assembly. (2015). Law No. 05/L-020 On Gender Equality. Retrieved from from http://www.assembly-kosova.org/common/docs/ligjet/05-L-020%20a.pdf.

Kosovo Assembly. (2013). Law No. 04/L-218 Law on Prevention and Combating of Trafficking with Persons and Protection of Victims of Trafficking. Retrieved from http://www.kuvendikosoves.org/common/docs/ligjet/Ligji%20per%20parandalimin%20dhe%20luftimin%20e%20trafikimit%20me%20njerez.pdf.

Kosovo Assembly. (2012). Code No. 04/L-082 The Criminal Code of the Republic of Kosovo. Retrieved from http://www.assembly-kosova.org/common/docs/ligjet/Criminal%20Code.pdf .

Kosovo Assembly. (2010). Law No. 03/L-182 On Protection against Domestic Violence. Retrieved from http://www.assembly-kosova.org/common/docs/ligjet/2010-182-eng.pdf.

Kosovo Assembly. (2008). Constitution of the Republic of Kosovo. Retrieved from from https://www.kuvendikosoves.org/common/docs/ligjet/2008_03-L073_en.pdf.

Kosovo Assembly. (2008). Law No. 03/L-073 On General Elections in the Republic of Kosovo, Article 27. Retrieved from https://www.kuvendikosoves.org/common/docs/ligjet/2008_03-L073_en.pdf.

Kosovo Assembly. (2008). Law No. 03/L-072 On Local Elections in the Republic of Kosovo, Article 7. Retrieved from http://www.kuvendikosoves.org/common/docs/ligjet/2008_03-L072_en.pdf.

Kosovo Assembly. (2004). Law No. 2004/2 On Gender Equality in Kosovo. Retrieved from from http://www.kuvendikosoves.org/common/docs/ligjet/2004_2_en.pdf.

Kosovo Assembly. (2004). Law No. 2004/3 The Anti-Discrimination Law. Retrieved from http://www.unmikonline.org/regulations/2004/re2004_32ale04_03.pdf.

Kosovo Assembly. (2004). Law No. 2004/32 Family law of Kosovo. Retrieved from http://www.kuvendikosoves.org/common/docs/ligjet/2004_32_en.pdf.

Kosovo Government. (2016). Strategjia Kombëtare e Republikës së Kosovës për Mbrojtje nga Dhuna në Familje dhe Plani i Veprimit 2016–2020 [National Strategy of the Government of Kosovo on Protection against Domestic Violence and Action Plan 2016–2020]. Retrieved from https://abgj.rks-gov.net/Portals/0/Strategjia%20Komb%C3%ABtare%20e%20RK%20p%C3%ABr%20mbrojtje%20nga%20dhuna%20ne%20familje%202016-2020.pdf.

Kosovo Women's Network. (2015). No More Excuses. An Analysis of Attitudes, Incidence, and Institutional Responses to Domestic Violence in Kosovo. Retrieved from https://www.womensnetwork.org/documents/20151124105025622.pdf.

Kosovo Women's Network. (2015). Kosovo Women's Network Strategy 2015–2018. Retrieved from Kosovo Women's Network. (2012). At What Cost? Budgeting for the Implementation of the Legal Framework against Domestic Violence in Kosovo. Retrieved from http://www.womensnetwork.org/documents/20130405120224756.pdf.

Kosovo Women's Network. (2009). More than Words on Paper: The Response of Justice Provider to Domestic Violence in Kosovo. Retrieved from http://www.womensnetwork.org/documents/20130120165443203.pdf.

Kosovo Women's Network. (2008). No Safe Place: An Assessment on Violence against Women in Kosovo. Retrieved from http://iknowpolitics.org/sites/default/files/nosafeplace_kosovo.pdf.

MacKinnon, A. C. (1989). Toward A Feminist Theory of the State. Cambridge Massachusetts: Harvard University Press.

Meyer, S. (2015). Still blaming the victim of intimate partner violence? Women's narratives of victim desistance and redemption when seeking support. Theoretical Criminology, 20 (1), 75–90.

Moore, H. (1988). Feminism and Anthropology. Cambridge: Polity Press.

Rai, S. (2003). Mainstreaming Gender: Democratizing the State? National Machineries for the Advancement of Women. Manchester: Manchester University Press. Sen, P. (1999). Enhancing Women's Choices in Responding to Domestic Violence in Calcutta: A Comparison of Employment and Education. European Journal of Development Research, 11 (2), 65–86.

UNMIK Regulation No. 2003/12 On Protection against Domestic Violence. Retrieved from http://www.unmikonline.org/regulations/unmikgazette/02english/E2003regs/RE2003_12.pdf.

Arno Heimgartner (University of Graz)

Biographies and Volunteering:
the Distribution of Social Time in the Society

Abstract

The distribution of time forms both biographies and societies. The distinction between work and everyday life does not take the variety of social tasks performed into account. The first part of the article thus deals with the questions of the existing contexts of supportive social work and the criteria for their definition. As meta-categories, family-related work, volunteering, paid work, and work on oneself are described. The individual biographical schema of life can be oriented toward a select, single work form or it can be pluralistic, meaning that the person combines different forms of work. On the level of the society, the coverage of social tasks results from this individual decision, together with existential security, and fairness in the distribution of paid and unpaid work between woman and men. Therefore, the distribution of responsibility for different social support issues among state, private enterprise, civil society, and family is important. The empirical study combines two qualitative methods (n= 50 volunteers, n= 12 experts) and two quantitative surveys (n= 100 volunteers, n= 45 institutional experts). The instruments reveal the different means of entry into volunteering, the dimensions of sense, and the needed resources and competencies. Moreover, the learning effects and the impact on life are presented. As a recent project, attention is paid to the development of a web tool, which offers a social time profile. Everybody can make a comparison to other people and reflect on the allotment of their own time.

Contexts of social work

Although the issue of the distribution of time is essential to biographies, there is uncertainty about the categories in which we distribute our time. The classical divisions between "work" and "leisure" or between "work" and "free time" are becoming increasingly inadequate. Heimgartner and Findenig (2017) and Heimgartner (2018) have therefore developed a list of categories of social contexts over which time is distributed. Five main categories are taken into account (cf. table 1):

a) *Personal growth related work:* So far, little attention has been paid to the question of time for oneself. The rarely used term *personal work* signals that the person needs phases of rejuvenation, self-care and education. Relationships in general can benefit from individuals working on themselves.

b) *Family-related work:* A second block is related to *family-related work*, which has different sub-types (e.g. education and caring for children, caring for one's partner or parents and grandparents, household tasks, etc.).

c) *Volunteering:* A third block of activities is related to *volunteering*, which is usually divided into two forms, formal (organisational) and informal (non-organisational) volunteering.

d) *Paid work:* For the economic wellbeing in our society, forms of *paid work* are essential. There are also various specific forms of work (i.e. depending on the degree of involvement in the social system).

e) *Other forms of work:* In addition, *other forms of work* are considered, e.g. practical training, bartering on a local basis, civil service obligations and compulsory military service.

In order to be able to determine differences and similarities in all the ways of spending time, the set of defining criteria (cf. Table 1) is correspondingly long, e.g. payment, obligation, integration into an organisation, family relationship, etc. The presented list is longer than the usually used defining criteria when only one main category is dealt with, e.g. volunteering is characterised as unpaid, aimed outside the household and voluntary. However, in regard to the complexity and the variety of needed distinctions, the number of defining criteria increases.

Singularistic vs. pluralistic biographies

In view of the multitude of ways one might spend time, we know relatively little about the time use distribution of people over their lifetimes. It is clear that different time uses are prevalent in different phases of life. It is exciting to presume that this is not only the consequence of individual decisions, rather it is also due to a recognition of social conditions and constraints, which leads to different biographical outcomes.

For our context the primary interesting question is whether it is possible to combine family-related work, paid work and volunteering. A biographical makeup combining these three work forms equally is labelled as a pluralistic biography. It differs from a singularistic biographical solution wherein only one form of work dominates, e.g. focusing only on paid work, only volunteering or positioning family-related work in the foreground.

Table 1: Categories of time distribution and defining criteria

Main Categories	Context of time distribution / defining criteria	Payment	Social assurance	Financial support	Obligation – not voluntary	Organisational	Documented units	Household	Family related	Education related	Focus on oneself
Personal time	work on oneself	no	no	no	no	no	no	no	no	no	yes
Family-related work	family-related work: care and raising of children	no	partly	yes	yes	no	no	partly	yes	no	no
	family-related work: taking care of parents	no	partly	possible	partly	no	no	partly	yes	no	no
	family-related work: taking care of partner	no	partly	no	no	no	no	yes	yes	no	no
	family-related work: household	no	partly	no	no	no	no	yes	yes	no	no
	family-related work: relatives	no	no	possible	partly	no	no	no	yes	no	no
Volunteering	informal volunteering	no	no	no	no	no	no	no	no	no	no
	formal volunteering	no	partly	no	no	yes	no	no	no	partly	no
Paid work	side employment	yes	partly	no	no	yes	no	no	no	no	no
	paid work with social security contribution	yes	yes	possible	no	yes	no	no	no	partly	no
	undocumented work	yes	no	no	no	partly	no	no	no	no	no
Other forms of work	exchange work	no	no	no	no	yes	yes	no	no	no	no
	compulsory civil and military service	no	partly	yes	yes	yes	no	no	no	no	no
	volunteer work	no	partly	yes	no	yes	no	no	no	no	no
	practical training	possible	no	no	yes	yes	no	no	no	yes	no

It is interesting to think about the different consequences biographical approaches collectively lead to (cf. Olk, 1992, Jakob, 1993, Hollstein, 2015). What are the effects for the society when some categories of work are encouraged and others are neglected? It is a question about the social support quality of our society and therefore elicits the question of which quality criteria we want to see realised. Security and safety, gender equality, and coverage of social support seem to be central criteria. Whereas security and social support are not easily to quantify and differ individually, the distribution of paid and unpaid work between men and women is clear (Statistik Austria, 2009, Statistisches Bundesamt, 2015). Currently, it can be said that the time spent in unpaid and paid work between women and men is unequally distributed (cf. Table 2). About half of the populace still does more unpaid work than the other half (cf. Funk, 1992, Wessels, 1993, Beher, Liebig & Rauschenbach, 2000).

Table 2: Distribution of paid and unpaid work between women and men (hours per week)

	Statistics Austria (2009) (covering more than 10 years)		Federal Statistical Office Germany (2015) (covering more than 18 years)	
	women	men	women	men
Paid work	19:42	30:42	16:09	25:13
Unpaid work	32:06	17:36	29:29	19:21

Unpaid volunteering activities in Austria are unequally distributed. There are some groups in the society that are more engaged in volunteer efforts than other groups (cf. Chart 1). In particular, it depends on age, rural or urban living, educational level and profession.

State, private enterprise, civil society or family

It is also important to consider the different activities performed by the state, the private sector, the civil society and the family system. Due to the heterogeneity and overlapping of these greater functional systems of the society, differences can only be defined in a goal-oriented manner.

However, it seems obvious to assume that the *private economy,* through its paradigms and structures, features specific services. As often require more cost-intensive face-to-face involvement.

The modes of *civil society* differ from for-profit on the basis of the liberation from monetary dependency. There is often a community-orientated process. In particular, the purpose, the common good and social wellbeing come to the fore. Human problems and needs initiate volunteering, although there is no financial compensation. Domains included in the civil society are disaster relief, culture activities, environment support, religion, social affairs, politics, community affairs, education and sport.

The *state,* with its special financial possibilities, has its own content priorities. It has specific tasks on the agenda; they are dependent on the recognition of problems. In addition, it is mainly material and thus limited in scope.

Finally, a relatively strong, emotional bond characterises the *family.* Moreover, in the family as a primary institution, there is a realisation pressure that is immedi-

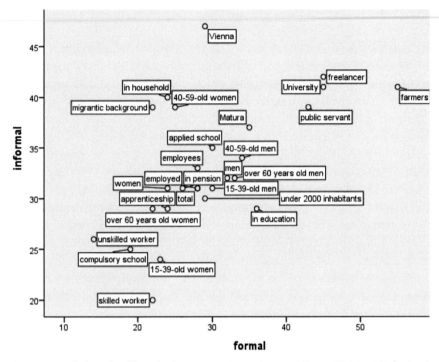

Chart 1: Rates of informal and formal volunteering in Austria (per cent) (Source IFES, 2013, Hofer, 2015)

ate and existential in everyday life. Therefore, they have to take care of such issues in any way they can, depending on the options available, as the family is the last line of support. In contrast, families and individuals carry the risk of excessive isolationism, so the individual and family interests do not necessarily have to encompass the social needs and concerns of the community.

Methods of the study

In a qualitative empirical study, volunteers (n = 50) and expert representatives of institutions (n = 20) distributed throughout Austria were asked about the biographical relevance of volunteering (cf. Heimgartner & Findenig, 2017). Two different guides were used for the interviews, and 13 main dimensions were included in the guide for the interviews with the volunteers: start and course, activities, figures of sense, participation possibilities, experiences, resources and competences, learning processes, value, relations, relationship to the addressees, supervision, limits, potential. After the transcription, a content analysis was performed (MAXQDA supported). These methods are quantitatively supplemented. Two differing surveys involved 100 volunteering persons (age: mean = 48.33; sex: 64.6% female) and 45 institutions, in which volunteers are working.

Results

First, the interviewed persons described their entry into volunteering. The hetero-geneity of the biographies is apparent from the very start. Social contexts, problem contexts and connections to individual personalities have been delineated. Some people note a familial background. The social milieu in which one is living can also lead to the decisive stimulus for commitment. Life changes are in the focus of other life descriptions, e.g. children in school, children moving out or retirement are examples of this content. There is additional access based on the issue or the prob-lem. On the one hand, individually experienced suffering gives the impetus for a wish to change something in society. Frequently, it is the individual need for social contact that triggers a volunteer commitment. This is true for people who are unem-ployed in particular. On the other hand, there is the perceived need or the aware-ness of the problems of other people. It is the desire to improve their life situations. Contexts are also the competencies that make you feel suited to a particular volun-tary activity. Here, references to internships and work are mentioned. Some peo-ple mention that volunteering is part of their life concept. Finally, simple research is also partially responsible for finding a way into volunteering.

Table 3: Entry paths to volunteering

Social context	Problem context	Personality context
family roots	individual problem	individual competencies
children in school, grown-up children, moving out of the children	solve problems	work experiences
social milieu and role models	individual unemployment	educational practice
start of retirement	social inclusion	life concept

Dimensions of sense

Volunteering is considered to be a stronghold of sense (cf. Peglow, 2002). In this study, 17 different meanings are specified. They have been coded into the following categories:

- Characteristics (e.g. social thinking)
- Altruistic sense constructions (e.g. pleasure, deficiencies in the lives of the others)
- Political meaning (e.g. empowering others, political position)
- Conceptual ideas and role-consciousness as a citizen (e.g. duty)
- Cross-life intercultural reconstructions (e.g. "because I have done well in life, I want to give something back")
- Social exchange situations (e.g. feedback, resonance)

- Need-related sense (e.g. change, curiosity, health, happiness)
- Meaningful dimensions of shaping the society (e.g. desire for change)
- Religious approaches (e.g. conveying faith)
- Self-referencing moments (e.g. individual mission)
- Egocentric considerations (e.g. deficits)
- Community-oriented orientation (e.g. positive coexistence)

People interpret their demands and perceptions very individually and integrate them into their life concepts in different ways. For example, the "change in a small world" is indicative of a modest approach that deliberately separates itself from a comprehensive world improvement or even omnipotence. Co-determination can be claimed in the individual organisation, as it refers to the choice of the services or to the freedom to opt out. This gives a feeling of power. An important background for those who volunteer can be a general want to shape and to transform society.

Resources and competencies for volunteering

The attention to the organisational conditions of formal volunteering has increased in the last decade, e.g. volunteering organisations, volunteering centres, education for volunteers, coordination of volunteering (cf. Rosenkranz & Weber, 2002, More-Hollerweger & Heimgartner, 2009, Hofer, 2015).

The results concerning the required resources for engagement are on the contrary surprisingly scarce. This corresponds to a want for spontaneity and independence. As an example of spontaneity, the following example may apply: "I am not a person who thinks a lot about things. I then started to raise money. We sat down there and, as I said, made some contacts, where we asked for cooperation and for financial help. We needed a car and a place. I didn't have anything at all. So nothing. I did not even have a car at the time. But we just needed it to go around and search for sponsors. We then went to the S. and K. and asked everywhere."(AI_10: 30). Engaged people refer to only four dimensions: the time, the space, the materials and an accompanying person(s). Although volunteering is subject to a more complex organisational model, this has to be taken as an inspiration when reflecting on the thresholds for the commitment.

The important competencies are first of all found in the interpersonal area. Emotional lines (e.g. "compassion") and communicative concepts (e.g. "eye-to-eye communicating", "approaching people") are connected with inner values (e.g. "personal optimism", "not the boss"). The communicative concepts are also relevant for organisational cooperation. As a starting point, personal care is mentioned (e.g. "to take care of oneself", "recognise one's own limitations"). In addition, the interviewed persons point out the fact that for some services, formal qualifications are necessary.

Learning and impacts in volunteering

Volunteering is a way of learning (cf. Düx, Prein, Sass & Tully, 2009). In our study, the primary outcome expressed is an emotional state. Volunteering is rewarding through contact with valuable people and institutions. It means the establishment of relationships, sometimes friendships. A further meta-statement is captured with "no stuck thinking". It is thus clear that volunteers are developing through their tasks and relationships. On the other hand, there is the avoidance of isolation and boredom. On a personal level, the establishing of borders is also mentioned. The experience with new settings is also a source of education. They are also regarded as being at the core of positive perception. To be successful, to be accepted, to be praised, to please others – these are important dimensions connected with the settings.

The support of volunteers includes a number of different offers for further training (e.g. meetings, seminars, courses). This continuing education also has a rewarding character. It is also interesting to note that prerequisite training can raise interest in volunteer issues. People appreciate being able to improve and test themselves via further education.

Volunteers talk about a fuller life, and also about friendships that have developed. Their own inclusion is important in everyday life-related situations such as the loneliness of older people, paid unemployment or migration, regardless whether it is regional or transnational migration. A relationship to one's own health is therefore introduced.

The quality of the connections between paid work, formal volunteering, informal volunteering, family-related work, personal work and paid work: conducive, neutral or conflicting

The gender perspective reveals that men in particular have a very cohesive interpretation of paid work and personal time. Women, on the other hand, are more likely to find paid employment conflicts with family-related work (33%), formal volunteering (32%), and also with time for oneself (25%). 41% of the men also confirm that formal volunteering and paid work conflict with each other. Many women, on the other hand, find informal volunteering and family-related work to be compatible (56%). They also say that formal volunteering and family-related work are positively associated (43%). For both sexes, formal volunteering and personal time are beneficial (56% women, 58% men). 18% of women and 11% of men experience a conflict between time for themselves and time for the family.

Table 4: Assessment of the relationship between work categories

Work Category	Women			Men		
	Beneficial	Neutral	Conflicting	Beneficial	Neutral	Conflicting
Formal to informal	46.3%	44.4%	9.3%	46.4%	46.4%	7.1%
Formal to family	43.3%	38.3%	18.3%	44.4%	33.3%	22.2%
Formal to paid	31.5%	37.0%	31.5%	37.0%	22.2%	40.7%
Formal to personal	56.4%	29.1%	14.5%	57.7%	34.6%	7.7%
Informal to family	57.9%	36.8%	5.3%	29.6%	59.3%	11.1%
Informal to paid	24.5%	54.7%	20.8%	19.2%	50.0%	30.8%
Informal to personal	47.4%	38.6%	14.0%	33.3%	63.0%	3.7%
Family to paid	25.9%	40.7%	33.3%	38.5%	38.5%	23.1%
Paid to personal	36.5%	38.5%	25.0%	64.0%	20.0%	16.0%
Family to personal	49.1%	32.7%	18.2%	44.4%	44.4%	11.1%

Connections between formal engagement and family

The explanations of the connections between formal volunteering and the family show a diverse picture (cf. Table 5). In some individual biographies volunteering has a compensatory function that replaces fragile family structures. A conceptual extension has also been found in this direction; some volunteers regard the people that they are helping as their family.

As a challenging management task, the compatibility between family, formal volunteering and paid work is described. It is considered to be a permanent struggle related to making temporal compromises. The long list of tasks in the family can also be an impediment for a voluntary commitment. However, constructive designs are also noted. Task-related, ideals and existence-assisted support of the partner are mentioned.

Criticism is introduced in relation to the lack of financial compensation for unpaid work. A family budget under the control of the partner does not mean having personal retirement savings; separations and divorces can worsen living situations. It is interesting to conclude that the family also benefits from a volunteering family member through that person's increased life satisfaction, learning processes, and positive experiences as a whole.

Table 5: Support, hindrance and compensation of family and volunteering

Support	Hindrance	Compensation
Learned as child	Compatibility as a task	Broken or missing family
Appreciation of the family	Family as hindrance	Family for the clients
Family financial situation		Family problems as starting point
Support of partner		
Family benefits		

Connections of formal volunteering, paid work and informal volunteering

The relationship between volunteering and paid work is difficult to see clearly in several aspects. On the one hand, it is noted that many voluntarily done tasks should be paid; on the other hand, respondents report difficulties on the side of employers to agree on a combination of formal volunteering and paid work. However, there are also positive experiences: improved compatibility and enrichment of life are mentioned. It is reported that some employers support volunteering in three ways; (a) as a volunteer; (b) with time for the volunteers; (c) with understanding and support for the creation of the time-compatibility. A transformation of formal commitment to paid work is also pointed out in some cases.

Informal and the formal engagement sometimes compete temporally, although both are characterised by a similar social style. Increased formal volunteering can thus lead to a decline in informal engagement on an individual basis.

Institutional developments in the years 2000 to 2016

Overall, according to the figures of the institutions involved, the number of volunteers in the social sector increased on average from 2000 to 2016. The percentage of over-60 participants is above the percentage of 24 year olds in the surveyed organisations, however the number of under-24 volunteers is growing gradually. In the interviews, a development of volunteering as pre-employment and post-employment and pre-family event and post-family event is stated. The number of pluralistic biographies, which consider volunteering over the lifetime, sees no changes. A U-curve is also to be found. This means that a higher participation rate among younger and older people and a relative decline in active participation in the family and professional phase is recognised. Participation in social support services has been taken on more by women, according to the surveyed organisations. In the interviews, the desire for more men contributing in the social sector is expressed. It points to the fundamental question of whether a balance of women and men in all sectors is called for, or if different domains in volunteering of women and men are acceptable.

Concerning gender, there is also a discussion about vertical discrimination. Women, relative to their involvement in woman-dominated sectors, still too rarely manage the organisations. It is difficult to say how gender equality can be achieved concerning the imbalance of unpaid and paid work. The starting point is that the acceptance of the taking on of paid work and the related training measures for both sexes have increased. One strategy is to redistribute family responsibilities to the state and to the private sector, so that the time is available for paid work. The evaluation of this shift depends on the extent to which a loss of quality of life results from this shift away from family life. In addition, men could work less on a paid basis and they could be more concerned with unpaid tasks. However, men must have the financial stability to be able to do so. Especially in view of the high level of identification that men have with paid work, this is unlikely – despite all the life quality and equality arguments.

The helping of refugees in recent years is considered to be a decisive phase in the development of voluntary commitment in Austria. In an almost entirely novel way, people have built up their own structures of engagement. With strong support from the new forms of media, and also with a new assumption of responsibility, initiatives have emerged in large numbers, which at least complement the traditional systems and organisational structures.

Such initiatives have shown different speeds of realisation. A threatening development in volunteering in this area is the polarisation about providing assistance. It revives the traditional debate surrounding the acceptance of problems and emergencies. Not all human problems are equally recognised (e.g. poverty, psychological problems and traumatisation) and volunteers in this field are therefore sometimes criticised.

Voluntary commitment is not just for some people (e.g. addressee, client); it also has an integrative relevance for the volunteers themselves (including people with mental problems, people searching for paid work, people with cognitive impairments, people of an advanced age) (cf. Munsch 2003). For all of them, their own volunteering and participation can be used to improve on their education and integration. Accompanying people in volunteering takes on a new quality, the intensity increases, linguistic skills have to be expanded, psychological skills are necessary, permanent support and assistance are to be introduced, all of which may exceed the current available resources.

Strategies to limit non-participation

The following strategies to prevent non-participation are mentioned by the interviewed persons:

a) Information and placement: At the basic level, information and placement work has to be accessed, for example, more volunteer centres and community projects should be established in Austria.

b) Project-oriented offers: The next element is "project-oriented offers", which give people the opportunity to get involved on a short-term basis. This corresponds to greater initial flexibility in terms of time and the trend of people seeking more concrete targets.

c) Financial security: The financial security of people is often mentioned as a basis for participation. Economic instability endangers the readiness of people to engage on a volunteer basis, and this makes the financial status of community members more questionable, reducing overall trust in institutions and the state.

d) Acceptance of time distribution: The acceptance of time distribution is another strategy element. Pluralistic biographies should be socially recognised and implemented. This already begins when children are in school, where the engagement in the community should start, and continues with higher education and paid work, where opportunities for community engagement should be provided.

The role of the state in formal volunteering and the future of volunteering

The state is seen as the authority, which in the end has to attend to the quality of human lives. Minimum support (basic income) is praised as an instrument that allows people to seek involved. For this reason, access thresholds for minimum social security should be kept low for all people in order to avoid absolute poverty and thus evoke secondary problems.

The state is often seen as the one to cover the material costs and the infrastructure for volunteering. Here, the state is actually supplemented by many donations that come from the private economic sector and from individuals. Furthermore, as a task of the state, it is noted that the state should involve the organisations in social planning. The Volunteer Council is a model in this area.

A detachment of the state is perceived in various areas in which the interviewed volunteers perceive serious problems. They ask for the state to share the load when it comes to responsibility. In this way, the people who are involved in the project have the role of discoverers of problems. They argue for an increased quality of life, they demand human rights and sometimes simply humanity. A continuous discourse should therefore be held concerning the decision about which services are paid by the state and which are left to civil society and committed individuals. In this sense, a "repolitisation" (Notz, 2012, 103) should always be reflected in voluntary commitment.

Some of the interviewed persons go beyond the present reality with more utopian perspectives. They demand, for example, complex monetary systems that also take account of the hitherto unpaid work. They are also considering the possibility of a flat-rate basic income.

However, the state itself is also confronted with limitations in terms of what it can do. Engaged people who support this position are fundamentally committed to the system of division into family, civil society, state and private economy. The consequence is that fair participation of all people in these systems should be realised. How such fairness looks and how it can be achieved cannot be stated in the light of the current individualistic design, because the consensus is that volunteering in Austria should remain voluntary, as it is defined by law.

For the future, interviewed persons expect varying developments. The role of volunteering in one's biography in terms of competence and occupation is growing.

In this context, an increase in the importance of training in the area of volunteering is also mentioned. Volunteering will be more often realised as projects – with more structured procedures, time clarifications, and clear goals. Overall, individual responsibility will gain importance for voluntary commitment. It is expected that people will be more independent from the organisation and will work in mediated initiatives based on personal resources. In addition, it is expected that incentive systems will develop; they will shift the voluntary commitment towards exchange. Balancing-measures of various kinds are envisaged (for example transportation services and public services). The model includes time-management systems, which are recorded in a database and handled like currency. On the social side, there is a certain uneasiness concerning demographic change. Older people are increasingly a target group, and potentially an active group. Refugee movement is another striking aspect of society. In this context, it is important to see migrants as potential volunteers, to address and encourage them, and to set up structures in such a way that they take care of the commitment of all groups of people. A change in the regional economy is also expected – with a stronger rise in local community structures (cf. Klöck, 1998, Elsen, 2007). The acceleration of human processes is also worth mentioning. Here, volunteering may play an important role as a perceptible and meaningful use of time.

In a further project, we look at the question of how much time people spend on paid work, formal and informal volunteering, family-related work and on personal work. In doing so, we are developing an electronic tool that enables people to measure their time budgets. The social time profile of the users displays an immediate comparison to other people – like a time footprint. Based on this, the possibility for comparison and reflection is created. Impulses for the optimal management of time should be given and developments for individual social engagement should be stimulated. Further tasks are the stability and distribution of the electronic tool, which should stimulate the discussion about time.

References

Beher, K., Liebig, R. & Rauschenbach, Th. (2000). Strukturwandel des Ehrenamts. Gemeinwohlorientierung im Modernisierungsprozeß. Weinheim und München: Juventa.

Düx, W., Prein, G., Sass, E. & Tully, C. J. (Hrsg.) (2009). Kompetenzenerwerb im freiwilligen Engagement. Eine empirische Studie zum informellen Lernen im Jugendalter. 2. Auflage. Wiesbaden: VS Verlag für Sozialwissenschaften.

Elsen, S., Müller, W. C., Lorenz, W., Staub-Bernasconi, S. & Tschanen-Hauser, A. (2007). Gemeinwesenentwicklung und lokale Ökonomie. Neu-Ulm: AG SPAK Bücher.

Funk, H. (1992). Das weibliche Ehrenamt im Patriarchat. In: Müller, S. & Rauschenbach, Th. (Hrsg.): Das soziale Ehrenamt. Nützliche Arbeit zum Nulltarif (pp. 119–126). Weinheim & München: Juventa.

Heimgartner, A. & Findenig, I. (2017). Biografien und freiwilliges Engagement. Herausgegeben vom Bundesministerium für Arbeit, Soziales und Konsumentenschutz. Wien.

Heimgartner, A. (2018). Arbeitskontexte und ihr Verhältnis zur Relevanzarbeit. In: Muckenhuber, J., Hödl, J. & Griesbacher, M. (Hrsg.): Normalarbeit. Nur Vergangenheit oder auch Zukunft (pp. 273–288). Bielefeld: Transcript.

Hofer, B. (2015). Bericht zur Lage und zu den Perspektiven des freiwilligen Engagements in Österreich. 2. Freiwilligenbericht. Hrsg. vom Bundesministerium für Arbeit, Soziales und Konsumentenschutz. Wien.

Hollstein, B. (2015). Ehrenamt verstehen: Eine handlungstheoretische Analyse: Frankfurt/M.: Campus.

IFES – Institut für empirische Sozialforschung (2013). Freiwilliges Engagement in Österreich. Bundesweite Bevölkerungsbefragung 2012. Hrsg. vom Bundesministerium für Arbeit, Soziales und Konsumentenschutz. Wien.

Jakob, G. (1993). Zwischen Dienst und Selbstbezug. Opladen: Leske + Budrich.

Klöck, T. (1998). Solidarische Ökonomie und Empowerment. Gemeinwesenarbeit Jahrbuch 6. Neu-Ulm: AG SPAK Bücher – M 133.

More-Hollerweger, E. & Heimgartner, A. (2009). 1. Bericht zum freiwilligen Engagement in Österreich. Hrsg. vom Bundesministerium für Arbeit, Soziales und Konsumentenschutz. Wien.

Munsch, Ch. (2003). Sozial Benachteiligte engagieren sich doch. Über lokales Engagement und soziale Ausgrenzung und die Schwierigkeiten der Gemeinwesenarbeit. Weinheim & München: Juventa.

Notz, G. (2012). „Freiwilligendienste" für alle. Von der ehrenamtlichen Tätigkeit zur Prekarisierung der „freiwilligen" Arbeit. Neu-Ulm: AG SPAK Bücher.

Olk, Th. (1992). Zwischen Hausarbeit und Beruf. Ehrenamtliches Engagement in der aktuellen sozialpolitischen Diskussion. In: Müller, S. & Rauschenbach, Th. (Hrsg.): Das soziale Ehrenamt. Nützliche Arbeit zum Nulltarif (pp. 19–36). Weinheim & München: Juventa.

Peglow, M. (2002). Das neue Ehrenamt. Erwartungen und Konsequenzen für die soziale Arbeit. Marburg: Tectum Verlag.

Rosenkranz, D. & Weber, A. (2002). Freiwilligenarbeit. Einführung in das Management von Ehrenamtlichen in der Sozialen Arbeit. Weinheim & München: Juventa.

Statistik Austria (Hrsg.) (2009). Zeitverwendung 2008/09. Ein Überblick über geschlechtsspezifische Unterschiede. Wien.

Statistisches Bundesamt (Hrsg.) (2015). Wie die Zeit vergeht. Ergebnisse zur Zeitverwendung in Deutschland 2012/13. Wiesbaden.

Wessels, Ch. (1993). Das soziale Engagement im Modernisierungsprozeß. Chancen und Risiken des Einsatzes beruflich qualifizierter Frauen. Pfaffenweiler: Centaurus Verlag.

Alma Pezerović (Center For Missing and Exploited Children), Jane McPherson (University of Georgia) and Marina Milić Babić (University of Zagreb)

Hearing the Voices of Refugee Parents: How Do They Evaluate the Quality of Humanitarian Assistance in Bulgaria?

Abstract

The current refugee crisis in Europe is a humanitarian disaster that requires our immediate attention. The number of individuals seeking international protection because of war, violence, and persecution experienced in their countries of origin has increased exponentially in the last few decades. The aim of this research is to focus on the experiences of refugee parents who have been resettled in Bulgaria, a host country that has been criticised for its poor treatment of refugees, as well as for the inadequate protection it provides to those who have been granted asylum in the country. This qualitative research study, which questions refugees about the quality of humanitarian assistance and support that they and their families receive, was conducted in 2016. As this study reveals, parents report that refugee families lack psychosocial as well as practical assistance. Additionally, refugee parents report a lack of goodwill from those Bulgarian authorities whose job it is to provide such support. This study explores multiple challenges and concerns regarding humanitarian assistance provided to refugee families in Bulgaria, and suggests the need for improved professional support and the implementation of psychosocial interventions. The authors also emphasize the need for Bulgarian authorities to act in accordance with international and national law with regard to humanitarian assistance.

Introduction

A humanitarian crisis, however it is triggered by different events and processes, will always dislocate families and create certain predictable needs – for example, for shelter, food, education, employment, and community – regardless of the nature of the event or the reason(s) for its occurrence (Martin, Weerasinghe & Taylor, 2014). Conflicts and insecurity predictably stimulate greater numbers of refugees to leave their home countries in search of secure places to live (The Home Affairs Committee, 2016). Globally, the number of migrants – that is, individuals living outside the borders of their natal countries – surpassed 251 million in 2015, and the number continues to rise (Migration and Remittances Factbook, 2016).

In 2016, 347,000 new refugees and migrants arrived in Europe, and, in 2017, 103,175 migrants and refugees had entered Europe before the year was half over (Overseas Development Institute, 2015; IOM, 2017). These new arrivals joined more than one million refugees and migrants who had successfully made the arduous journey across the Mediterranean in 2015. This population surge is the largest and most challenging that Europe has faced since the Second World War. As has been widely reported, the number of migrants who arrived in 2015 and 2016 severely taxed the capacity of European nations to absorb their numbers and provide basic services. The resultant burden on public services has also become a highly sensitive political issue, generating intense debate about migration and aggravating preexisting weaknesses in immigration systems across Europe (Overseas Development Institute, 2015).

Many of the migrants who complete the dangerous Mediterranean crossing are entitled to international protection as they are fleeing war, violence and persecution in their countries of origin. In 2016, almost 60 percent of European arrivals were from the world's top 10 refugee-producing countries, coming chiefly from the Syrian Arab Republic (Syria), Afghanistan, and Iraq (UNHCR, 2016a).

The Refugee Crisis in Bulgaria

Bulgaria is one of many European countries that has been challenged by the refugee crisis. Although the Bulgarian Constitution guarantees the rights to freedom of movement and choice of residence within the country's territory and outside its borders, Bulgaria has been accused of restricting the entry of refugees by limiting applicants' access to the asylum process within its territory and also enforcing inappropriate and inhumane detention policies (Hajdinak, 2011; UNHCR, 2016a). In 2016, Bulgaria received 19,418 asylum claims for review, but granted asylum (also known as refugee status or subsidiary protection) to only 1351 people. Similarly, in 2015, with 20,391 asylum applications, Bulgaria granted refugee status or subsidiary protection to only 5597 people. Also, in 2016 Bulgaria had 2,772 asylum applications submitted by unaccompanied children (AIDA, 2016).

Although the UNHCR has demanded that Bulgaria implement the protectionsensitive entry system in compliance with international standards for humanitarian programs, there continue to be credible reports of refugees experiencing intimidation, physical abuse, and hindrance of entry at the Bulgarian border (Roberts, 2016). International law does not recognize "illegal entry" into a country in the context of asylum seekers and refugees, and although the provisions of the Geneva Convention, duly ratified by Bulgaria, state that refugees may not be sanctioned for fleeing countries where their lives were in danger, Bulgaria has been found to ignore these rules and principles (Ilareva, 2016). Moreover, Bulgaria is continually called out for instances of brutal and inhuman treatment of refugees at its borders, as well as for inadequate protection of refugees who have been granted asylum in the country (Gómez de Larrain, 2016).

Bulgarian law explicitly states that refugee children whose parents have filed asylum applications are guaranteed access to education. This provision not only warrants access to free education in public schools, but it also offers opportunities for schooling in line with the rules and the conditions that apply to all Bulgarian children (AIDA, 2015). Still, most refugee children are denied access to school in Bulgaria due to their inability to pass a Bulgarian language test. Their lack of language proficiency is a direct result of the government's failure to provide appropriate instruction. Responding to this gap in government services, CARITAS, an NGO, has taken over second language instruction for refugees in 2014 (UNHCR, 2014).

The Importance of Formal Support in the Context of Family Stress and Trauma

Refugee families face many challenges before arriving in their new host countries. They have experienced life in a conflict zone and survived often-harrowing journeys before arriving in a new country where they must start their lives again. Many refugees have experienced physical, sexual, and/or psychosocial trauma, lost their homes, and been separated temporarily or permanently from family members. Beyond these initial losses, they are now faced with adapting to a new culture, a new language, a new climate, and a new way of life (Mock, 1998; Kamya, 2004). Relationships with loved ones as well as the ability to form new relationships with others are affected, and entire families can experience the primary effects of mass trauma. Refugees, therefore, are at a high risk for developing mental health problems; although some individuals are more vulnerable to stress than others, no one is immune to suffering in such extreme situations (Walsh, 2007; Bäärnhielm et al., 2014). It is crucial to provide organized and professional mental health services and social supports for refugees upon arrival. Formal, professional support can help in overcoming barriers in the refugees' integration process as well as promote trust that others will be there for them when needed. Such support can reduce feelings of insecurity, helplessness, and meaninglessness, and even exert a positive influence on the mental and physical health of refugees (Walsh, 2007; Stewart et al., 2010; Watson, Pichler, & Wallace, 2010). In refugee populations, the perception that support will be available can alleviate the fear of failure and danger (Sarafino, 2002; Sarason & Sarason, 2009). Balter (2002) suggests that formal support is also a protective factor for parents and their children, and that parents who receive sufficient support from social networks have the least chance of experiencing unfortunate events in their parenting (Horton & Wallander, 2001).

In summary, the existence of social and professional support generates a sense of well-being, produces beneficial effects on the mental health of parents (resulting in their ability to provide better parenting), contributes to personal well-being, and alleviates the negative effects of socioeconomic hardships (Bornstein, 2002; Hampton, 2001; Watson, Pichler, & Wallace, 2010). Previous research shows that social support significantly contributes to the mental health and well-being of parents and also promotes positive parenting (Bornstein, 2002). Parents who perceive psychosocial support in their communities show higher levels of life satisfaction compared to parents who lack that support (Hampton, 2001). Refugees find that a supportive environment alleviates loneliness and despair, while inadequate support both negatively affects their health and reduces their access to health care services (Stewart et al., 2010). Several studies on refugees support the interconnectedness of psychosocial support and post-traumatic stress disorder, in particular by identifying poor psychosocial support as a predictor of PTSD (Milenković et al., 2010; Nelson et al., 2004).

The UNHCR emphasizes that formal support in the form of access to education is absolutely crucial to giving a child a sense that life is (or is returning to) 'normal'. For refugee children, education can also foster social cohesion, address psychosocial needs, and offer a stable and safe environment, and this is especially true for children at risk of abuse, for those who have experienced sexual or gender-based violence, and for those who are reintegrating after forced recruitment (UNHCR, 2016c; Skovdal & Campbell, 2015). Schools also play an important role in empowering children to seek help, and at the same time, in building their own strategies to help themselves (UNHCR, 2016c). Conversely, not enrolling promptly in school puts refugee children at increased risk of permanently withdrawing from any form of schooling. In spite of the importance of school in their lives, only 50 percent of refugee children have access to primary education, and refugee children are five times more likely to be out of school than their non-refugee peers (UNHCR, 2016c). The situation is even more dire for refugee adolescents: compared to 84% of children in the general population, only 22% of adolescent refugees attend high school programs, and only 1% of refugees attend universities (UNHCR, 2016c).

Methodology

Research aim

The aim of this research is to examine refugee parents' experiences in seeking and receiving mental health care, social services, and other professional support for themselves and for their families in Bulgaria. In line with the research aim, the following **research questions** were defined:

1. How do parents describe their experiences with receiving professional support services in Bulgaria?

2. What are the key issues and concerns identified by refugee parents with regard to receiving formal support in Bulgaria?

Study design

Qualitative interviews were chosen as the best method for this study because the authors seek to understand the experiences of receiving humanitarian assistance from the perspective of those who are actually receiving that aid, and the strength of qualitative research is its ability to capture participants' lived experiences. Interviews provide information about the "human" side of an issue – that is, the "often contradictory behaviors, beliefs, opinions, emotions, and relationships of individuals" (Mack et al., 2005, p. 1). Qualitative approaches, which privilege the voices of research participants, are considered especially appropriate for sensitive topics such as exile, trauma, and the refugee experience.

Recruitment, data collection and analysis procedures

Study participants were recruited from among Arabic-speaking refugees living in Sofia (Bulgaria's capital city) or in Harmanli, Bulgaria (a city close to the Turkish border) during the spring of 2016. Refugee parents who had migrated with at least one child and had been living in Bulgaria for a minimum of 6 weeks were recruited for the study. Potential participants were excluded from the study who (1) had not migrated with at least one child, (2) had not been living in Bulgaria for 6 weeks, and (3) were not native Arabic speakers. Refugees residing in the camp where the first author of this research was based were also excluded in order to eliminate the risk of coercion. Additionally, one mother was removed from the sample because she expressed that the interview process itself was too traumatizing for her.

Participants gave oral consent for the interviews to be conducted and audio-recorded after the study procedures and goals were fully explained to them. Data was collected using individual, semi-structured interviews, and participants were asked the same twelve, open-ended questions focusing on their experiences as refugees in Bulgaria. Each participant was allowed to tell his or her particular story, highlighting points of importance that were relevant to their individual experiences. Participants were also given the option to skip any question or to withdraw from the interview at any point. All interviews were conducted in English and Arabic, specifically by the first author of this paper with the assistance of trained Arabic-language interpreters. Prior to the interviews, the interpreters were trained in research ethics and were counselled on how to handle participant distress. The interviews were completed in approximately 45 minutes and were conducted in the refugee camps where participants were living or in the office of CARITAS, a non-governmental agency providing refugee assistance services in Sofia, Bulgaria.

Participants were guaranteed anonymity and the confidentiality in terms of the information they were providing, and those who expressed interest in the research results shared their e-mail addresses with the interviewer, and this article will be shared with them. After the interviews, the recordings of the interviews were transcribed. Participants' names were eliminated from the transcribed data, and each interview was given an alphanumeric identifier: fathers' interviews were labeled as F1, F2, F3, F4, and F5; mothers' interviews were identified by M1, M2, and M3. Content analysis, a method for systematically classifying data, coding themes, and identifying patterns, was used to analyze the interview transcripts (Zhang & Wildemuth, 2005). Qualitative content analysis allows researchers to understand social reality in a subjective but scientific manner. Each of the 12 research questions was analyzed separately, and researchers returned iteratively to the original research questions as they coded each question and each interview for themes.

Findings

Eight individuals – 5 men and 3 women – were recruited to participate in the study. Participants ranged in age from 21 to 53. They were all married or widowed, and they were all parents. All study participants had fled their countries of origin and/or resettlement due to violence. The four Syrian participants fled the Syrian war; three participants left Iraq due to threats of violence from the Islamic State of Iraq and the Levant (ISIL); and one participant migrated initially from Palestine to Syria and later to Bulgaria from Syria because of the Syrian civil war. All participants were seeking or had received asylum in Bulgaria, and they had been in Bulgaria for periods ranging from 6 weeks to just over 2 years. Collectively, the interview participants were parents of 22 children ranging in age from infancy to adulthood.

Content analysis of the interview data revealed three major themes, which will be addressed here in order. In this sample refugee parents resettled in Bulgaria reported on their (1) psychosocial support; (2) informational support; and (3) practical support in the educational system. In all cases, refugee parents reported the support they received to be inadequate to their needs, as is reported below.

Psychosocial support

Participants in this study frequently lamented their lack of psychosocial support. When asked who supported or assisted the family in difficult situations, one mother responded:

M1, mother of three: "No one ... before we talked a lot with our families, but now connections are very bad, and we cannot talk much and often."

Interviewer: "And when you want to talk with someone ... with whom do you talk?"

Mother of three: "No one ... there is no one with whom I could talk."

For refugees, social support represents a mechanism for coping with the stress and the challenges of displacement. The support of a local community can produce a beneficial influence on mental health, whereas the lack of support has an adverse effect (Palinkas et al., 2003; Lindencrona, Ekblad, & Hauff, 2008; Kirmayer et al., 2012). A Syrian father addressed the issue of social isolation this way:

F4, father of one: "I am the oldest son in my family, so I am taking care of myself."

Interviewer: "And when you feel bad, who helps you?"

F4, father of one: "No one, I am totally on my own … and these days no one is helping us because the situation is bad for everyone."

Another participant claimed that she is relying only on herself:

Interviewer: "Who supports you in hard times? Who would you ask for an advice or help?"

M3, mother of two: "My self … I rely on myself … I work very hard … illegally … because you don't have right to work … so I rely on myself … I had gold, I sold all of my gold … and my work is very hard so I don't have free time for myself …"

With regard to insufficient psychosocial support, the participants in this study also indicated difficulties in coping with their present life circumstances. Only one participant reported that he received support from someone outside his family circle, which helped him cope with current life circumstances. In his case, the support came from a psychologist who worked in one of the camps in Bulgaria. F3, father of one: "Here, there is a doctor, a psychologist, I see her. Whatever is on my chest, I go and see her, and she lets me talk … she gives me a chance to say it. It is all the help I get …"

The stress of migration is often exacerbated by abrupt changes in both language and culture, and the social context of these stressors is frequently as significant as the stressors themselves (Brough, et al., 2003). In this research, two fathers spoke of feeling inadequate to manage their current life difficulties, and in turn, they felt powerless and oppressed by this burden. Here is how the situation is described by our participants: F5, father of five: "So far, I was working all my life … here I have nothing … each child wants different things, and sometimes I want to cry … but I say, now it is not the time … and maybe we live to a happy day and get another chance, but not now. You must wait … sometimes when I see the faces of my children … I cannot look at them like that … sometimes when I remember everything, I want to cry, but I do not want to cry in front of my family." F2, father of four: "It is very hard … it is very, very hard … sometimes I just sit inside [the room]. I do not want to go outside. I do not want to hear anyone's problems … I just want to stay here because, you know, I am my own person as well."

Refugees and migrants often feel overwhelmed, confused and sad. They suffer from high levels of fear and anxiety, emotional outbursts of anger and sorrow, as well as nightmares and other sleeping disorders (UNHCR, IOM, & MHPSS, 2015). Furthermore, refugees who experience difficulties in coping with daily life often feel socially isolated and less motivated to (1) engage in activities that would facilitate their integration; (2) establish relationships with the local community; or (3) to engage in language acquisition (Phillimore, 2011). Different forms of social support are central to this effect as are the high-quality public services that may offset the disadvantageous effects of socioeconomic hardships and advance the subjective well-being of refugees (Watson, Pichler, & Wallace, 2010).

Informational support

Informational support refers to the provision of necessary information for applying for asylum, settling into a new community, and resolving problems or difficulties (Cohen, 2004). Informational support is very important because it is the knowledge that can assist a person with problem solving during a time of stress (Peterson & Bredow, 2009). Examples of informational support include advice, guidance, suggestions, directives, and other factual information. The participants in this research study all spoke of the insufficient informational support that had been provided to them.

> F5, father of five: "I don't know anything about school here … but my daughter is 16 years old, she must go to school. When I asked a social worker why she is not going to school, she said: "No, she can't go to school" … why not? I don't know, no one is saying anything to me … I don't understand …"

Moreover, informational support reduces refugees' uncertainty and confusion by explaining culturally-appropriate behaviors in the host country, and, therefore, helps the refugees develop sensitivity towards cultural norms (Caligiuri & Lazarova, 2003). Participants complained about their misunderstanding of Bulgarian culture.

> M3, mother of two: "I don't understand it here … in schools in my country teachers are very strict and children don't have such a freedom … in Bulgaria they have more freedom and teachers don't have any right to say anything to them … when I saw my daughter going to school without a school bag and I went to meet a teacher and she said that there is no need for her to do a homework because she is very smart … it is enough what she is studying here … I don't like the system of education … the children have too much freedom … at

any time they don't want to go to school there is a easy way not to go to school ... it is easy to get some documents that they are sick ... they are running away from the school ... I don't like that way ... they have to be more strict because this is a future of the children ..."

Moreover, refugees who participated in this study asserted that they were given neither explanation for decisions made about their asylum process nor any understanding of what the impact of those decisions would be:

M3, mother of two: "Oh, what if I get a negative answer [to my asylum application]? Then I will have to return to my country ... and if I go back to my country, I may be killed and my children may be killed."

F1, father of two: "I don't know what will happen ... how long I will stay here, I don't know ... 3 months, 6 months? I don't know."

Many parents decide to leave their home countries primarily because of concerns over the safety of their children. For them it is crucial to gain some information about their future, especially regarding the asylum process (Hynie, Guruge, & Shakya, 2012). Information helps reduce the stress associated with applying for and being accepted as a refugee and assists refugees in mentally preparing for life in a new country. Concrete and accurate information about a destination and about what to expect in terms of housing, employment, and education is a significant type of formal support and can mitigate the impact of traumatic experiences (Simic, Morton, & Mawani, 2003). One father spoke of the inadequacy of his family's housing situation and his confusion over what will happen for his family in the future:

F5, father of five: "We need to live ... with my family ... we need to rest. Now we are in the room, 3.5 [meters] by 4 [meters], and 7 people are living in this room ... why? If they cannot give a normal life to us, why did they ask for us to come to Bulgaria? Why is here so different? It's also European country ... here is not good for the refugees."

Lack of information can also cause frustration and vulnerability, especially when refugee parents have a strong sense of responsibility for their children, their relatives and the family members who stayed in their home countries and who may still be in danger (Stewart et al., 2010; Bala, Mooren, & Kramer, 2014). Research also suggests that refugees lack information on the larger EU asylum process, and the requirement that they seek asylum in one of the countries on the route to the country where they had intended settle (Thielemann, 2004; Gómez de Larrain, 2016).

Practical support in the educational system

In the interviews for this study, respondents reported anger and frustration at the exclusion of their children from schools.

> *F5, father of five: "I came here to the camp and said to the people who are working here that my children needed to go to school, but no one did anything. Last time, I spoke with a woman working here, a social worker, and asked her why my children were not going to school … I do not want them to stay in the room. She said she would try … but no one came."*

Previous research in Bulgaria has documented refugee parents' frustration over denied educational opportunities for their children, with some parents reporting their children were excluded from school for as long as three years (Maine, Rico-Martinez, & Kalaydzihieva, 2014). Parents also complained about children being placed in school settings that did not correspond to their age groups, therefore disrupting their peer socialization (Maine, Rico-Martinez, & Kalaydzihieva, 2014). One of the mothers who participated in this research study expressed her dissatisfaction with the lack of schooling for her children: M2, mother of three: "Because of the war in Syria, they could not go to school there … then they could not go to school on our journey to come here, now also they cannot go to school here because we need to see first how our asylum request would be solved … so now we have to wait for asylum to have rights and to see what would happen later … I do not know now what will happen … I hope they will go to school."
Another participant said:

> *M3, mother of two: "I got some support … I used that money and decided to pay for the teacher to teach my daughter Bulgarian language in order to enroll my daughter at school."*

There are no preparatory classes in Bulgaria that facilitate access to the national system of education, nor to the specialized programs that offer tailored support to refugee children with disabilities (AIDA, 2015). One participant in this study confirmed that her son attended university in their country of origin, Syria; however, upon arrival in Bulgaria, he was obliged to seek employment due to their poor financial situation and insufficient support from the state. Other participants equally stressed the need for education and regular school attendance: F3, father of one: "I see it like … Bulgaria is in Europe, and it should do everything for the kids, especially for the kids without parents. We are in Europe. We are not in Afghanistan, or Iraq or Syria … I have been here in this camp for three months … the UK government asked me if the children were going to school here in Bulgaria … I said they were not … they asked why not. I replied that they should not ask me, they should ask the government here ... it is not up to me ... I want the kids to go to school, a Bulgarian school, a normal school ... the government says no, to stay in the camp. They are not allowed to go to school."

Another father reported a similar inability to send his children to school.

F5, father of five: "I don't know anything about school here. When I decided to leave Iraq I decided to go far away from my country ... so we left to Finland ... the Finish Red Cross came to my house and sent my children to school, and here in Bulgaria no one does anything. My children are not going to school."

Regular school attendance is particularly beneficial to children recovering from traumatic experiences. Above all, it offers children a sense of normalcy by providing support for psychological healing and recovery from traumatic events through structured activities in a safe place in which they can acquire new skills and learn about conflict resolution, gender equality, and disease prevention. Schooling equally protects marginalized groups, in particular the groups who are at higher risk of exploitation and precarious work conditions (Sinclair, 2007). According to the Migrant Integration Policy Index (MIPEX) 2011, Bulgaria provided the second worst services in the area of refugee education in a ranking of 31 assessed countries. Bulgaria fulfilled only 15% of the international standards in the area of migrant education (Brown & Krasteva, 2013). In light of these facts, the government priorities in all countries should improve inclusion of refugee children in national educational systems and provide multi-annual educational strategies. Education offers refugees a positive orientation toward their future prospects, both in the receiving country and in their home country upon their return (UNHCR, 2016c).

Conclusion

This paper presents the results of a small, qualitative study that asks refugee parents to reflect on and assess the support they have received as they have applied for (and in some cases received) asylum in Bulgaria. The refugee parents in this study commonly report receiving insufficient or no access to formal educational, informational, and psychosocial support in their Bulgarian host country. Additionally, they expressed concern about a perceived lack of goodwill from the Bulgarian authorities to provide the support needed. Indeed, these participants identified insufficient support from public authorities as one of the biggest challenges they face in Bulgaria. According to these interviews, the lack of governmental support causes anxiety, anger and frustration for parents and creates additional difficulties for them as they seek to integrate into Bulgarian society and cope with their present life circumstances. This lack of available support services together with their personal anxieties over the future prospects of their children represent the key factors of stress for refugee parents, as reported in this study. Refugees who lack formal support stated that they feel less motivated to engage in activities that would facilitate their own integration into Bulgarian society, and that this served to heighten their sense of social isolation. Further investigation is needed to understand what is happening with these isolated refugee families in Bulgaria. Certainly, the findings of this study support the need for increased efforts to reach out to them. These findings suggest the need for continuous professional support and the implementation of psychosocial interventions to help refugee families cope with the stress and the challenges of displacement. Importantly, refugee parents expressed anger and frustration over denied opportunities for their children in the Bulgarian educational system. It is thus equally important to conduct further investigation into the resulting outcomes for children who have been excluded from the educational system for longer periods of time. Targeted educational interventions are critically needed for this group of vulnerable youth, who are currently out of school. Also, there is a need to identify responsible professionals who are dedicated to supporting children once they are involved in the Bulgarian educational system. This research has demonstrated some of the many challenges and issues faced by refugee parents in Bulgaria, as well as the inadequate response to their humanitarian concerns from the Bulgarian authorities. This study calls on the government of Bulgaria – and the governments of all host countries – to provide support and protection for refugee families – both parents and children – who have experienced traumatic events and exile from their countries of origin. There is a strong need for Bulgarian authorities to act responsibly in accordance with international and national law.

Limitations

The principal limitation of this study is the small sample size. Recruitment for this study was complicated by the fact that many refugee parents were concerned that participation in the study might negatively affect their asylum applications, and therefore they chose not to participate. Potential participants expressed the fear that "talking about what is not good" could affect the Bulgarian government's decision on their individual asylum petitions, and this was the reason they gave for refusing to participate in the research. Therefore, we are extremely grateful to the eight parents who agreed to participate, and we see their voices as particularly valuable. Future studies should certainly aim for larger and more varied samples of refugee parents.

A second limitation is that several of our interviews were accomplished using a translator, who translated from Arabic to English. It is possible that in his role as bridge between the researcher and participants, he also exerted some influence on the participants' responses. In order to minimize this risk, the research team trained translators in advance. Training focused on methods for conducting and translating interviews, stressed the importance of confidentiality, and also prepared the translators for their own potential emotional reactions to the participants' traumatic stories. Once the research began, there was time for briefing/debriefing the translator both before and after the interview, in order to clarify ambiguities in the discussion and to assess the translator's need to support.

The pool of potential research participants was reduced by our inability to find translators for the Farsi, Pashto and Kurdish languages. The lack of translators required that our research be limited to parents from Arabic-speaking areas, and therefore – another limitation – this research only sheds light on the experiences of Arabic-speaking refugees. It should be noted that this absence of translators likely affects the access that refugee speakers of those languages have to the psychosocial, informational, and educational support that are the subject of this article. Future research should focus on the well-being of these minority language groups in Bulgaria.

A further strength and limitation of our study is the diversity of its participants. Our small sample brings together 8 refugees parents and we hope that we have used this study to elevate their voices. It should be noted, however, that our sample is not uniform. Among our participants, we have mothers as well as fathers, asylum holders along with asylum seekers, residents of Sofia combined residents of Harmanli. In our small sample, we have not sought to compare these disparate voices, but only to hear them. Future studies should focus in on these sub-populations, and draw large enough samples to compare them one to another.

A final limitation is that the qualitative methods used in this study combined with the small sample size limit the generalization of our study conclusions. The researchers have chosen to publish this initial study now in order to draw attention to the conditions which refugee families are now experiencing in Bulgaria.

Declaration of Conflicting Interests

The authors declared no potential conflicts of interest with respect to the research, authorship, and/or publication of this article.

References

Asylum Informational Database (2015) Country report – Bulgaria. Report, European Council on Refugees and Exiles, October.

Asylum Informational Database (2016) Country report – Bulgaria. Report, Bulgarian Helsinki Committee, December.

Bäärnhielm S, Edlund AS, Ioannou M. and Dahlin M. (2014) Approaching the vulnerability of refugees: evaluation of cross-cultural psychiatric training of staff in mental health care and refugee reception in Sweden. *BMC Medical Education*, 14(207): 1–10.

Bala J, Mooren T and Kramer S (2014) Cultural Competence in the treatment of political refugees based on system approacher. *Clinical Neuropsychiarty, 11*(1): 32–39.

Balter L (2002) *Parenthood in America: an encyclopedia.* Santa Barbara: California.

Bornstein MH (2002) *Handbook of Parenting: Volume 1, Children and Parenting.* New Jersey: Lawrence Erlbaum Associates.

Brough MK, Gorman D, Ramirez E and Westoby P (2003) Young refugees talk about well-being: A qualitative analysis of refugee youth mental health from three states. *Australian Journal of Social Issues, 38*(2): 193–208.

Brown LE and Krasteva A (2013) *Migrants and refugees equitable education for displaced populations.* Charlotte, NC: Information age publishing, INC.

Caligiuri P and Lazarova M (2003) A model for the influence of social interaction and social support on female expatriates' cross-cultural adjustment. *International Journal of Human Resource Management, 13*(5): 761–772.

Cohen S (2004) Social relationships and health. *American Psychologist, 59*(1): 676–730.

Global Knowledge Partnership on Migration and Development (2016) *Migration and Remittances Factbook 2016.* The World Bank: Washington.

Gómez de Larrain F (2016) *Refugee Policies in the European Union: Why do asylum recognition rates vary across Member States? A case study of Bulgaria and Hungary.* University Münster: Hamburg.

Hajdinak, M. (Ed.). (2011) *Migrations, gender and intercultural interactions in Bulgaria.* Sofia: International Center for Minority Studies and Intercultural Relations.

Hampton NZ (2001) Disability Status, Perceived Health, Social Support, Self-Efficacy, and Quality of Life among People with Spinal Cord Injury in the People's Republic of China. *International Journal of Rehabilitation Research, 24*(2): 69–71.

Horton TV and Wallander JL (2001) Hope and social support as resilience factors against psychological distress of mothers who care for children with chronic physical conditions. *Rehabilitation Psychology, 46*: 382–399.

Hynie M, S Guruge and Shakya BY (2012) "Family Relationships of Afgan, Karen and Sudanese Refugee Youth". *Canadian Ethnic Studies, 44*(3): 11–28.

Ilareva V (2016) Bulgaria's treatment of asylum seekers. In M. Couldrey (Eds.), *Forced Migration Review.* Oxford: Refugee Studies Centre.

International Organization for Migration. (2017). Humanitarian Emergencies, Missing Migrants. Available at: https://www.iom.int/news/mediterranean-migrant-arrivals-reach-103175-2017-2357-deaths (accessed 01 January 2018).

Kamya H (2004) The impact of war on children and families: Their stories, my stories. *AFTA Monograph Series, 1*: 29–32.

Kirmayer LJ, Dandeneau S, Marshall E, Phillips K and Williamson K. (2012) Toward an ecology of stories: Indigenous perspectives on resilience. In M. Ungar (Ed.), *The social ecology of resilience: A handbook of theory and practice.* New York: Springer.

Kugler EG (2009) *Partnering With Parents and Families to Support Immigrant and Refugee Children at School.* The Center for Health and Health Care in Schools: Washington, DC.

Lindencrona F, Ekblad S and Hauff E (2008) Mental health of recently resettled refugees from the Middle East in Sweden: the impact of pre-resettlement trauma, resettlement stress and capacity to handle stress. *Social Psychiatry and Psychiatric Epidemiology, 43*: 121–131.

Mack N, Woodsong C, Macqueen K, Guest G and Namey E (2005) *Qualitative Research Methods: A Data Collector's Field Guide.* Family Health International: USA.

Maine N, Rico-Martinez F and Kalaydzhieva V (2014) Syrian Refugees in Bulgaria: A Double Edged Sword. Toronto ON: FCJ Refugee Centre.

Martin SF, Weerasinghe S and Taylor A (2014) *Humanitarian Crises and Migration: Causes, Consequences and Responses.* Routledge: New York.

Milenković T, Simonović M, Samardžić Lj, Nikolić G, Grbeša G and Stanković M (2012) Impact of Social Support on severity of Posttraumatic stress disorder. *Acta Medica Medianae, 49*(4): 31–35.

Miller WV and Affolter WF (2002) *Helping children outgrow war.* Washington: Bureau for Africa.

MIPEX. 2011. *Key findings: Bulgaria.* Migrant Integration Policy Index. Available at: http://www.mipex.eu/bulgaria (accessed 15 March 2017).

Mock M (1998) *Clinical reflections on refugee families: Transforming crises into opportunities.* In M. McGoldrick (Ed.), Re-visioning family therapy (pp. 347–359). New York: Guilford.

Nelson BD, Fernandez WG, Galea S, Sisco S, Dierberg K, Subaric-Gorieva G, Nandi A, Hern J, Mitrovic M and VanRooyen M (2004) War-related psychological sequelae among emergency department patients in the former Republic of Yugoslavia. BMC Medicine, 2: 22.

Overseas Development Institute (2015) The migration crisis? Facts, challenges and possible solutions. Available at: https://www.odi.org/sites/odi.org.uk/files/odi-assets/publications-opinion-files/9913.pdf (accessed 02 February 2017).

Palinkas L, Pickwell S, Brandstein K, Clark T, Moser R and Osman A (2003). The journey to wellness: stages of refugee health promotion and disease prevention. *Journal of Immigrant Health, 5:* 19–28.

Petrson SJ and Bredow ST (2009) *Middle Range Theories: Application to Nursing Research.* Lippincott Williams Wilkins: USA.

Phillimore J (2011) Refugees, acculturation strategies, stress and integration. *Journal of Social Policy, 40:* 575–593.

Roberts EE (2016) Bulgaria's struggle at the frontline. In M. Couldrey (Eds.), *Forced Migration Review.* Oxford: Refugee Studies Centre.

Sarafino E (2002) *Health Psychology.* New York: Wiley.

Sarason IG and Sarason BR (2009) Social Support: Mapping the construct. *Journal of social and Personal Relationships, 26:* 113–120.

Simic L, Morton B and Mawani F (2003) Social Support and the Significance of Shared Experience in Refugee Migration and Resettlement. *Western Journal of Nursing Research, 25*(7): 872–891.

Sinclair M (2007) Education in Emergencies. In Nexus Strategic Partnerships (Eds.), *Commonwealth Education Partnerships 2007.* London: Commonwealth Secretariat.

Skovdal M and Campbell C (2015) Beyond education: what role can schools play in the support and protection of children in extreme settings? *International Journal of Educational Development, 41:* 175–183.

Stewart MJ, Makwarimba E, Beiser M, Neufeld A, Simich and Spitzer D (2010) Social support and health: immigrants' and refugees' perspectives. *Diversity in Health and Care, 7*(2): 91–103.

The Home Affairs Committee (2016) *The Migration Crisis: Seventh Report of Session 2016–17.* Available at: https://www.publications.parliament.uk/pa/cm201617/cmselect/cmhaff/24/24.pdf (accessed 10 March 2017).

Thielemann E (2004) *Does Policy Matter? On Governments' Attempts to Control Unwanted Migration.* California: The Center of Comparative Immigration Studies.

United Nations High Commissioner for Refugees, International Organization for Migration, & Mental Health and Psychosocial Support Network. (2015). Mental Health and Psychosocial Support for Refugees, Asylum Seekers and Migrants on the Move in Europe. Available at: http://www.euro.who.int/en/health-topics/health-determinants/migration-and-health/publications/2016/mental-health-and-psychosocial-support-for-refugees,-asylum-seekers-and-migrants-on-the-move-in-europe.-a-multi-agency-guidance-note-2015 (accessed 03 February 2017).

United Nations High Commissioner for Refugees. (2014). Bulgaria as a country of asylum. Available at: http://www.refworld.org/pdfid/52c598354.pdf (accessed 03 February 2017).

United Nations High Commissioner for Refugees. (2016a). Regional Refugee and Migrant Response plan for Europe. Available at: https://data2.unhcr.org/en/documents/download/52619 (accessed 03 February 2017).

United Nations High Commissioner for Refugees. (2016c). *UNHCR reports crisis in refugee education.* Available at: http://www.unhcr.org/news/press/2016/9/57d7d6f34/unhcr-reports-crisis-refugee-education.html (accessed 03 February 2017).

Walsh F (2007) Traumatic Loss and Major Disasters: Strengthening Family and Community Resilience. *Family Process, 46*(2): 207–227.

Watson D, Pichler F and Wallace C (2010) *Second European Quality of Life Survey: Subjective well-being in Europe.* Dublin: European Foundation for the Improvement of Living and Working Conditions.

Zhang Y and Wildemuth BM (2005) Qualitative Analysis of Content. *Analysis, 1*(2): 1–12.

Sabine Klinger (University of Graz),
Ines Findenig and Thomas Buchner (SOS Kinderdorf)

Unaccompanied Minor Refugees and Work with Transnationally Dislocated Families: Challenges Faced by Professionals within the Field of Child and Youth Care in Austria

Abstract

This paper focuses on work with unaccompanied children and adolescents who have experienced forced migration, and the challenges for social workers within this field. It is derived from a larger research project examining life worlds, needs and perspectives of unaccompanied refugee minors in the context of residential housing services such as group homes and assisted living with a maximum size of 20 individuals. From three semi-structured one-on-one interviews with social workers, we will present an analysis of the challenges these experts have identified in their work. To describe and better understand the life world of unaccompanied refugee minors, we combine the results of the interviews with data from an online survey targeting unaccompanied refugee minors (n=157) who are permanently being housed in Austrian child and youth welfare facilities. Besides a variety of challenges faced by the experts, dislocated family relations are one of the most pressing concerns within refugee child and youth welfare work. This paper concludes by summarizing challenges as well as opportunities and limitations of dislocated family-oriented social work within the field of unaccompanied refugee minors.

Unaccompanied minors with experiences of forced migration as recipients of child and youth welfare services

Migration and flight have represented challenges for societies throughout history. Today, these topics are particularly relevant in the child and youth welfare system on all levels (Müller, Stauf & Teupe, 2010). Over the last five years, global flight movements have tremendously increased the demand for residential care in Austria for unaccompanied minors with experiences of forced migration. Due to their needs and a shortage of time, organizations had to focus primarily on finding (student) housing for young refugees instead of doing evidence based social work. This happened because of – aside from the extent of practical experience – the general lack of research within this field. Therefore this article, which is based on a 2017 research project, focuses on examining challenges faced by professionals who work within the Austrian child and youth care sector with unaccompanied minors in the context of residential care.

The research project uses methodological triangulation to outline the life worlds, needs and perspectives of unaccompanied minors who have experienced forced displacement in permanent housing settings (with a maximum group size of 20 children or adolescents per housing unit). It was conducted through cooperation between Austrian SOS Children Villages' (i.e. SOS-Kinderdorf Austria) department of research & development and the University of Graz. We also conducted an online questionnaire (N = 157) and participatory photovoice workshops with young refugees (N = 12) utilizing auto photography (Deinet & Krisch, 2009) and one-on-one interviews with social workers (N = 3). The quantitative part of the research was based on the population of all minor refugees who lived in residential care provided by SOS Kinderdorf Austria in May 2017. The research was performed on the population itself, in this case with 301 young people. We tried to perform a census and reached a response rate of 53.4%. The descriptive data analysis was made in the form of an explorative analysis. In this paper, the center of the content interpretation presented here, are the outcomes of three qualitative interviews, which will be outlined as E1, E2 and E3. The results provide insight into the specific situations and challenges of social workers, and concrete recommendations for needs-based support are also identified, as well as anticipated implications for the development of migration-pedagogical and refugee-sensitive child and youth welfare services (personnel).

Seen through a historic lens, refugee movements affecting Austria – and all of Europe – are not novel. The reasons why individuals have to leave their homes are manifold and can be identified as "mixed migration flows" (Scheipl, 2017). Independent from motives to flee, there were 75,000 minors among the world's refugees in 2016.[1] 4,551 unaccompanied children and adolescents under the age of 18 arrived in Austria and applied for asylum (BMI, 2017). With the application for asylum, the responsibility for them lies in the child and youth welfare system. Within this system there is a variety of diverse (social pedagogical) services. There is evidence that especially in the sector of permanent housing facilities, some of the services do not match the actual needs of unaccompanied minors who were forcibly displaced (Graßhoff, 2017).

The Austrian landscape of housing facilities for young refugees ranges from large-scale group homes to shared apartments with (social) pedagogical assistance. The legally mandated youth-to-staff ratio of 1 to 10 (RIS, 2017a) is interpreted differently. For instance, this can mean one person (40 hours of social work) per week for ten minors, or 24/7 guidance hours in the form of one person for ten minors. To illustrate the non-transparent living outcomes as a comparison, in the federal province of Lower Austria the legally mandated ratio for children with an Austrian cit-

---

1   No data is currently available for 2017.

izenship is 1 to 3.5 (RIS, 2017b). Housing and especially guidance ratios for unaccompanied minor refugees have various consequences, at least until the young people turn 18. The daily life worlds and the effectiveness of social services depend on the staff ratio, as well as their job satisfaction and their possibilities for agency on the job. General structural and individual problems often surface in social pedagogical work settings through limiting the capacity of professionals to do their jobs, for example boundary and relationship work, capacity overload, stress, financial limitations, lack of power, etc. Besides that, the highly charged field of work with young individuals after their forced migration needs to be examined and developed. Even though there is a high demand for service development for this group, very few concepts exist for systematic social work in this area, likewise for professional transnational family systems. Simultaneously, there is little professional exchange concerning how services might be developed using a cooperative approach involving unaccompanied refugee minors (Grasshoff, 2017). Additionally, the child and youth welfare system is challenged by the fact that with this field of work, (unresolved) old structural issues are resurfacing in new ways (ibid.).

Human resources are directly affected by a lack of resources that stem from the financing system of basic benefits, in contrast to financing via child and youth welfare budgeting. Thus, experiences of powerlessness with serious consequences can occur in social work with unaccompanied minors, affecting all participants and including the social workers. Personnel doing hands-on social/pedagogical work experience complex challenges and demands, which play out in their daily routines. In this context, Baros and Otto (2017) highlight capability deprivation due to growing austerity policies according to Sen (1999) which "[manifests] (…) in poverty as lack of opportunities for self-realization, in precariousness as the embodied experience of ambivalence (…) and in disqualification processes as external interference with the life of the subjects."[2] Unaccompanied minors experiencing forced displacement are exposed to systemic power mechanisms in addition to flight-specific and social-psychological challenges.

Months can pass before an individual is provided with long-term accommodations (often still inadequate), beginning with the months-long escape, long waiting periods and clearing processes in the host country. This is also evident in the data of the interviewed adolescents: They had been travelling for an average of 4.8 months. Before they were admitted to the social service institution they lived in at the time of the interview, the adolescents lived in various types of accommodations within Austria for an average of 5.2 months. An equally drawn out "pending" path of asylum proceedings takes place after that. As a result, the prospects and opportunities of minors with experience of forced displacement are decidedly curtailed. This uncertainty, stagnation, and precariousness present multi-dimensional barriers for

---

2   Freely translated by the authors from the German original on page 9.

those affected (Peucker & Seckinger, 2014) and have an immense impact on the the life worlds of youth, and consequently their cooperation with pedagogical professionals. Social work that takes issues of diversity and intersectionality seriously thus requires a critical-reflexive stance of migration pedagogy that shapes decision-making and attitude (Polat, 2017). This attitude is particularly necessary in order to meet the demands of the vulnerable and highly complex group of unaccompanied minors who have experienced forced displacement, who oscillate between being children and adolescents – and similarly the contradictory poles of independence and need for help (Detemple, 2015). Accordingly, the professional requirements of professionals in social work with underage refugee children and adolescents seem highly complex, difficult and demanding.

Challenges and requirements in working with unaccompanied refugee minors and adolescents from the perspective of social workers

A variety of topics emerged in the analysis of the interviews, as social workers expressed important requirements and their implementation as well as challenges in their work. These challenges and demands are described and discussed here. The complexity and interconnectedness becomes evident in the data. Pedagogical work with young people after forced displacement requires the **establishment of a daily routine** and a structure for everyday life. This serves to create stability in terms of living environments (E1, E2 & E3[3]). However, the establishment of this daily structure is experienced as very challenging because the group of children and adolescents with a history of forced displacement is very heterogeneous. From the point of view of E1, the employees within the social service institutions need "confidence and ease when dealing with different nationalities and different cultures" (E1, line 134f.), Also, they should possess "good judgment and a very empathic perspective" (E1, line 142). In this context, the experts emphasize the need for **relationship building** with the young people, since one-on-one support is considered to be of great importance for the establishment of a daily structure. However, due to group sizes, good relationship work can still be difficult to realize (E1, E2 & E3). Here is an example: "This is certainly a challenge, that you actively pay attention to them all and also try to be there for the quiet and shy ones (…) and it's just important that you really take care of their needs in a timely manner. Yes, when they all meet together, then it is crowded" (E1, line 150ff.). The opportunity to do **educational work in small groups,** and thus to constructively address the aforementioned challenge, seems to be an important factor in the caring support and guidance of unaccompanied refugee minors that needs to be strengthened (E1, E2 & E3). In addition, the diversity

---

3   For reasons of confidentiality, we have identified the three professionals as E1, E2, and E3 in this paper. We indicate line numbers of verbatim transcripts when directly quoting from data material.

in terms of children and adolescents age range plays a major role. The challenge of creating daily routines seems to be an easier task for unaccompanied refugee children under the age of 15 as they have school access. 97.8% of the children under the age of 15 said they were attending school. The creation of a meaningful daytime structure for over 15 year-olds seems slightly more difficult. Since the end of compulsory schooling in Austria also signifies the end of the right to school access, only 49.4% of young people above the age of 15 attend a school, and 6.5% are employed in vocational training. Another 31% of those over 15 are in differing educational courses, but their duration and intensity vary greatly. This means that around 15% of youth over the age of 15 in the sample do not have any daytime structure, and 31% of respondents do not have a long-term structure. The concepts of "meaningful employment" and "**tailor-made support**" (E2, line 87ff.) are repeatedly emphasized by the experts with regard to the creation of a daily structure; they also state that the supply of daily structure (courses, events, work activities, etc.), while important, has its limits and cannot replace the psychotherapeutic supervision of traumatized adolescents (E1, E2 & E3). Against this background, the fundamentally **ambivalent and precarious life world** of these children and adolescents is seen as a challenge in terms of everyday professional action (E1, E2 & E3). The experts often conclude that many of their clients would need more intensive support and services, which cannot be provided due to financial limitations. In addition, there is a lack of professional exchange and communication among institutions and service providers – considered necessary by the experts. In their pedagogical work, the experts especially emphasize the participatory decision making of the young people about their own lives. In their opinion, the participation of young people should be even more intensified. In particular, they brought up life areas such as clothing, events and travel destinations, educational goals, and also the participatory determination of place and form of residence.

Another major challenge is the **aftercare** of young people as soon as they reach their 18th birthday or have to leave the institution for other reasons (ibid.). Austrian asylum legislation stipulates that as soon as adolescents turn 18 they must leave the facility and have to move to large-scale adult accommodations, even if they receive a negative asylum decision. This makes meaningful follow-up care almost impossible. The interviewed professionals identified challenges in regard to contacting and to **cooperating with physically absent families of origin** of the children and adolescents (ibid.). Cooperation with the family system of origin is particularly important, as 85% of the young people interviewed stated that they were in contact with their family. The development of these contacts, in the sense of integrating the system of origin into the social work, is further complicated by the fact that the young people's situations and their families are very diverse, and secondly, experience and clear professional guidelines in regard to working with transnational caregivers are lacking. In practical terms, it does not appear to be a well-established practice among professionals to have online parent conversations, for example via Skype.

However, this would be important as working with parents also facilitates the work with young people (E3, line 333). From the experts' point of view, it would be important to professionalize and to financially equip the "work with the system of origin" (E3, line 743).

Finally, we would like to address the challenge posed by the physically absent families of origin and emphasize the relevance of transnational family work in child and youth welfare services. In this context we highlight the need for conceptual and technological prerequisites that need to be in place for successful transnational family work.

Transnational family work as a challenge for child and youth welfare

As a primary agent of socialization, family offers the framework and stage for mutual influences, learning processes and conflict resolution over the lifespan like no other place (Westphal, 2018). It represents influential symbolic and subjective bonds for children and adolescents as well as an influential social space, which is continuously recreated between all participants. This concept of "doing family" (Jurczyk, 2015) adds additional complexity to the lives of children and adolescents in the context of unaccompanied forced migration. The social space of family is not conceptually limited to physical encounters, but also includes transnational communication and virtual opportunities as well as difficulties. Familial networks or transnational family contexts (including aunts, uncles, etc.) play a central role for young refugees – whether accompanied or unaccompanied (Lechner & Huber, 2017). The everyday life of unaccompanied children and adolescents thus revolves around 'family' in different ways. Whether it is the concern for the family's whereabouts and wellbeing, the yearning for family reunification in the host country, or whether young refugees exert a certain expectations to support family members financially in the country of origin, seems to vary among the unaccompanied children and adolescents. However, family issues tend to be burdensome for them (Lechner et al., 2017) and determine their lifestyles in a variety of ways (Westphal, 2018). In addition, in the socialpedagogical discourse, families are hardly considered or discussed as a positive space for education in the context of migration (Westphal, 2018).

In the child and youth welfare context, Graßhoff and Schröer (2018) emphasize that even though family systems might not be in geographical proximity, their impact on support and 'healing' processes is not reduced. This is also clearly visible and confirmed by the results of the quantitative survey: families are the number one issue occupying the minds and dreams of refugee children and adolescents, in addition to (professional) education. For example, 40.4% of respondents said that they "think a lot about their family." A further 18% stated that wishes for the future are centered on their families. On the other hand, only 3.1% said that they needed help with their family. At the same time, 85.1% of respondents have contact with their family. Other studies (Lechner & Huber, 2017; Kutscher & Kreß, 2015) also conclude that the majority of young people have regular contact with their family systems of origin through various tools (WhatsApp, Facebook, Skype, etc.). As a result, the Internet, with its many facets, seems to offer places for creating social family spaces, and is widely used as such. Only with modern information and communication technologies have transnational practices and social processes become an everyday lived social reality for many families dealing with migration (Westphal, 2018). In this way, family and kin networks can also form stable communities and maintain their social and emotional ties in diverse ways across transnational spaces, care commitments, and loyalties (ibid.). The everyday social construction and representation of family in migration thus takes place more or less densely and intensively in a transnational and virtual environment.

Transnational family contexts and dynamics encompass processes and border crossing practices transcending nation-state territories, which are a social reality for many of the respondents of children and youth welfare services (Westphal, 2018). However, there is still no consensus in practice concerning how to work with transnational family structures, thus there are a number of interpretations. It oscillates between the extremes of perception as a threat to resource-oriented work (Graßhoff & Schröer, 2018).

Social workers are thus in a field of tension characterized by a lack of pedagogical practices and guidelines for transnational family work and their social/pedagogical everyday work, in which the cooperation with the physically absent families of origin represents a lived reality. This poses a major challenge for social workers, which in our view can be seen as an overload and an imposition. Our research makes clear that it is essential to acknowledge that transnational family work is indispensable – moreover, the conditions to make it possible have to be improved. Because, as also emphasized by Kindler (2014), the path to the well-being of the child inevitably leads from the well-being of families or family relationships, which can often also strengthen resilient behavior among children and adolescents (ibid.). According to this, it is essential for social work in the context of forced displacement to highlight the common resources of social family spaces in a transnational and virtual context together with all those involved. This surpasses the method of transnational biography work, as detailed by Schmitt and Homfeldt (2014). Transnational biography work centers around the stories of children and adolescents and accentuates the importance of recognizing and processing them, including their burdens, perspectives and needs, with the sensitive lens of a transnational social space. It also supports new (old) networks transcending national borders and should help them cope (ibid.). The goal is to bring all involved parties on board and collaboratively process different transitions, such as the arrival, confusing life experiences, (educational) questions, networks of children and adolescents, etc. with social pedagogical support. However, such a resource-oriented and strengthening transnational – virtual as well as physical – design of familial spaces requires increased personnel and understanding. It also requires digital prerequisites and structural conditions.

These can still be expanded in Austrian child and youth welfare services and can be regarded as an immense future opportunity.

In conclusion, the requirements and challenges for social workers within the Austrian field of child and youth welfare and in the context of unaccompanied minor refugees who experienced forced displacement are manifold. They differ on many levels and first require a social and academic understanding, which starts with this paper.

In summary, multi-dimensional challenges and requirements can be identified on a structural and individual level of analysis in regard to specialized staff, and we summarized the outcomes in Table 1. Seen as interactional elements, these require professional and reflexive action. Thus, for the professionals who work with the vulnerable group of unaccompanied minors with experiences of forced migration and their transnational contexts, the challenges will continue to be complex and require further analysis and research as well as structural changes.

Table 1. Multidimensional challenges and requirements for social workers

Multidimensional challenges and requirements for social workers	
Challenges	**Requirements**
Work with heterogeneous groups in terms of age, origin, culture, social class, educational attainment level, family background, etc.	• Tolerance of ambiguity, sensitivity for migration experiences and intercultural competence • Social and emotional competence • Reflexive agency
Reduce work in large groups	• Encourage pedagogical work in and with small groups • Offer individual mentoring and tailor-made support • Strengthen intense relationship building
Confusing and precarious life worlds of the children and adolescents	• Establishment of daily routines and structures to establish stability in living environment • Creation of meaningful daily structure for clients at the age of 15 and above • Establish and intensify guidelines for aftercare • Facilitate active participation and inclusion of kids and adolescents voices when it comes to topics like choice of clothing, places to visit, pedagogical goals, and housing options.
Missing professional networking across organizations	• More time and resources for professional networking and exchange • Establishment of working groups • Advocate professionalization
Collaboration with physically remote and geographically distant families of origin	• Intensify work with the family system of origin • Professionalize transnational family work, e.g. clear guidelines for transnational parent participation (conceptual work) • Create required technological and digital environments

References

Baros, W., & Otto, H.-U. (2017). Migration und Soziale Arbeit. *Sozialpädagogische Impulse*, 2, 7–11.

BMI (2017). Asylstatistik Dezember 2016. Retrieved from http://www.bmi.gv.at/301/Statistiken/files/2016/Asylstatistik_Dezember_2016.pdf [13 July 2017].

Detemple, K. (2015). *Zwischen autonomiebestreben und Hilfebedarf. Unbegleitete minderjährige Flüchtlinge in der Jugendhilfe.* Baltmannsweiler: Schneider-Verlag Hohengehren.

Deinet, U. & Krisch, R. (2009). Autofotografie. sozialraum.de 1(1). Retrieved from http://www.sozialraum.de/autofotografie.php [10 April 2017].

Graßhoff, Gunther (2017): Junge Flüchtlinge. Eine neue Herausforderung für die Kinder- und Jugendhilfe?. In: *Sozialmagazin. Zeitschrift für Soziale Arbeit*: 42 Jh., H. 3-4., pp. 56-61.

Graßhoff, G. & Schröer, W. (2018). Hilfen zur Erziehung für junge Menschen, die als Geflüchtete in Deutschland leben – "muddling through" als Dauerlösung? *Forum Erziehungshilfe*, 24(1) 16–21.

Hiebl, J. (2017). Hilfe für unbegleitete Kinderflüchtlinge. *Sozialpädagogische Impulse*, 2, 47–49.

Jurczyk, K. (2015). Doing Family – Zur Herstellung von Familie in spätmodernen Gesellschaften. Beitrag an Fachtagung Kindheits- und Familienwissenschaften in Hamburg. Retrieved from https://familienfachtagung.files.wordpress.com/2015/03/blog_jurczyk_doing-family.pdf [09 May 2017].

Kindler, H. (2014). Flüchtlingskinder, Jugendhilfe und Kinderschutz. *DJI Impulse*, 1, 9–11.

Kutscher, N. & Kreß, L.-M. (2015). „Internet ist gleich mit Essen" Empirische Studie zur Nutzung digitaler Medien durch unbegleitete minderjährige Flüchtlinge. Retrieved from [13 March 2018].

Lechner, C. & Huber, A. (2017). *Ankommen nach der Flucht. Die Sicht begleiteter und unbegleiteter junger Geflüchteter auf ihre Lebenslagen in Deutschland.* München: Deutsches Jugendinstitut e.V.

Lechner, C., Huber, A. & Holthusen, B. (2017). „Familie, Schule, Freunde – Ich wünsche mir ein ganz normales Leben!" – Die Sicht begleiteter und unbegleiteter junger Geflüchteter auf ihre Lebenslagen. In: *Jugendhilfe*, 1(55), 11–19.

Müller, H.; Stauf, E. & Teupe, U. (2010). Migrationssensible Jugendhilfeplanung. In S. Maykus, & R. Schone, R (Eds.). *Handbuch Jugendhilfeplanung* (pp. 359–374). Wiesbaden: VS Verlag für Sozialwissenschaften.

Peucker, C. & Seckinger, M. (2014). Flüchtlingskinder: eine vergessene Zielgruppe der Kinder- und Jugendhilfe. *DJI Impulse*, 105, 12–14.

Polat, A. (2017). Migration als „normative Kraft des Faktischen". Pädagogisches Handeln in der Migrationsgesellschaft. *Sozialpädagogische Impulse*, 2, 16–18.

RIS (2017a). Retrieved from https://www.ris.bka.gv.at/GeltendeFassung.wxe?Abfrage=Bundesnormen&Gesetzesnummer=20003460 [13 July 2017].

RIS (2017b). Retrieved from https://www.ris.bka.gv.at/GeltendeFassung.wxe?Abfrage=LrNO&Gesetzesnummer=20001076 [13 July 2017].

Scheipl, J. (2017). Mixed migration flows. *Sozialpädagogische Impulse*, 2, 4–6.

UNHCR (2017). Global Trends. Forced Displacement in 2016. Retrieved from http://www.
    unhcr.org/5943e8a34 [05 July 2017].

Schmitt, C. & Homfeldt, H. G. (2014). Flüchtlingskinder besser verstehen: Die „Transnatio-
    nale Biografiearbeit". *DJI Impulse*, 1, 15–17.

Westphal, M. (2018). Transnationaler Bildungsort Familie: Elterliche Erziehung und Bil-
    dung in der Migration. In E. Glaser; H.-C. Koller; W. Thole & S. Krumme (Eds).
    Räume für Bildung – Räume der Bildung (pp. 161–171). Verlag Barbara Budrich.

Martin Auferbauer (University College of Teacher Education Styria)

How to Enhance the Field of Youth Information: Focus on Actual Information Needs of Young People and Intensified Cooperation in Youth Work

Abstract

Youth information services became a more and more important aspect of the field of youth work. A differentiation of youth information work into formal, non-formal and informal youth information is proposed for a better understanding of the activities involved and deeper cooperation between the involved institutions. Formal youth information work is carried out by specialised institutions. The article presents information needs of young people based on data from a standardised online survey (n=1.811) among Styrian (a region in Austria) pupils of all school types from the seventh grade on (aged 12 to 18 years). Statements by the pupils were openly encoded and grouped into 24 categories. These categories were examined for significant correlations considering gender, age, social stratification, and migration background. As a result, gender and age proved to be revealing, while there are hardly any significant observations with regard to social stratification and migration background.

In a second step, the different institutional contexts of youth information are related to the topics of the highest demand articulated by the pupils: schools as a context of non-formal youth information and adults in the family (informal youth information) are the most important sources of information for young people.

Introduction: What is *youth information*?

In our postmodern environment with its growing complexity and the existence of more and more options – as well as more threats and risks in terms of coping with life (Beck, 1986) – services for young people should provide support and orientation for them (Böhnisch, 2003). Youth information services became a more important part of the field of youth work in (central and western) Europe.

> *"These institutions were established to provide access for young people to reliable, neutral and accurate information on all areas concerning them and exist now in almost every European country." (Cangelosi, 2012, p. 1).*

Youth information is of course not only provided by these specialised services, but they have a key role to play in order to multiply impacts and be capable of dealing with networks. For a better understanding of the activities in the field of youth information and in order to establish a deeper cooperation between the involved institutions, I suggest a terminology to distinguish the types of youth information: formal, non-formal and informal youth information (Auferbauer, 2017).

Formal youth information is provided by specialised institutions. Their aim is to cover young people's information needs directly. These institutions are organised under the heading of the European network ERYICA (The European Youth Information and Counselling Agency). Since the beginning of their work in the late 1960s and early 1970s in the BeNeLux-countries, these kinds of institutions now exist in all member states of the European Union and most countries of the Council of Europe (Auferbauer, 2017). The Council of Europe plays an important role in promoting the services of Youth Information in its member countries:

> "(...) young people have a right to full, comprehensible and reliable information, without reservations, and to counseling on all problems concerning them in all sectors, without exception, so that they may have complete freedom of choice, without any discrimination or ideological or other influence" (Council of Europe, 1990)

Even with the rise of new information technologies, the Council of Europe emphasises the importance of these institutions as growing up and integrating into social systems is considered a more and more challenging process for young people:

> "Guidance and counseling is even more important today than for previous generations, due to the fact that social inclusion of young people is now a lengthier and more complex process." (Council of Europe, 2010)

These institutions should meet the demand of young people when it comes to information needs concerning all areas of their lives:

> "One of the reasons those services were introduced was the demand from young people for access to reliable, neutral and accurate information on all areas concerning them; information that was comprehensive and reflected the reality of their lives." (Cangelosi, 2012, p. 1)

Ulrike Schriefl (2015) defines three means of communication for the Styrian center for youth information: personal interaction, online communication and printed media.

Institutions of formal youth information typically provide a location where young people can get personal advice, brochures, access to the Internet and so on.

They also create their own media (e.g. in the form of printed brochures and magazines, that are sent to young people or as online content on social media platforms like Facebook, Snapchat, Instagram etc) about current topics, conduct workshops and organise fairs for young people.

Illustration 1: Demonstration of formal youth information: direct interaction between youth information worker and young people.

Non-formal youth information is provided by professionals from other institutions (e.g. teachers, youth workers, health professionals). These professionals could also have the function of a multiplier and amplifier for formal youth information services. They often have special know-how (e.g. about sexually transmitted diseases, financial literacy or specific demands of certain groups of young people) and/or they function as a gatekeeper to certain groups. Institutions of formal and non-formal youth information should seek organised exchange and cooperation in order to optimise their services, deepen their knowledge and expand their reach.

Informal youth information means the communication of content without the direct involvement of representatives of institutions – such as in peer groups and families.

Illustration 2: Demonstration of informal youth information: interaction between youth information worker and professionals (e.g. teachers and youth workers).

Illustration 3: Demonstration of non-formal youth information: direct interaction between young people, while one of them is participating in a peer programme of a youth information institution.

Some institutions of formal youth information developed specific programs to address young people as *info-peers* (aha Vorarlberg, n.s.), so that they can spread information in their groups.

Regardless of the institutional context, professionals – as well as parents or other responsible parties – should be aware of the specific information needs of young people. The provided information should be comprehensive and accurately match the reality of the lives of young people. Until now there has hardly been any empirical look at the actual information needs of young people and there is no scientific research on youth information (Auferbauer, 2017), so the aim and purpose of the research was to gain more insight into the characteristics of the information needs of young people and their preferred information channels.

Methodology

Sponsored and supported by the regional government of Styria, an evaluation of the work in the field of youth information and possible further perspectives has been carried out (Lederer-Hutsteiner, Auferbauer, Polanz & Diwoky, 2014; Auferbauer & Lederer-Hutsteiner 2015). Key issues were the degree of familiarity of young people with the institutions of Youth Information and their actual information needs (in connection with their preferred information channel). In this study, several research methods (group discussions with young people, interviews with youth work professionals and a standardised online survey among pupils from the seventh grade) have been triangulated. The standardised survey was conducted in schools whose classes were chosen randomly. In order to collect reliable data and to be able to make representative statements, 106 school classes were drawn from. In coordination with the financier and client, young people from the age of 13 in were questioned in all existing school forms. The area of investigation was limited to Styria as part of the responsibility of the local government. 101 school classes of this sample could be included for participation in the study (Lederer-Hutsteiner et al., 2014).

In a further analysis (Auferbauer, 2017) the data was subjected to more in-depth study: Answers to an open question about current issues in their lives (from the standardised online survey, n=1.811) have been coded into 24 categories. The process of coding permits data to be "segregated, grouped, regrouped and relinked in order to consolidate meaning and explanation" (Grbich, 2007, p. 21). In a next step, these categories were analysed with t-tests in order to find correlations with dependent variables like age, gender, social stratification and migration background.

What information needs do young people in Styria (Austria) actually articulate?

So far there is hardly any empirical research on the actual information needs of young people and there is no scientific research on youth information (Auferbauer, 2017). The following table shows the ten most frequently mentioned topics (of course it was possible that some pupils mentioned more than one topic in their response to the open question):

Table 1: The ten most frequently mentioned topics (categorised)

Category	Percentage of statements
School	42.5%
Professional orientation and jobs	30.7%
Sports and exercise	13.9%
Future	13.6%
Peer group and friends	12.6%
Family	11.4%
Politics	9.9%
Partnership	8.7%
Economic challenges	8.3%
Pessimistic statements, acute problems	7.6%

It is not surprising that *school* is a very important matter for young people: more than four out of ten mentioned school-related issues. As the survey was carried out in school classes, there could be also a response bias due to priming, i.e. being asked in the setting of the school could lead to more answers concerning this issue. Almost every third respondent made references to *professional orientation and jobs*. About one out of eight pupils mentioned matters concerning *future* prospects and relations with *peer group and friends* and/or *familiy*. The other 18 categories were not mentioned by more than 10% of pupils.

When it comes to the correlation with gender, there have been several significant correlations in the t-tests as the following table shows:

Table 2: Categories with correlations with gender (** =highly significant correlation (P<.001); * = very signifi-cant correlation (P≤.01); without asterisk = significant correlation (P≤.05)). Categories are listed in order of fre-quency of the response. For further details (χ2, p, Cramér's V) see Auferbauer, 2017, pp. 198–231)

Female pupils	Male pupils
Categories (with significant correlation to gender in order of frequency of the response)	
School**; Family**; Relationships*; Economic challenges*; Pessimistic statements, acute problems; Nature, animals, environmental protection**; Health and mental wellbeing*; International mobility**	Sports**; Politics; Mobility**; Media consumption**; Criticism of the survey, bizarre and obscene answers**

Female pupils responded more often and at greater length to this question in the survey and consequently mentioned more issues (Auferbauer, 2017, p. 233). They referred significantly more often to social contexts like family and relationships. They also addressed economic challenges and other acute problems as well as their (mental) health status. The cliché that women put more effort into addressing their social surroundings (including natural environment and animals) and talk more openly about their challenges has been confirmed here.

The male pupils skipped this question more often than their female classmates and they criticise the survey itself (sometimes by entering strange and/or obscene statements) significantly more often. Topics like sports, politics and mobility are, as might be expected, typical *male* categories, while it may be a surprise that also media consumption was highly significant and more often mentioned by the young men.

Age groups turned out as a good predictor of certain fields of interest, as there are several specific correlations with categories, as the following table shows:

Table 3: Categories with correlations to *age groups* (** =highly significant correlation (P<.001); * = very signifi-cant correlation (P≤.01); without asterisk = significant correlation (P≤.05)). Categories are listed in order of fre-quency of the response. For further details (χ^2, p, Cramér's V) see Auferbauer, 2017, pp. 198–231)

Age-Group	Categories (in order of frequency of the response)
12–13	Sports and exercise; Media consumption; Nature, animals, environmental protection*; Positive and optimistic statements
14–15	School**; Peer group and friends**; Family**; Sexuality*
16–17	Professional direction and jobs; Politics**; Economic challenges**
18+	Politics**; Economic challenges**; International mobility

The youngest respondents showed a significant higher affinity to the categories *Sports and exercise*, *Media consumption* and to matters concerning nature and animals. Moreover there were significantly more *Positive and optimistic statements*.

Pupils aged 14 to 15 years old mention significantly more often *School*, *Peer group and friends* and *Family*. These matters show the increased importance of social contexts in this age group. Statements concerning the topic *Sexuality* are also mentioned significant more often.

Pupils at the age of 16 to 17 make many more statements about the issue of *Professional direction and jobs*. Like in the group of the oldest participants (18 years and above) there is a significant higher reference to *Politics* and to *Economic challenges* (e.g. lack of money) they feel in their life. In this group, there is also a significantly higher prevalence of questions and ideas concerning *International mobility* (cf. table 3).

According to an index of social stratification from the most important youth survey for Germany (Shell, 2015), the respondents were divided into three groups. There were quite a few correlations between the social status of the pupils with the statements they made: The third with the lowest score in this stratification index showed a very significant correlation with the category *Economic challenges*. In contrast, the third with the highest score (where we can assume that their parents' economic situation is much better) mentioned significantly more often the categories *Sports and exercise* and other individual activities. Also the matter of *School-life balance* (this category sums up statements concerning difficulties to combine school obligations with other commitments) is mentioned significantly more often by this group (Auferbauer, 2017, p. 235).

According to an index from Schenk et al. (2006) the possible migration background of the contestants has been assessed. Based on these criteria, no significant correlation between migrant background and the mentioning of certain categories could be found (Auferbauer, 2017, p. 236).

The age and gender of the pupils are more likely to determine the demand for certain information than their (parents') social status and migration aspects in their biography.

Professionals in different fields of youth work should anticipate the likely demand (or at least acceptance) of information with the data above in order to present suitable offers and to be prepared for certain requests for information. Age groups as well as gender proved to be revealing, while there are hardly any significant tendencies with regard to migration background.

As a second step, the link between information demand and the preferred information channel was examined.

What are the preferred information channels for specific information needs?

While the categorisation of the pupils' answers to the open question in the standardised online survey concerning their actual information needs should function in an explorative way, we also asked them using 32 response options (Lederer-Hutsteiner et al., 2014). The pupils rated the level of importance in their present life. When the topic was rated with the option *"I would like to have more information on that matter"*, they were then asked what information channel they would prefer for this topic. Out of group of 17 possibilities, they could choose their preferred information context. These options included different types of media (journals, brochures, social media, internet pages), talks with different family members, peers or professionals (teachers, school social workers, psychologists and medical staff in schools, counsellors inside or outside the school context, coaches in sports clubs or cultural workers, specialists from the local formal youth information center and telephone hotlines).

The following presentation of the results concerning the preferred information channels is clustered by the differentiation of the institutional contexts of Youth Information: formal youth information (here: the local institution for Youth Information in Styria), non-formal (here: professionals in the school context) and informal youth information (here: adults in their own families). For every context, the five most often mentioned issues are presented.

Table 4: Top five expectations on information in the context of the institution of formal youth information, Logo-Jugendinformation Steiermark

Top five expectations in the context of formal youth information	Percentage
Voluntary work for the benefit of others	5%
Side jobs, summer jobs and internships	4%
Participation and codetermination	3%
Possibilities for political engagement	3%
Financial support	3%

The local institution for formal youth information is not very well known among the respondents (cf. Lederer-Hutsteiner et al., 2014, p. 69f.). Therefore it is not surprising that only a few per cent of the pupils declare that this institution is their preferred information channel for certain topics. Besides the factor of the rather low recognition of this institution and therefore low expectations surrounding this service, it is interesting that the mentioned topics are mostly related with participation and politics or financial support (via support payments or placement services for side jobs). Due to the close connection to administrative programs, the institutions of formal youth information actually are adequate for these kinds of concerns and reflect their offerings.

The expectations concerning professionals in the context of schools (as a form of non-formal youth information) are much more numerous:

Table 5: Top five expectations on information in the context of schools (as a form of non-formal youth information)

Top five expectations in the context of schools	Percentage
Bullying and violence	54%
Development and prevention of mental disease	51%
Addiction and risks of (legal and illegal) drugs	50%
Political education	48%
Crisis intervention and support	47%

Except the matter of political education as a core task of schools, it is eye catching that most of the expectations in the school context are related to health topics (in a broader sense). Schools, as an institution of non-formal youth information, are considered to be the most important channel for information. Topics like bullying and violence, risks of substance use, mental health issues and their prevention as well as support in the case of crisis are the most expected topics for professionals in the context of schools. When we think about professionals in this context, we should not only focus on teachers but also on additional personnel resources like social workers, psychologists, medical staff and external professionals providing workshops in schools.

When it comes to informal settings, adults in their own families (parents, grandparents, stepparents, partners of one parent, etc.) are generally considered a very important support. The most important expectations are:

Table 6: Top five expectations for information for adults in the family (as a channel of informal youth information)

Top five expectations regarding adults in respondent's own family	Percentage
Military and civil service	42%
Finding an adequate job/apprenticeship	41%
Finding an adequate school/college/university	38%
Side jobs, summer jobs and internships	36%
Receiving support for learning/extra tuition	32%

As in Austria there is still compulsory military service for young men (with the possibility of alternatively doing a longer civil service), this issue is of high interest for at least the male respondents. While the decision between military and civil service is only indirectly relevant for further education and/or job opportunities, the other four mentioned topics are very closely linked to job direction and education. *To find an adequate job/apprenticeship* as well as the category *To find an adequate school/ college/university* is something that about four out of ten pupils expect (or at least hope) to be informed about by family members. To get a link to possible employers for side or summer jobs or for internships is also highly related with the family context. Those young people who feel the need for extra instruction or any other support for learning also expect this from the family context.

Discussion

The information needs of young people are diverse and differ along certain categories (gender, age and social status of their parents are important predictors, while in contrast migration background is not). With this empirical data, it is possible to determine the perceived information needs of young people and to establish accurate programs (e.g. workshops in schools or in youth clubs) according to group characteristics like age, gender and social background.

Most correlations could be found with gender. Therefore it seems advisable to orient the offers according to gender-related interests. In this way, the young people's attention can be captured in order to be able to go beyond these gender-related topics, when the link to offers of Youth Information is established.

When it comes to the age of the respondents, it is noticeable that there is a shift from rather self-orientated topics that were most important for the youngest pupils (12 to 13 years old) to an increase in the importance of social relationships and questions of professional or educational direction. Along with the increase in responsibility, that young people have to take, economic challenges become more and more important.

While questions concerning sexuality tend to decrease with age (without this having to mean that in fact all the questions are resolved, as experts emphasise; cf. Auferbauer & Lederer-Hutsteiner, 2015), matters like politics and international mobility become important for the older pupils (age 16 years and above). Therefore, some thematic connections are segmented according to the age groups because new or changed requirements or developmental tasks are constantly being asked of the young people. Especially for age-heterogeneous groups (such as in school classes) it is therefore advisable to focus on a corresponding guiding theme.

Along the contexts of information transfer, we can see a certain thematic assignment.

- Topics with aspects of political participation are linked with the institution of formal youth information.
- Information about different aspects of health is expected from professionals in the school context.
- When it comes to questions of educational or professional direction, young people especially mentioned adults in their family as their preferred source of information (i.e. non-formal youth information). This is especially challenging when the parents are not able to provide this information, e.g. because they do not know the educational landscape and the job opportunities very well because of their educational backgrounds or due to their migration biographies.

Services of formal youth information therefore should emphasise the work with multipliers and outreach workers from disadvantaged communities in order to strengthen the adult's knowledge, so that they can support their children with information regarding education and job outlook.

Face-to-face interviews with youth information workers (n=15) showed that certain issues (like sex education or work on their information and media competences) are very important for young people, even if they do not ask more for it directly (Lederer-Hutsteiner et al., 2014, p. 174). In order to prevent young people from possible harm, in addition to the expressed information needs, other topics have to be addressed. In that sense, it would be an interesting challenge to expand the topics preferred by young people to aspects that they might not be interested in themselves. The interest in media thus could be enriched by the aspect of media literacy. Sport could be addressed as a topic of health and mental wellbeing, etc.

When it comes to young people at risk and/or those with fewer resources and opportunities, we see a paradox: These people would have the most urgent needs for Youth Information, but it is very difficult for these institutions to get it in touch with kids at risk (e.g. young people with any kind of disabilities, children with a different cultural background, youth struggling with substance abuse and/or young people who are currently not taking part in formal education, employment nor training). So there is the challenge to intervene as early as possible and to reinforce the cooperation between formal and informal youth information with sectors like school (also school social work), youth work, youth welfare and institutions that support parents. In particular, youth information should be a strong partner for schools, as young people in this setting are easily accessible and formulate the most expectations for this context.

On the basis of interviews with representatives of formal youth information services (n=6), some innovative approaches to connect young audiences and topics could be detected (cf. Lederer-Hutsteiner et al., 2014, p. 171). These models of good practice often have in common that they address young people quite broadly and then provide strong support for those in need. Furthermore, they often establish good cooperation with people who are suitable to act as multipliers and gatekeepers to young people that are hard to reach. They often manage to combine high-demand topics with those deemed most important to professionals (e.g. combining street soccer tournaments with literacy training or hip hop dance workshops with integrated health literacy skills training).

So various aspects are needed to make youth information a useful support for young people and to strengthen social cohesion in a postmodern society that offers more options and fewer restrictions for some on the one hand – but on the other hand also threats and self-responsibility without security networks for most.

References

aha Vorarlberg (n.s.). *Info-Team*. Retrieved from: http://www.aha.or.at/ueber-aha/team/check-in-1/videoteam [05 June 2018].

Auferbauer, M. (2017). *Informationsbedürfnisse von steirischen Jugendlichen. Ein bildungssoziologischer Beitrag zum sozialpädagogischen Handlungsfeld der Jugendinformationsarbeit*. Unpublished dissertation at Karl-Franzens-University Graz.

Auferbauer, M. & Lederer-Hutsteiner, T. (2015). Vielfältigkeit als Herausforderung in der Jugendinformation. Ein Einblick in empirische Untersuchungsergebnisse zu Informationsbedürfnissen steirischer Jugendlicher. In Land Steiermark, Referat Jugend (Ed.), *Jugendarbeit: bewusst vielfältig. Versuch einer interdisziplinären Auseinandersetzung* (S. 9–24). Graz: Verlag für Jugendarbeit und Jugendpolitik.

Beck, U. (1986). *Risikogesellschaft. Auf dem Weg in eine andere Moderne.* Frankfurt/Main: Suhrkamp.

Böhnisch, L. (2003). *Pädagogische Soziologie. Eine Einführung.* Weinheim und München: Juventa.

Cangelosi, A. (2012). *Youth Information – Historical reminder & main achievements.* Retrieved from https://www.coe.int/t/dg4/youth/Source/Resources/PR_material/2012_ Compendium_Youth_Information_text_en.pdf [05 June 2018].

Council of Europe (1990). *Recommendation 90 (7).* Retrieved from http://eryica.org/files/Council%20of%20Europe%20-%20Recommendation%2090_7_EN.pdf [05 June 2018].

Council of Europe (2010). *Recommendation 2010 (8).* Retrieved from http://eryica.org/sites/default/files/Recommendation%20CM%3ARec%282010%298%20on%20Youth%20Information_EN_0.pdf [05 June 2018].

Grbich, C. (2007). *Qualitative Data Analysis: An Introduction.* Thousand Oaks: Sage Publications.

Lederer-Hutsteiner, T., Auferbauer, M., Polanz, G. & Diwoky, T. (2014). *Jugendinformation in der Steiermark. Status quo, Bedarf und Innovationspotenziale.* Retrieved from http://www.x-sample.at/pdf/Bericht_Jugendinformation%20in%20der%20Steiermark_Druckfassung.pdf [05 June 2018].

LOGO Jugendmanagement. (2016). *Jugendinfo. Angebot.* Retrieved from https://www.logo.at/jugendinfo/jugendinfo-angebot [05 June 2018].

Shell Deutschland Holding. (2015). *17. Shell Jugendstudie. Jugend 2015.* Frankfurt/Main: Fischer Taschenbuch.

Schriefl, U. (2015). *Jugendinformationsarbeit in der Steiermark.* Retrieved from https://prezi.com/o0vpbon2ylsr/jugendinformationsarbeit-in-der-steiermark/?utm_campaign=share&utm_medium=copy [05 June 2018].

Schenk L., Bau, A., Borde, T., Butler, J., Lampert, T., Neuhauser, H., Razum, O., Weilandt, C. (2006). *Mindestindikatorensatz zur Erfassung des Migrationsstatus. Empfehlungen für die epidemiologische Praxis.* In: Bundesgesundheitsblatt, Gesundheitsforschung, Gesundheitsschutz Vo. 49 (9), pp. 853–860. Berlin: Springer Medizin Verlag.

Geir Hyrve and Joachim Vogt Isaksen
(Norwegian University of Science and Technology)

Reframing Child Welfare Education in Norway

Abstract

Even if the government in Norway has the primary responsibility for child protection, volunteer and private organizations also make a substantial and important contribution to the field. In this chapter, we take a closer look at the Norwegian volunteer organization called Change Factory.[1] This organization has broadly influenced social services, such as policy and lawmakers, practitioners within the social services, in addition to educational institutions. We will first give a brief review of user involvement in children's services in Norway. We will then we give a description of the role of Change Factory, before we move on to evaluate their impact on the political and educational arena. We discuss opportunities and challenges with the implementation of user experiences in the educational system.

Introduction

User involvement in the child welfare system is measured according to how children and their parents can achieve greater influence in their interaction with the services. Although Norway has traditionally put emphasis on the principle of the children's best interests, there has been a debate on whether there has been a shift from a focus on child protection towards what is called family-focused welfare. From attention directed towards protection of the child, it is argued that there has been a shift to a more family-oriented child welfare system. We will analyze the organization Change Factory, which has broadly influenced the Norwegian child welfare services. We discuss how the inclusion of children's user experiences can be managed at different levels, with our main focus being child welfare education. In recent years, there has been a great expansion in user involvement in social work, both from a government driven policy perspective and a liberal democratic perspective (McLaughlin, 2006). The Change Factory, representing the involvement of children with experience with the child welfare system, *can* potentially develop the child welfare system in a more "child friendly" way. We discuss how user involvement may encompass a cultural shift in Norway's child welfare promotion, both within the social services, and within the education system. Even if user involvement is con-

---

1   This is an English translation of the Norwegian name "Forandringsfabrikken".

sidered an important ideal, the increased influence from children can also challenge the dominant knowledgebase, as well as the traditional discourses. The child welfare problems involve complex judgments and debates, and several actors argue from different positions and perspectives. In this field of conflict of interests, the weakest party may often end up as the least influential. As such, the complexity and potential consequences of decisions has led to a wider debate around the necessity of involving children at a deeper level in these processes.

Traditionally the evaluation and investigation of the child's problems involved a set of negotiations between stakeholders with knowledge of the child's situation, including professional actors, family members and the child. In the Norwegian context, the main goal of the child welfare services is to ensure that children and adolescents, who are living under conditions that represent a risk to their health and/ or psychological-social development, receive the help they need *when* they need it, and to contribute to children growing up in safe and caring conditions. We argue that the children, who have personal in-depth knowledge of their situation, can be involved on several levels when developing policy, practice and education within child welfare. We offer concrete examples of how user involvement has taken an innovative turn through the user organization Change Factory, and we discuss specific opportunities and challenges with this new approach.

Rethinking the creation of knowledge in child welfare education

Although there has been increased attention on the implementation of user involvement in the field of social work, it has been pointed out that it is not as efficient or extensive as it ideally could be. The interpretation of this concept, as well as the practical implementation, is a potential problem among professionals, institutions and educators. Despite the fact that user involvement is both a political and professional goal, studies have shown a lack of sufficient communication between children, families and the social workers (Clifford, Fauske, Lichtwarck, & Marthinsen, 2015). It is therefore essential to improve the dialogue between educators, social workers, and the children and their families. User experiences can help better inform practice as well as contribute to new solutions, which may improve outcomes.

Arnstein (1969) has constructed a ladder of citizen participation consisting of eight steps, from *nonparticipation* to *citizen control*, with each step corresponding to the extent of citizen power in determining the result of the negotiations between professionals and users. At the lowest step, the objectives are not to enable citizens to participate in the planning or decisions, but rather to enable a child welfare worker to "educate" or "cure" the participants. Further up the ladder, we find levels of citizen power, with increasing degrees of decision-making influence, that enable them to negotiate and engage in discussion with the child welfare worker. At the top of the ladder, the citizens gain the main control and can determine the outcome of the complicated problem. Because of the relatively autonomous position and strategies of the different stakeholders, and the complexity of the decision-making processes that follows, it is difficult to achieve satisfactory outcomes without extensive networking between the child welfare services and involved actors. Placing the focus on children and youth in the decision-making processes can have broad implications in the education of social workers.

Traditional knowledge is easy to legitimize within the system. The traditional definition of knowledge is "justified true belief" (Nonaka & Takeuchi, 1995). While traditional epistemology emphasizes the absolute and static, the non-human nature of knowledge is typically expressed in propositions and formal logic. On the contrary, knowledge can also be considered as a dynamic human process of justifying personal belief towards the "truth". The consequences of this knowledge are context-specific, relative and humanistic, having a practical, active and a subjective dimension. For child welfare students, it means that learning is a question of engaging in and contributing to the practices of child welfare. For example, this can be illustrated in the training of communication skills, through interaction between student and child. In the education of social workers, this means that learning is an issue of refining practice and ensuring development. Heino (2007) calls relationships known from within a special type of knowledge. It is not only knowing from the child or youth's own relationship; it is also about knowing from within the larger family and from within the culture. At the same time, the education systems also have their own knowing created and expanded upon through the social interaction between tacit and explicit knowledge (Nonaka & Takeuchi, 1995). For the education system, it means that the quality of learning depends on sustaining a practice that is interconnected with the professional communities. Ideally this takes place when the students get the opportunity to share experiences with users, while at the same taking part in the process of converting new explicit and tacit knowledge.

In child welfare services, educators need to take the complex processes of co-creation between the social workers and the users of the service into account. Benington and Moore (2011) discuss the process of creating public value, the idea that citizens could debate the role of the government in the society and contribute to deciding which individual circumstances and social conditions they want. The concept of public value highlights the importance of focusing on the process and outcomes, and the child welfare services can be considered more in terms of an open system. When users take an active part in defining professional values, they may become co-producers and partners in the creation of services. Consequently, the users can contribute to the creation of public value.

Reflecting the voices of youth

In this section we will look more closely at the Change Factory, which defines itself as a social enterprise. This is an ideal organization and is legally registered as a foundation. The point of departure is that it is through the children and youth, the child welfare and researchers/educators gain more insight into user experiences. The methods are inspired by Participatory Learning and Action (PLA). PLA is a strategy applied to advance both science and practice, and is an approach for learning about and engaging within communities. It combines a toolkit of participatory and visual methods with natural interviewing techniques, and it is intended to facilitate a process of collective analysis and learning. As it is a powerful consultation tool, it offers the opportunity to go beyond mere consultation and promote the active participation of communities in the issues and interventions that shape their lives.[2] Understanding how the children evaluate the services, as seen from their own perspectives and words, may improve the services in a direction that also has more legitimacy among the users. The user's insights may be implemented both in child welfare services and in professional training of social workers, and it represents a bottom-up strategy. Jacobsen (2012) has operationalized strategies that social development can be understood through. The bottom-up model, which he named strategy O (i.e. organization), is based on cooperation and consultation, motivation of local communities, and expansion of learning opportunities, which requires time, increased communication and exchange, as well as cultural acceptance of participatory processes. For practitioners using the bottom-up model as structured by social development theory, participation in discussions with youth and their families give opportunities to improve and learn, and the sense of empowerment that follows knowledge are the necessary precursors to accomplishing goals within community development. Approaching a problem with knowledge from user experiences can represent a bottom-up strategy, as this may increase participation from the community simultaneously as it provides new learning opportunities among social work students. It has managed to increase the communication, not only between users and practitioners, but also between research and practice.

Lately, there has been an increased focus on innovation, change and knowledge production in terms of children and youth involvement within child welfare services (Smith, 2009). The Change Factory is innovative in that it recruits children and youth to convey stories from their own experienced vulnerable life situations. As part of their activities they also give advice, and try to influence public institutions; not only within the child welfare service, but also within criminal justice, mental healthcare, drug treatment and schools. This innovation mainly started as a response to dissatisfaction among users with certain practices within the services.[3] Child Welfare Professionals (CWPs)[4] is the title of the young people working in the organization within the field of child welfare. They suggest changes and reforms within the profession, and reach out to politicians, practitioners and educators. As

---

2   http://idp-key-resources.org/documents/0000/d04267/000.pdf.
3   http://www.forandringsfabrikken.no/om-oss/.
4   This is a translation of the Norwegian

an example, the CWPs have claimed that child welfare workers often use words and concepts that many children and young people do not understand, or that they experience as alienating. In this case, the Change Factory introduced new words and concepts that could more easily convey information in an easy and more "child-friendly" way. Even if this may be understood primarily as a rhetorical innovation, it may still have practical consequences concerning how the practitioners understand and treat the youth, as well as on how the youth perceive themselves.

The impact of Change Factory at a political level

Official government reports have shown that the child welfare services in Norway need to improve communication with children. One official Norwegian report (NOU, 2017: 12) concludes that the dialogue with children is missing or too poor in quality. Identifying a common problem is a chance to improve the institutions, as well as to examine and rethink the child welfare education system. Political authorities have directed their attention toward innovation and adjustments within the services, and education in order to meet the challenges linked to the changing needs of the population (Meld. St. 13, 2011–2012). An increased demand for user involvement challenges social workers, both when it comes to ethical considerations, personal judgments, and increased communication with users. In order to increase the quality in education and in the service providers, the politicians want to strengthen the research at the educational institutions, and want the research to be thematically more closely linked to the field of practice (for more, see Meld. St. 18, 2012–2013). In public documents there is, for example, a demand for increased knowledge within child welfare services, both when it comes to the children's needs, increased focus on user involvement, multicultural competence, and leadership (Prop. 106 L. (2012–13). It is also maintained that the disciplines must build on a combination of available scientific knowledge, alongside user experiences and preferences, and ethical assessments (Barne- og likestillingsdepartementet, 2009). In order to strengthen the development of knowledge and competence in the field of practice, the Ministry of Children and Equality ordered a report by an appointed group of experts called The Befring Group. One of the conclusions of the report was that it was important to increase and improve the cooperation between the educational professions and the field of practice (NOU 2009:8). This goal is also in line with the international professional community's emphasis on knowledge production. One important aspect is improved cooperation between the field of practice and the educational professions; something that is often referred to as "bridging the gap" between research and practice (The Salisbury Forum Group, 2011). In order to bridge the gap, it is necessary to have a closer link between the education of proffessionals and the field of practice.

The Change Factory has managed to broadly influence social services, such as policy and lawmakers, practitioners within welfare services, and educational institutions. As a response to insufficient communication between the government and young people, the Change Factory has worked on the developmental proj-ect "My life: Child welfare service" together with the child welfare services.[5] Since 2013 more than 150 child welfare service institutions have taken part in this proj-ect. Child welfare workers and CWPs have together developed practical advice for more reliable quality assurance tools for use in the municipalities. The recommen-dations were passed on to the the Norwegian Directorate for Children, Youth and Family Affairs (Bufdir). In the fall of 2016, Change Factory broadened their scope, as they started with the project "My life: Child welfare institutions",[6] with 21 insti-tutions as pilots.[7] In cooperation with the CWPs, the institutions discover values and working methods that may lead to more purposeful practices within institu-tions. This project is an illustration of how the Change Factory both works at a local and a governmental level. Several of the CWP's suggestions have been discussed at the highest political level and have been integrated into legal proposals. Since 2013, proposals from the Change factory have achieved wide impact for the preparation of the government's proposed new child protection law.[8] The CWPs have, for exam-ple, suggested that children's user involvement must be translated into a more con-crete language, and it must be expressed formally that the child is the most impor-tant cooperative partner. Another important proposal is that the child always must have the opportunity to talk directly to those caseworkers who are making the deci-sions concerning their situation. The users have also influenced social workers to change parts of the terminology and concepts used in the child welfare services. For example, the word *caseworker* is about to be replaced by the word *contact person*, from which the children's perspective is a more "humane" description of the role of the social worker who provides help. During the fall of 2016, the Norwegian govern-ment presented a new legal proposal in child welfare, where several proposals from the CWPs were included. The CWPs now work with hearing proposals, in addition to a large number of national amendment processes within the child welfare service. They also visit most of the child welfare and education programs, and the young people's knowledge has become part of the professional code among child welfare workers in some institutions. Overall, at several levels the CWPs have managed to influence the child welfare system to shape its thinking more in terms of the chil-dren's interests.

---

5   Translated from Norwegian: "Mitt Liv: Barnevern".

6   Translated from Norwegian: "Mitt Liv: Barnevernsinstitusjon".

7   http://www.forandringsfabrikken.no/er-du-var-nye-prosjektarbeider-pa-barnevern/.

8   http://www.forandringsfabrikken.no/files/Horingsinnspill-til-ny-barnevernlov-fra-Barnev-ernsProffene-i-Forandringsfabrikken.pdf.

Ways of turning to practice in child welfare education

In recent decades, the established scientific community has arguably been one important force behind reform within the child welfare services. Practice has been guided by the kind of knowledge that seems to work in a professional context. Scientific knowledge is regarded as a guide for practical social work, and scientifically valid solutions for social problems are often sought. Embedded in this view of practice is a pervasive notion of instrumental rationality, and it can be regarded as an objective, *and* as a means. Based on this idea, there is an implicit skepticism regarding any practice that cannot be scientifically proven. More obvious is the notion that scientific knowledge is of instrumental use to practice; practice can be repaired and improved by the application of the "right" kind of knowledge. In order to implement and legitimate the ideas from the Change Factory in the child welfare system, they must undergo scientific evaluation, and the user experiences must arguably be translated into theories or methods.

Nonetheless, there are different perspectives surrounding what foundation the child welfare services should build on. A narrow definition, such as methods in evidence-based practice, at least implies that social and educational practices must be updated and need reform. Høgsbro (2015) argues that we need a broader definition of evidence-based practice, and suggests that practice is more than a site or context for the application of scientific knowledge. He writes:

> We have to investigate the whole process of the contact between citizens and social services and identify possible systematic obstacles, which might render it difficult for the users to get access to help. We have to identify the factors in the organization of social work and the collaboration between different agents that make the total structure difficult to access and comprehend for both users and professionals (Høgsbro 2015, p. 65–66).

This implies that practice can be the foundation for knowledge. In order to identify problems, the students must understand the source of the problems. Already at an early stage, the students can gain training in how to work together with children and families. Knowledge in the form of instrumental evidence of "what works" is important, but it also poses a variety of methodological, practical and ethical challenges that can undermine the benefits of the approach (Eikeland & Nicolini, 2011). An instrumental approach may also function as a barrier towards identifying the unique situations that may not "fit" into scientific theories or methods. However, one could argue that students, through meetings with children and families, can better decide how and when to draw on scientific knowledge, in combination with an understandings of their specific needs. Regarding practice primarily as a matter of the local and situational, a consequence of this view is that the knowledge provided for practice must be adjusted or adapted to fit the circumstances. Practice in this view demands a dialectic process of working back and forth from the specific case over to established knowledge, values and commitments. This way of reasoning is hermeneutic, where interpretation of the situation is based on grasping the relevant features of the case at hand in combination with values, principles and standing commitments.

It seems difficult to include children, youth and their families in the decision-making processes in the child welfare services. The formal accountability rules are taken care of by the services as the families are allowed to express their opinions and to use their rights for appeal. Still, this does not seem to have a large influence on the content (Smith, Fulcher, & Doran, 2013). Despite Norway's welfare system being highly developed, many stakeholders do not communicate sufficiently with the children and their families (Clifford et al., 2015). The CWPs argue that there is a lack of opportunity for users to be involved within institutions. Public programs working with children and youth are often adult-led, and the design and functioning of public policies and institutions do not allow sufficiently for the opinions of users. Even if families and children's knowledge are important for the welfare system to work, the systems do not interact sufficiently with users in order to gather information that can lead to more relevant and qualitatively based decisions (Clifford et al., 2015).

Reframing child welfare education in Norway

The translation of practice poses a variety of methodological, practical, and ethical challenges that can undermine the benefits of the approach. The Change Factory aims to get young people to identify system-changing ideas, build consensus around them, and open direct communication between users and policy makers in order to implement change (Dønnestad, Sanner & Brun, 2006). According to evaluations, there are several factors that may lead to failure in child welfare service. These include lack of knowledge and expertise, absence of strategies and planning in knowledge and competence work, weak mechanisms for multi-level cooperation and coordination, unclear control mechanisms, missing standards and guidelines, weak management, or an absence of multilevel management.

The idea of systematic feedback being transmitted more directly from users to the profession may open up a wide range of opportunities. There are different ways to respond to the challenges the Change Factory have defined, and different interventionist traditions have developed different understandings of how these can be met. Using representation practices to stimulate change also creates theoretical and methodological challenges that need to be taken into account. Eikeland and Nicolini (2011) have introduced a classification of ways of putting practice at the center of the concern of social scientists (see Table 1). We will use this model to discuss the educational consequences of the Change Factory's methodology. Our starting point is that the people who are most competent in the workings of the child welfare system are those within that system, and that they have unique experiences which can be applied when identifying problems, as well as suggesting solutions. The Change Factory has officially argued that the ultimate goal of the organization is to provide public institutions with a proven way to listen to children in a respectful way. Furthermore, they use a participatory change methodology to encourage young people aged 8 to 20 to honestly talk about and evaluate their situations[9]. Through their experiences, they can contribute with important insights into the landscape, which Schwandt (2003) characterizes as the "rough ground", where stakeholders constantly struggle to get along and cooperate. In this environment, actors with different interpretations of social practices unfold. The sharing of experiences from the users to the educational system makes it possible for the students to understand how children and young people make sense of their experiences.

Table 1: Ways of turning to practice in social science – an illustration of the direction of interest

Starting point	Broadly practical	Broadly theoretical
From outside and above	1 Develop specialized techniques/applied research	2 Normal science (explanatory and interpretative approaches)
From within and below	3 Informed deliberation	4 Trigger critical dialogue – Immanent critique

Table 1 above is a simplified version of the model presented by Eikeland & Nicolini (2011, p. 166). We have chosen to use this model in a generalist manner in order to illustrate our point. For example, the actors within the child welfare educational system can broadly be seen as either practically or theoretically motivated. A broadly practical interest in the field can be motivated by wishes to produce changes and improvement, such as improved decision-making models (cell 1). In the educational institutions, lecturers who use established theory to understand, explain, develop or create changes in practice may arguably fit into cell 1. Students are perhaps prepared for practice through literature and theory, even though they have practical internship phases as part of their studies. A broadly theoretical motivation can be filled with a desire to gain theoretical knowledge, or explanations according to detached research (cell 2). The interests can start from a spectator position outside the action concerned, or it can start from within the practice that is studied. According to this classification, the Change Factory would fall in cell 3 as the user's competence can improve the child welfare system since they have been part of the system. By listening to their experiences, it is possible to identify dysfunction within the system that otherwise may have gone unnoticed. Empirical social researchers, who normally gather data and test theories imaginatively from an outside and above perspective,

---

9   http://forandringsfabrikken.no/article/about-us-english.

would ideally fit in cell 2. Among other universities, the Norwegian University of Science and Technology (NTNU) has integrated Change Factory philosophy as a part of the examination and grading in the bachelor's degree program in child welfare education. One important advantage for the educational system to reach cell 4 is that it can open up more for the use of actionable knowledge from user organizations. Theory can also be developed from practical experiences gathered from the child welfare system.

One of the most important aims of user organizations is empowerment in the process of conveying and respecting the users' own knowledge. This can take place when there is a bridge between knowledge, power and control. Freire (1999) used the notion of "conscientization" to describe this process. By involving users in the education process, you create the experience of influence and empowerment, while the students gain insights in the field of practice through interaction with users.

One important challenge is to relate user experiences to scientific knowledge. Eikeland and Nicolini (2011) use grammar as a metaphor to explain why user experiences have to communicate with scientific knowledge. Grammar is descriptive and analytical, but it is also normative, since it sets standards for correct speech and writing. In the same way as a grammar organizes and structures language, the professionals within a certain field structure scientific knowledge. From a scientific point of view, the young people's interpretation of the child welfare system has to be transformed into the scientific "language and structure", so it can be related to the theoretic tradition within the field. This is different from the traditionally applied way of understanding theory and practice from outside. There is an inbuilt potential of conflict when the children's experiences of the system may stand in opposition to the scientific knowledge. While the active use of such organizations opens up new possibilities, it also requires an informed and prudent implementation by the educational system.

Conclusion

In a field that is a becoming increasingly complex, the educational system needs to adjust to new guidance from national curriculum plans, evidence-based practices, performance measurement systems, and other new demands in order to understand what lies behind variations among users. In child welfare education, central themes are to identify standardized patterns of childhood, the workings of the family, and formalize methods such as family group conferences. However, many of these traditional objects in the curriculum plans, which are the target in education, are being destabilized. How can we deal with and better understand practice, and how can education provide education that is more consistent with practice?

We point out that one way is through practice-based studies, but there are in fact many different ways of turning to practice in child welfare education. The advantage of user organizations such as the Change Factory is that they make their experiences more available through their active participation on several levels. Through social interaction between the young users of services and the education system, it is possible to gain a new understanding of the "rough ground" of child welfare. One example of this is the use of CWPs in the practice of developing student communication skills.

Educators stand in a demanding position between practice and theory. Schwandt (1999) argues that understanding requires an openness to experiences, including a willingness to engage in a dialogue on challenges of our understanding of ourselves. In the educational system, there are clear advantages to actionable knowledge that students can easily apply. The knowledge can favorably be presented in a way that makes it possible to implement it in an efficient manner (Argyris, 1996). The educational system needs to convey pragmatic knowledge, and user organizations contribute with social knowledge. This knowledge can be used through critical dialogue among the actors, and may increase the understanding and mutual respect towards the users. We have pointed out that it can be advantageous for the educational system if it strengthens the critical dialogue with the users in the field, and develops actionable knowledge by cooperating with user organizations. We have pointed out that the most prominent challenge is to treat these user experiences in a reflective way. We argue that there are advantages for the educational system to develop actionable knowledge from user organizations. Theory may also be developed from practical experiences gathered from the child welfare system.

Educators stand in a challenging position between practice and theory, and the sharing of user experiences with the educational system provides both opportunities and challenges. Traditionally, the first-time child welfare students are introduced to the users in a professional setting is in their roles as trainees. A more systematic implementation of CWPs at the universities in an educational setting can potentially give more legitimacy to the user experiences, as they are invited into an arena they are normally excluded from. A more active involvement of users in the universities can also give more legitimacy to the child welfare profession by increasing contact between educators and users. Ultimately academia can function as a unifying actor that strengthens the cooperation between professionals and users, and create a more negotiated and mutual understanding of what is in the users' interests.

References

Argyris, C. (1996). Actionable knowledge: Intent versus actuality. *The Journal of Applied Behavioral Science, 32*(4), 441–444.

Arnstein, S. R. (1969). A ladder of citizen participation. *Journal of the American Institute of planners, 35*(4), 216–224.

Barne- og likestillings-departementet (2009). *Forskningsstrategi 2009–2012.* Barne- og likestillingsdepartementet.

Benington, J., & Moore, M. H. (2011). *Public value: theory and practice.* Palgrave Macmillan.

Clifford, G., Fauske, H., Lichtwarck, W., & Marthinsen, E. (2015). *Minst hjelp til dem som trenger det mest* (Vol. NF-rapport nr. 6/2015). Bodø: Nordlandsforskning.

Dønnestad, E., Sanner, M., & Brun, M. (2006). *Håndbok for forandrere: om verdighet i møte med de som vokser opp og de som vil vokse*. Kristiansand: Forandringsfabrikken.

Eikeland, O., & Nicolini, D. (2011). Turning practically: broadening the horizon. *Journal of Organizational Change Management, 24*(2), 164–174. doi:10.1108/09534811111119744.

Freire, P. (1999). *De undertryktes pedagogikk* (2. utg. ed.). Oslo: Ad notam Gyldendal.

Heino, T. (2007). Knowledge-Creating Process in Family Group Conference. In L. Schjelderup & C. Omre (Eds.), *Veiviseren for et fremtidig barnervern* (pp. 55–74). Trondheim: Tapir Akademiske Forlag.

Høgsbro, K. (2015). Evidence and research designs in applied sociology and social work research. *Nordic Social Work Research, 5*, 56–70. doi:10.1080/2156857X.2015.1066706.

Jacobsen, D. I. (2012). *Organisasjonsendringer og endringsledelse* (2. utg. ed.). Bergen: Fagbokforl.

McLaughlin, H. (2006). Involving young service users as co-researchers: possibilities, benefits and costs. British Journal of Social Work, 36(8), 1395–1410.

Meld. St. 13 (2011–2012) (2012). *Utdanning for velferd*. Kunnskapsdepartementet.

Meld. St. 18 (2012–2013) (2013). *Lange linjer – kunnskap gir muligheter*. Kunnskapsdepartementet.

NOU 2009:08 (2009). *Kompetanseutvikling i barnevernet -Kvalifisering til arbeid i barnevernet gjennom praksisnær og forskningsbasert utdanning*. Barne- og likestillingsdepartementet.

NOU 2017:12 (2017). *Svikt og svik – Gjennomgang av saker hvor barn har vært utsatt for vold, seksuelle overgrep og omsorgssvikt*. Barne- og likestillingsdepartementet.

Nonaka, I., & Takeuchi, H. (1995). *The knowledge-creating company: how Japanese companies create the dynamics of innovation*. New York: Oxford University Press.

Prop. 106 L (2012–2013) (2013). *Endringer i barnevernloven*. Barne- og likestillingsdepartementet

Schwandt, T. A. (1999). On understanding understanding. *Qualitative Inquiry, 5*(4), 451–464.

Schwandt, T. A. (2003). 'Back to the Rough Ground!' Beyond Theory to Practice in Evaluation. *Evaluation, 9*(3), 353–364. doi:10.1177/13563890030093008.

Smith, M. (2009). *Rethinking residential child care: positive perspectives*. Bristol: Policy.

Smith, M., Fulcher, L. C., & Doran, P. (2013). *Residential child care in practice: Making a difference*: Policy Press.

The Salisbury Forum Group (2011). The Salisbury Statement. Social Work & Society Volume 9 (1), 1–9.

Whyte, W. F. (Ed.). (1991). Sage focus editions, Vol. 123. *Participatory action research*. Thousand Oaks, CA, US: Sage Publications, Inc.

Anne Grytbakk, Berit Skauge and Roar Sundby
(Norwegian University of Science and Technology, NTNU)

From Client to Partner:
Children Changing the Child Welfare Services
and the Education of Child Welfare Workers

Abstract

The innovation and research projects *My Life Cooperation* and *My Life Education* are joint projects between children in the Change Factory, six child welfare services in the central part of Norway and NTNU (Norwegian University of Science and Technology) and HSN (University College of Southeast Norway), financed by NTNU and BUF-dir (The Norwegian Directorate for Children, Youth and Family Affairs) and HSN. The innovative elements of the projects are the implementation of new working methods in child welfare services with the aim of strengthening the cooperation between children, child welfare services, social work and child welfare education programs. The children are giving advice and they ask to be listened to in order to improve the quality of the casework, family support, foster families, care work in institutions, psychiatric institutions, etc. A process evaluation of these innovations is included in the projects. The methodology in the projects is influenced by the principles of participatory action research.

Child welfare workers involved in the innovation process toward enhanced communication with children express great satisfaction with the change in their working routines, which they interpret as a more meaningful practice. They also point to the importance of values and relational skills in their work routines as distinct from the previous, more rigid manual-based and method-based routines frequently identified as the methods taught in the social work and child welfare education system. The innovation can be seen as a paradigmatic change in child welfare services, pointing towards a more humanistic practice.

Introduction

Do child welfare services and the competence of their social workers change when they really listen to children's experience with these services? A child welfare service that is more focused on cooperation and communication with children than advanced behavior therapy or formal bureaucratic proceedings seems to be one of the outcomes. This paper will focus on social workers in the child welfare services and their experience in an innovation project that prioritized listening to children.

The innovation projects *My Life Cooperation* and *My Life Education* involve cooperation between the following: children in the *Change Factory*, six child welfare units

(CWS) in central Norway and NTNU (Norwegian University of Science and Technology) and HSN (The University College of southeastern Norway). The work was funded by the universities NTNU and HSN and by BUF-dir (The Norwegian Directorate for Children, Youth and Family Affairs).

The projects set out to include the young people's voice in public services for children and to demonstrate experience-based best practices in the field of communication and cooperation in child welfare. Communication theories were applied, for example Seikkula's *open dialogue* approach as outlined in Seikkula (2006). Development of routines and models for better cooperation with children were also central features of this innovation (Andersen & Hygum Espersen, 2017). The methodology in the innovation projects is heavily influenced by the principles in *participatory action research* as described in research by Whyte (1991), including group meetings for planning and reporting, instruction through discussions and lectures, structured qualitative interviews with the involved partners in child welfare, student involvement, evaluations and documentation and observation of new routines in the services.

The research project presented in this paper is a result of this cooperation. It must be understood in the context of the work initiated by the Change Factory where children describe their experience with the child welfare services in Norway and offer advice. In light of this advice, a number of child welfare services have revised their working methods and values. It should also be mentioned that the third party in this cooperation is the professional education serving the CWS, which revised their education curricula with an increased focus on communication and cooperation skills. The resulting changes in the education system will not be further elaborated upon here.

This paper will give a general overview of the background for the project, first by briefly describing child welfare services in Norway and the social movement initiated by the Change Factory and introducing some of the advice given by children and the resulting innovations. In the second part of the paper, we describe the experience of the child welfare workers with the implementation of new principles and methods in child welfare work that were generated in the project.

The overall user value is expected to be that children in contact with public services such as CWS should feel that they are listened to through improved quality in the communication with children, their families and the civil society in general, and reduced conflict levels and reduced case processing time due to improved cooperation. The lessons learned should also be applicable to other fields such social work in schools and in centers for child and adolescent mental health (BUP) and family therapy related work.

Background: The child welfare services

The child welfare services in Norway are highly professionalized, legally regulated with set protocols, and there is a child welfare service qualification. The work is also associated with conflict, extreme workloads and frequent staff turnover.

In 2014, 9982 children aged 0 to 17 years were placed in the care of child welfare services in Norway. In relation to the general population in the age category 0 to 17 years old, this represents 7.9 children per 1000 population. A care order is only made if the child's situation is considered to be of serious concern and when it cannot be remedied using voluntary measures; for example when a child is subjected to serious neglect, physical maltreatment or other serious abuse or neglect in the home. Cases are investigated and prepared by the municipal child welfare service.

43,370 children receive other forms of help from child welfare services, which is mainly support for children living at home.

Criticism of child welfare services

A care order sometimes represents a conflict of interest between children, parents and the child welfare services. These conflicts are regularly aired in the media by one of the parties. Immigrants are overrepresented in the child welfare services mainly due to different cultural understanding of what constitutes acceptable care for children and problems of integration into Norwegian society. Lately such cases have resulted in concern in some immigrant families' countries of origin; the Norwegian child welfare system is accused of "stealing" children. One assumption is that absence of or low quality communication with the parties, parents or children in the welfare services is one of the main reasons for a generally high conflict level. As a foster mother put it: "I feel quite powerless in the face of a rigid system" (Fosterhjemsforening, 2017).

A recurrent complaint about child welfare services in Norway is that they do not communicate adequately with children (Clausen and Tiller 1997, Gulbrandsen 2014, NOU 2017:12 Svikt og svik), that the child's opinion is only mediated through the case worker (Næss et al. 1998) and that matters are not improving; children's voices were less evident in case records in 2009 (40%) than in 2000 (70%) (Skauge, 2010). Children feel that they are not involved in the process, and not consulted about their opinion on decisions concerning their future (Christiansen 2012).

There is an ongoing discussion about communication methods in the child welfare services. Standardized, alienating and often instrument-based methods in use in child welfare services have been very criticized by the Change Factory and by children with experience with the CWS. Jorange (2016), looking to Habermas' liberating understanding, challenges the social services to critically reflect on their practices.

One of the reasons advanced for this bias is that caseworkers do not feel that their competence and skills in communication and cooperation are adequate (Gamst, 2011). Other explanations are found in the contradiction in the child welfare services between, on the one hand, evidence and manual based practice and the need for "proof" to support a care order, and on the other hand the overall aim of "good enough care" as the main objective for the services (Martinsen 2012). The dilemma may be expressed as an evidence and instrumentalist approach versus a communicative and relational approach. There is a general impression of a patronizing attitude by public agents representing legal power. This inherent contradiction in the child welfare services may account for the service having relatively high conflict levels, high levels of stress among caseworkers, sometimes lengthy processing times and an increase in resorting to emergency placements. A reasonable assumption in this project is that improved communication and cooperation with children and parents will affect the overall functioning of the child welfare services.

"Change Factory"

The *Change Factory* is an NGO that organizes children with experience from the child welfare services, as well as children with experience with other services such as psychiatric care, the education system, or children with experience with poverty, violence, or those with non-Norwegian cultural backgrounds. These children, calling themselves child welfare professionals (children with experience with the child welfare services), have been long-term partners and a source of inspiration for child welfare education. Recently they have exerted a good deal of influence and have gained an enhanced reputation in the child welfare services and in child policy in general. Their work is based on Article 12 in the UN Convention on the Rights of the Child, dealing with children's right to expression and to be heard.

The children are recruited through networking connections and by word of mouth, and they are encouraged to speak freely about their experiences with the services or institutions they have been part of. More than 1,100 children from the child welfare services have been in contact with the Change Factory and give their opinion about the services. They provide presentations for large audiences ranging from the Ministry of Children and Equality to employees in the child welfare services, as well as teachers or students in social work or child welfare education. The impact has been quite dramatic, and the children often tell stories that challenge the assumptions of some of the common methods used in social welfare work or the principles taught in social work methods or in psychiatric treatment. The quotes in these presentations are from the child professionals' participation in the training of students in the child welfare education in NTNU 2016–2017 and the advices they give to the child welfare services and with their consent.

The Change Factory can be seen as a value-based social movement working for the democratisation of the child welfare services.

What are the children's experiences?

These children tell stories about difficult childhoods where violence and other traumatizing experiences are part of their daily lives. One of the recurrent themes is that these experiences remain secret for a long time during their childhood because they find nobody to listen to their story, nobody asks about what is going on at home, and they find nobody to trust. Some of the children have been in the care of the child welfare since they were born; others have lived most of their childhood with their families without anybody knowing about their circumstance. Another typical story is that the child's frustrations and traumatic experiences are expressed in challenging or provocative behavior, criminality or drug abuse. The resulting feedback from the teachers is that these children are "difficult", they don't "behave" or they bully their classmates, or they withdraw. The normal reaction of the teacher is that they report the child to the parents and that the child is punished when returning home. From the child's perspective, the dilemma is that "nobody asked me what my perception of the situation is."

Advice from children

They talk to children almost never but they are still called child protection, says Gloria (18). The children in the Change Factory offer advice to child welfare, and other services working with children, in discussions about their experiences. Their views are very varied: those mentioned here are those that seem to have had the greatest impact on the child welfare services.

Changing the terminology

As academics and social workers seem to prefer scientific terminology, often with an alienating effect, to describe children's situation or problems, the children are clearly inclined towards low-key, everyday language and non-stigmatizing communication terms.

> "We are not clients, patients or users (my father was a "user"), I am the child, the young person, or just use my name."

> Never use "behavior" to characterize the child, if I do not "behave" it is because I do not feel well inside (or I have some really bad experiences). Talk about that."

Another important comment is about the common use of diagnostics and medication in child psychiatry, psychology, pedagogics and child welfare. *"When they put a label or a diagnosis on my head, they also stop talking about my real problem." (Italicized text above are quotes from presentations from the child welfare professionals.)*

Values

Values in this context means the attitude the children want the care worker to meet them with. Through the histories told from the children in the Change Factory they have singled out four main values representing their summary of the children's experiences.

The social workers in the municipalities together with the child welfare professionals propose the following four basic values openness, love, humility, and cooperation.

1. We work with children by being open an honest, and by providing all relevant Information.
2. Working with love means caring and showing human warmth.
3. Show humility by believing children, listening and being engaged.
4. Cooperation involves including children in decisions and asking the children for feedback. (Forandringsfabrikken, 2015).

These basic values should also be reflected in child welfare education.

Implementing new working methods in the child welfare system

190 child welfare services in the municipalities have now adopted a common basis for working with children and have adopted common values that imply that 1) children know a lot about their own lives; 2) they have the same values as adults and 3) they need love and to be believed and taken seriously.

Children promoting changes in the education of child welfare workers

The aim of educational and training is to prepare students of child welfare education to work providing social services, including implementing changes in working methods, especially in cooperating and communicating with children. The development of methods for assessment and new approaches to practical work training will be a core challenge in the project and an expected contribution of research.

Experience from recent revisions of practical communication training in child welfare education will be used as a basis for development of communication and cooperation training programs for students in their practical field placements and for possible application for child welfare workers in counseling work. The principles for learning communication skills are based on an awareness of one's own life story and communication in real life contexts with children from child welfare as being crucial for realistic training and replacing the former methods of role-play and constructed situations.

Exposing traumatic histories in public: legal and ethical challenges

Cooperation with children with a background in the child welfare services, often with traumatic experiences, has been met with some objections and reservations.

There has been some concern regarding burdens and the consequences and vulnerability of children when they reveal their history of often violent family settings and traumatic events in their past. These concerns are most evident among therapeutic staff. Psychologists and social workers are concerned about the effect such exposure can have on children's heath and recovery. The children themselves, without exception, think differently. They feel liberated and justified when given the chance to tell their story. When this is provided, they experience enhanced self-confidence and competence. Some concern has also been raised concerning the stigmatizing effect these stories might have in the local community.

The second group of concerns mainly attach to privacy and the issue of whether the children can give legal consent to participate in cooperation with the child welfare services and the education of social workers. There is concern about the right of protection for those who are the presumed perpetrators of abuse, e.g. parents, other relatives or other persons.

The basic assumption of the project group is that freedom of expression also includes children, particularly as expressed in the Convention on the Rights of the Child (CRC) (UN 1991) article 12:1, and that the right to expression overrules these concerns Article 12:1 states *That Parties shall assure to the child who is capable of forming his or her own views the right to express those views freely in all matters affecting the child, the views of the child being given due weight in accordance with the age and maturity of the child. 2. For this purpose, the child shall in particular be provided the opportunity to be heard in any judicial and administrative proceedings affecting the child, either directly, or through a representative or an appropriate body, in a manner consistent with the procedural rules of national law.*

Experience of Child Welfare Workers

Problem formulation: How is innovation in the child welfare services, which is aimed at improving cooperation and the communication with the children in the CWS, experienced by the social workers who work in in the services?

Methodology: Open, semi-structured interviews with social workers and social educators employed in the CWS

Representatives from six municipal CWS units involved in the project have been interviewed with the following focus:

1. A description of the changes they have made regarding new working methods
2. The process of change, including the role of the leader of the organisation
3. Their perception and understanding of the focus on values connected to the change

4. Their views on competencies needed for the social services working within the new paradigm
5. Some narratives describing benefits associated with the change

It is important to bear in mind that the selection of social worker for these interviews represented CWS units that are the most ambitious in implementing the new working methods and that the selection of quotes is made with a focus on understanding best practices in this process. As far as possible, we will let the voice of the social workers be expressed directly. The combination of and succession of quotes in the next section has also been organized to represent a logical progression.

Changing working methods

The motivation to change routines and working methods will, in most cases, come from the experience that one's work does not produce the expected results or that it is not satisfactory in some other way, for example in terms of ethics. As we have outlined above, a general objection to CWS has been that communication with the child has not been satisfactory and that levels of conflict have been too high.

> "It is really extremely tragic to say it, but we were almost not talking to children at all. Working for change with the parents but forgetting to check if it was really working for the children, who are the most important people." "And it was there that we saw that we had to work differently in the child welfare services in Norway today,(...) and if this is a project to try out something different, joining in must be a great opportunity (...) and we were looking at this as exciting and we wanted to do things differently"

From working with case records and procedures to working together with the child

When doing social work in public bureaucratic organization, one risks getting lost in routines, forms, and regulation to the degree that the real people involved simply disappear.

> "Earlier we just worked with routines, now we are expected to be in a process with the child, (...) I do think there has been too much focus on the formalities around child protection cases"

> "And then there was a lot of emphasis on meeting deadlines, action plans and care plans, and seeing that all the legal requirements were fulfilled so you lost sight of what you really should work with, I think."

"So it has, to a great extent, been part of a change of routines and attitudes in the service, it really has."

"Use the time, I said. What does it mean? Yes maybe to use the time more directly with the child, and the other thing is to work more in process with the family."

"So we changed everything in the documentation, no more child welfare officer, now it is your contact person."

Working methods

Work in child welfare services has been dominated by methods and programs such as MST, as well as manuals and rote communication techniques. These methods can sometimes, if used mechanically, produce alienation or aggression. The child may experience the child welfare worker as more interested in the question or the method than the person and that the worker is playing a role as professional.

"Yes, when you are sitting and repeating questions, or as I have said all the time, then we understand that this is a method that you have learned. And that is something that you should not use; be yourself, be a fellow human being. (…) The parents have such great challenges and complex challenges, that a method that you are following rigidly, it is not suitable. So therefore it's as if these values, they are the method, and that is assumed to be good enough."

"So now we are maybe a little more inclined to think that the first step will be to just build confidence and a relationship, and then meet the parents when it comes to what they think the challenges are, and then we start there. And then we can come in and say what we think are the challenges. Just to be connected and build the confidence that we need."

Advantages of cooperation / change of perspective

Problem definitions are mostly external accounts and descriptions. Taking the child's perspective yields another kind of information and it means that you have to look for solutions together:

"There was this meeting where the boy participated, and the health service described the situation, and everybody described just problems and then the parents went silent and the boy became silent. Then I said OK, we'll stop now and find a new date for a meeting. Meanwhile I talked with the boy and we agreed how we, he and I, should start the meeting. Then we were talking, and

*it became like a kind of interview, he wanted things to be like this. And every-
body was listening to me, in a kind of reflecting team you know, and then they
said 'Oh my god, we have never heard you say these things before, you know.'
Then everything became much brighter and the parents and the boy clearly
connected. And I think we have to have more meetings like this to show what
this is all about.(...) In this way we have to be really conscious of how we can
have an okay conversation."*

Change needs good leadership

There are some fundamental preconditions for success in a changing process.

> *"That the leader, the child welfare leader was so positive. That has been like the
> alpha and omega for me; that the time you should use for this is recognized
> and that its importance is recognized and top priority, and that she has also
> kept her leader informed."*

This is one of our most consistent findings; the support of the leader is crucial and
lack of interest or indifference from the leader makes real change impossible. In
addition, one of the fruits of the efforts put into changing the processes is recognition from outside. It is very hard to put energy in a process that nobody sees:

> *"We have some recognition out there. Some hints from time to time. There has
> been something about us in the newspaper, and we have gotten good references,
> these kinds of things, and on the municipality barometer (...) and yes the
> county governor has boasted a lot, so in a way saying 'look to this community!'"*

Working value base instead of or in addition to methodology base

So what does it mean to work in a value-based way, and to have a common understanding of value? Is this in opposition to being rigidly attached to a method or
methodical thinking as formerly expressed by one of the workers in the services?

> *"It is about being open and caring about the child, these things about being lov-
> ing and love is the thing that has challenged me the most."*

> *"For some, it is totally weird to call it love, because we put something else in the
> concept than the child welfare pro's do now. For them it's about that (...) as we
> have finally interpreted, that we are more compassionate, we are not so profes-
> sional (...) showing feelings, we can show that what they are telling is touching
> us, that we can be a bit warm and meet them and show with our eyes as they
> are talking, that we understand and that we, yes, listen to them (...) So we*

have put a lot of time into clarifying what it is, in the meeting with those we are working with."

Most of the services emphasized that it takes time to adjust to the concept of love in professional work, and continually try to substitute it with other words. Nonetheless, the children keep on saying that you cannot use other words because then you are moving away from the whole idea. It is also challenging because it places an emphasis on the personality of the social worker;

"I think it was fun just this thing about love (…) it was very interesting to discuss this concept, because we had, and maybe I said it before, some colleagues that are somehow impersonal in a way."

Obviously some social skills and aptitude is needed to work as a social worker, and sometimes it is difficult or too personal to discuss this. It is easier to talk about formal qualifications, also because we do not have a clear concept of how to train people for this kind of social work.

Humility

"So, I have a case where I think that two years ago we did some bad work, and I have no problem being humble about that. It is only honest to admit these failings, for example in respect to letters that were sent, and also about the case being worked in a way that I could not accept today.

"But … therefore … that you apologize and are a bit humble regarding that … and I can see that it does something with the person. It is in a way to hear that because she is sitting there today being afraid that the same thing could happen again, you know. She experienced that time as so traumatic. To be humble; to say you know I understand that that experience … it was totally wrong. It is important for the relationship …"

Is the education system dysfunctional (in terms of value-based social work)?

"What I think is so well put by the child welfare pro's is that you enter this profession with the desire to help the kids. You have the focus on the kids. That's the reason you want to be a child welfare worker or a social worker, and want to work in the child welfare services. And then after three years of education, it is gets so difficult. So we are leaving the original goal and the desire we had with this profession."

"As the child welfare professionals are saying; why do those who really have a sincere wish to work for us, the kids and the young people come out (from the education system) being afraid to talk to us?"

"I'm very skeptical about that entire manual based thing that we should jump on that too. We should instead meet the parents with these values and that is a method that's as good as any. "

Not all are skeptical about traditional methods, but they are looking for a compromise:

"We must of course take with us these theories and methods, to have them back there and then you should be yourself and use yourself, and I think we can do both. I believe we can do both things."

Emotions

Some of the social workers have a striking ability to express how they have changed and their ability to be open, expressing their feelings and closeness to the child in these meetings.

"I cry in the meetings with these kids (…) and I have been much, much more secure that that it is totally okay. Once upon a time we learned that we should not show these things. We are done with that, and that I can see, it does something with the relationship, it does a lot with the relationship. And that thing, we have been talking a lot about that lately, if you are insecure in a conversation, dread something or whatever, so just say it, this is the way it is, now I do not know what to do now somehow. Be honest."

"So we are working with these kind of power symbols, yes. And to dare to let the meeting be a dance, as I like to call it, then they roll their eyes you know. But it means to put away the power and be in the meeting and then you do not know where it ends up, but that's what is exciting too."

"I think it is great fun, I think it is so inspiring (…) it has never been so much fun to work with child welfare, and I have been in this work for a long time. I have been head of the child welfare service for 16 years and I am still on fire, and it's getting more and more fun, because I know that we are on the right track. It is so good when we can have a focus on those that are really affected."

"I have such belief, and you know, I feel that to work on this basis, together with these kids and young people, it just gives a fantastic energy. Then you go home

*and are really happy when the day is over, when you really had such chat with
a young person so that you see it when they feel that they have been seen, and
it is really, really incredible. So it is fun, yes."*

Necessary competencies

The education system for child welfare workers, social workers and social peda-
gogues has a bias toward evidence-based methods and theories, but the practical
field seems to demand social competence and practical skills.

The social service workers have, from time to time, been involved in discussions
with representatives from child welfare education who are more attached to traditional methods, and these meeting have sometimes been a little tense:

> *"It was that belief in methods. It was a bit, now I say it plainly, but it became
> very much like 'No, I believe in methods, and I will continue to teach methods.'
> It was this, it was a little bit arrogant if you understand."*

> *"How can educators show that it is not the methods themselves that are impor-
> tant, but it is you as a person (...) I cannot accept that somebody is coming
> here and working according to a specific method that they have learned in
> school. It's almost an impossibility, because you must go out in practical work
> to learn, it is there that you are learning, it is then you feel (in your body) how
> you will be as a professional."*

"To use yourself" is recurrent in interviews with the majority of the social workers
and it is presented as being in opposition to science, methods and the education
system.

> *"The education system ought to have a lot of focus on attitude and values. One's
> use of oneself, that's the point."*

> *"We really wish that social work students could be as up to date as the child
> protection students (...) and it is important that when we talk about My Life
> (the project), they know what we are talking about."*

Discussion

The process of changing routines and working methods is complex and depends on
both personal factors and the organiszational context. We leave a familiar landscape,
with recognized rules and methods, and move into a more complex context that
depends more the professional as a person than a predictable order of routines and

methods. This new terrain apparently also has some rewards: the work is more "fun", the relationship with the child is improved and the child feels that he or she is seen.

The selection of quotes above has, as stated earlier, been made to illustrate examples of best practices that can give an impression of the core ideas of the innovation. Another guiding idea is that the quotes should give meaning themselves, and together form a contextual account and a coherent narrative about the core ideas of the project.

One striking impression from the child welfare workers is their enthusiasm about the changes; their understanding about the way they are working now as distinct from before gives an impression that the changes are experienced as real. The focus on value communication and social skills is underlined and seems to give meaning to the work in another way than the manual-oriented work.

Personal skills are sometimes difficult to define, and they are often defined as being opposed to academic or scientific or evidence-based knowledge. The skills are acquired through practice. It seems to be a decisive point as to whether the workers perceive good practice as incompatible with "manuals and methods" taught in training, or something that can be combined. At the very least, it seems that the education system has some work to do to fill the gap between the actual working methods in the child welfare services and the approaches promoted in universities.

The reports from the field seem to have implications for the scientific paradigm in education, suggesting a stronger focus on reflective and discursive methods and practical training in communication as post-positivist approaches.

Another objection discussed in this context is the question of productivity. Can the outcome of good communication and relational practice be perceived as more productive in any meaning of the word? The experience of meeting somebody who really cares about your situation and listens to your problem is both a method and a final goal in child welfare.

Finally, it is also a question of power; including the children in the decision-making regarding their own situation and future is obviously a good idea that makes the help offered more relevant and appropriate for the child. Still, other considerations such as the legal principles and the other family members' interests must also be balanced in this context.

The inclusion of children in the decision processes of child welfare services is a move towards recognition of children as individual members of a democratic society with their own voices, and this can be seen as part of the general democratisation of society.

Conclusion

Innovation in the child welfare services in Norway has been, to a considerable extent, influenced and initiated by the Change Factory and the child welfare professionals (i.e. children with experience with the child welfare services) and has focused on more and improved communication with the children and inclusion of the children in the process of decision-making.

Child welfare workers involved in the innovation are making progress toward extended communication with the children and express great satisfaction with the change in their working routines as they interpret them as being a more meaningful practice. They also point to the importance of values and social skills in their work routines as distinct from the previous, more rigid manual and method-based routines frequently identified as the methods taught in the social work and child welfare education system. The innovation can bee seen as a paradigmatic change in the child welfare services, pointing towards a more humanistic practice.

References

Andersen, L. L. & Hygum Espersen, H. (2017). Samskabelse, samproduktion og partnerskaber – teoretiske perspektiver. (Co-creation, co-production and partership; theoretical perspectives) I Partnerskaber og samarbejder mellem det offentlige og civilsamfundet (pp. 107–137). Odense: Socialstyrelsen.

BUFdir. (2017). Children under the care of the Child Welfare Services.

Christiansen, Ø. (2012). Hvorfor har barnevernet problemer med å se og behandle barn som aktører? (Why does the child welfare services have problem to view children as subjects) Tidsskriftet Norges Barnevern, 89 (01–02), 16–30.

Clausen, C. J. & og Tiller, P.O. (1997). Barnevern og barns ytringsfrihet. (Child protection and Forandringsfabrikken. (2015). Fra Meny til utprøving (Change factory; from menue to trial).

Fosterhjemsforening, N. (2017). Samarbeidsklima mellom fosterforeldre og barnevern. (Cooperation climate between foster parents and the child protection services) (http://www.fosterhjemsforening.no/fagkunnskap/temasider/samarbeid-mellom-fosterforeldre-og-barnevern/) [25 September 2017].

Gamst, K. T. (2011). Profesjonelle barnesamtaler: å ta barn på alvor (Professsional conversations with children) Oslo: Universitetsforl.

Gulbrandsen, L. M. (ed) (2014). Barns deltakelse i hverdagsliv og profesjonell praksis: en utforskende tilnærming. (Children's participation in everyday life and in professional practice) Oslo: Universitetsforl.

Haarakangas, K., Seikkula, J., Alakare, B., & Aaltonen, J. (2007). Open dialogue: An approach to psychotherapeutic treatment of psychosis in northern Finland. In H. A. D. Gehart (Ed.), Collaborative therapy: Relationships and conversations that make a difference (pp. 221–233). New York: Routledge.

Joranger, L. (2016). "Hvorfor gjentar dere siste ordet vi sier hele tida?" ("Why do you repeat the last word we are saying all the time?"). Fontene forskning, 1.

Martinsen, L. J. (2012). Barnets beste ved fastsettelse av fast bosted for barn. (The childs best in determining the permanent living place for children) Tidsskrift for familierett, arverett og barnevernrettslige spørsmål 01 / 2013 (Vol. 11)

NOU. (2017). Svikt og svik: gjennomgang av saker hvor barn har vært utsatt for vold, seksuelle overgrep og omsorgssvikt. (Failure and betrayal in cases where children have been subject to violence, abuse or care failure) (NOU 2017:12). BLD.

Næss S., H. T. & Offerdal A., Wærness K., (1998). *Erfaringer med barnevernloven i kommunene – dokumentasjonsrapport fra en landsomfattende undersøkelse.* (Experience with the child protection legislation) Bergen: SEFOS.

Seikkula, J. (2006). Dialogical meetings in social networks.

Skauge, B. (2010). Er det noen som vil høre på meg? (Is there somebody who wants to listen to me?) Master thesis, NTNU Institutt for sosialt arbeid.

UN. (1991). *Convention on the rights of the child.* New York: United Nations.

Whyte, W. F. (1991). *Participatory Action Research* Sage

Marijana Majdak (University of Zagreb) and
Zrinka Leko (Social Welfare Centre Vinkovci)

Characteristics of Risky Sexual Behaviour
of the Student Population in the Capital of Croatia

Abstract

This paper is focused on research among first year students (N=222) from two academic institutions in the capital city of Croatia (Zagreb). The main goal was to investigate the characteristics of risky sexual behaviour of students and to determine the correlation between peer pressure and alcohol consumption with risky sexual behaviour. The research was conducted through web survey using a questionnaire that consisted of three parts: a questionnaire about peer pressure, questions from the European School Survey Project on Alcohol and Other Drugs, and a questionnaire covering AIDS-related knowledge, attitudes and sexual behaviour as predictors of condom use among young adults in Croatia. Data were analysed with descriptive statistic and Pearson's correlation coefficient. The results show that the student population in Zagreb can generally not be described as a risky sexual behaviour population. According to the results, peers do not have much influence on risky sexual behaviour among the student population, but they do influence alcohol consumption by students. Although the student population is a specific population, and probably more responsible than youth in general, prevention and education about the danger of risky sexual behaviour is needed, as well as alcohol consumption prevention. This is a task for the media and school programs as well as social support and health care services.

Introduction

During adolescence, multiple changes characterise the physiological, emotional and psychological area of functioning in young people. Adolescence is therefore very intense and stressful (Kuzman, 2009). The duration of adolescence is defined differently by different authors[1] and it is evident that age borders are flexible and that the beginning and the end of adolescence varies from person to person. There are many theories explaining risk behaviour during adolescence. According to *biological theories,* adolescence is specified as a period during which fast physical and sexual maturation is happening, which results in a variety of psychological and social consequences (Lacković-Grgin, 2006). According to *psychoanalytical theories,* there

---

1   Rudan (2004) defines the duration of adolescence from 10 to 22 years of age. Kuzman (2009) sets the age borders for adolescence from 11 or 13 until 18 or 20, while Lacković-Grgin (2006) describes adolescence as lasting from 10 to 25 years of age.

are three important elements of personality for observing the development of adolescence: id (represents biological aspects, instincts), ego (represents psychological aspects, mechanisms of defence) and superego (represents social aspects, process of liberation from crises in earlier developmental stages). In adolescence, the sexual dirve is appearing and it needs to be integrated into each individual personality. Often the sexual instinct is in conflict with religious, moral and social attitudes of the individuals and therefore young people experience conflicts and tensions (Lacković-Grgin, 2006). Adolescents use different mechanisms of defence and these mechanisms differ according to efficiency and maturity (repression, regression, projection, rationalisation, identification). Moreover, adolescents form new relationships with their peers and at the same time they liberate themselves from confining familial relationships (Lacković-Grgin, 2006). According to *psychosocial theories,* the emphasis is on interaction between the personality structure and the surroundings. In the adolescence phase of life, the psychological aspect is unstable because of the dual roles of adolescence; in some situations they act like children and in others as adults. Also, the environment is treating them as children in some situations and in others as adults. Because of this mixed treatment, adolescent behaviour is also mixed (Lacković-Grgin, 2006). *Developmental-cognitive theories* are directed at researching the development of knowledge processes in adolescence. As for thinking in adolescence, the formal operations like combinatorics, experimental proving, propositional operation and abstract reasoning are typical. Cognitive development allows adolescents to perceive the physical and social world that is surrounding them. That is why in adolescence young people start to change their relationships towards authority figures, and they also start to plan the future (Lacković-Grgin, 2006). *Learning theories* explain adolescence through learning processes, or more precisely through learning by modelling. Individuals observe the model, become aware of the consequences of its behaviour, understand what is positive and what is negative, and after that individuals accept or reject certain patterns of behaviour (Lacković-Grgin, 2006). *Ecological-conceptualistic theories* are based on the exploring interaction between the individual and the system; how the individual develops according to his or her surroundings. The surroundings closest to the individual is his or her microsystem (e.g. family, school, church). The mesosystem consists of different components of microsystems, exosystem represents the wider surroundings of the individual while macro system represents the culture and subculture (Lacković-Grgin, 2006).

In adolescence, aside from parents, who until than were the most important role models for children, the influence of peers is increasing. Young people observe their peers directly and form their own behaviour, and also peers set some norms, so it is not necessary for adolescents to observe peers behaviour directly; they can also form their own behaviour according to the perception of what certain groups consider to be acceptable. To this end, adolescents form their behaviour in order to be liked by their peers and be socially accepted (Tome and Gaspar de Matos, 2012).

Sexuality in adolescence

Sexual maturation in adolescence is characterised by higher interest in sexuality followed by changes in the body and changing attitudes toward the sexual characteristics of others in their surroundings (Lacković-Grgin, 2006). Human sexuality includes not only physical characteristics, but also psychosocial features, norms, attitudes and contextual factors, all of which have an influence on sexual behaviour (Kuzman, Pavić Šimetin & Pejanović Franelić, 2007; according to Rajhvajn Bulat, 2011). The sexual behaviour of youth is determined by environmental factors, mostly family members, peers and school (Boden and Horwood, 2006; according to Rajhvajn Bulat, 2011). Fingerson (2005) explains youth sexuality using the term "sexual socialization", where the term means that sexuality and attitudes towards sexuality are developed in young peoples' immediate surroundings (family and peers).

Sexual initiation[2] is an important life event for each person and can influence future sexual behaviour (Lacković-Grgin, 2006). The average age for entering into a sexual relationship in the Republic of Croatia is 17 (for both genders), but some research show that boys enter into sexual relationships one year earlier (at 16) (Kuzman et al., 2007)[3]. Motives for entering into sexual relationships differ according to gender. Girls note that their motives are mostly the need for emotional closeness (with their relationship partner) while boys mostly enter their first sexual relationships as an adventure (single encounters) (Lacković-Grgin, 2006). For girls, they generally enter into their first sexual relationships with an older partner with whom they are in serious emotional relationship, while boys mostly have their first sexual experience with girls who are their peers through so-called "one-night stands" (Hodžić and Bijelić, 2003). Personal motives for entering into a sexual relationship are a wish to achieve higher self-respect, reduction of feelings of loneliness, seeking to get revenge on parents or partners, and jealousy (Lacković-Grgin, 2006).

In addition to personal motives for early sexual activity, structural features of the family, parenting style, parental standards about sexuality as well as peers' standards and expectations are important (Lacković-Grgin, 2006). Different aspects of parental behaviour are connected to the psychosocial adjustment of youth and their relationship with peers. Also, parental behaviours are connected to adolescents' leisure time activities and risk behaviours (Raboteg-Šarić, Sakoman & Brajša-Žganec, 2002). Parental acceptance or rejection of certain youth behaviour will be understood by young people as a subjective social norm, so number of partners, age

---

2   Sexual initiation is the first sexual experience.
3   Similar results were also attained by Božičević and associates (2006) on a sample of 1093 of young people aged between 18 and 24. The results showed that an averige age for entering into sex is 17.2 for boys and 17.6 for girls. Research conducted by Hodžićandi Bijelić (2003) on a sample of 995 middle school students in Zagreb, Osijek and Split showed that an averige age for entering into a sexual relationship is 15 years for boys and 15.7 years for girls.

for entering into a sexual relationship and use of protection will depend on parental attitudes and conversation about sex between parents and children (Fingerson, 2005). Conversation about sex between parents and children is of great importance because parents give children more correct and complete information in comparison to information provided by peers (Whitaker and Miller, 2000). Conversely, during adolescence adolescents do not want to lose peers and be rejected, which is why they often adjust to certain peer groups and accept some sexual activities that might be risky for them (Bastašić, 1995). Peers have a stronger influence on young people if they do not talk to their parents about responsible sexual behaviour (Whitaker and Miller, 2000), and therefore in future preventive programs it is necessary to place emphasis on open and sincere communication between parents and children about responsible sexual behaviour and protection.

Risk sexual behaviours and possible consequences

Risk sexual behaviours[4] in adolescents are connected to psychological structure and experiences: individual characteristics, general tendency toward risky behaviours, low self-esteem, feelings of lack of control over one's life, exposure to sexual violence and mood disturbance (Štulhofer, 2009).

Besides the above psychosocial aspects, there are many other reasons why young people expose themselves to the negative consequences of sexuality: lack of sexual experience tends to lead to experimenting, lack of information and lack of exchange of information lead to minimization of risks (Lacković-Grgin, 2006), gender stereotypes, dual sexual standards (for women and men) which brings uneven power in making decisions. Social differences and religion can influence the age of the first sexual experience and the number of partners (Štulhofer, 2009).

Exposure to sexual risks is greater for younger adolescents because the younger they are, the greater the tendency for experimenting. Youths' decisions in terms of irrational or risky sexual behaviours are often influenced by emotions (Galligan and Terry, 1991; according to Štulhofer, Jureša & Mamula, 1999), lacking awareness of possible dangers, lack of communication skills and peer conformism (Dacey and Kenny, 1994; according to Štulhofer et al., 1999).

The consequences of risky sexual behaviours are unwanted pregnancy, sexual disease and sexual victimization (Štulhofer et al., 1999).

Many adolescent pregnancies are considered to be unwanted and risky because girls are not physically and psychologically developed enough so the risk for mis-

---

4   Risky sexual behaviours are behaviours which include no or irregular use of protection, frequent shifting between sexual partners, consumption of psychoactive substances before sexual intercourse and unwanted sexual experiences (Moon, Fornili and O'Briant, 2007).

carriage, premature birth and poor child development is high (Đepina and Posavec, 2012). According to research, there are many reasons for juvenile pregnancies[5].

Data for 2015 (Croatian Department of Public Health) show that there were 306 girls younger than 17 and 826 girls in the age of 18 and 19 who became pregnant. The total number of juvenile births in 2015 was 1.132. The birth rate for girls younger than 20 for the year 2015 was 9.5/1000. In the year 2015 there were 226 girls younger than 19 years who asked for termination of pregnancy (Stevanović, Capak & Benjak, 2016).

Sexual illnesses[6] are infectious diseases that are transmitted during vaginal, oral or anal sexual contact (Lazarus and associates, 2010). Every year worldwide, more than 400 million people contract a sexual disease, of which 60% are people younger than 25 years (Dabo, Malatesterinić, Janković, Bolf Malović & Kosanović, 2008). Sexual diseases can damage health, cause infertility and even death.

According to data from Croatian Department of Public Health, in the period from 1985 to 2015 in the Republic of Croatia, 1.321 person were infected with the HIV virus, of this number 458 developed AIDS, and 201 persons died from AIDS (Stevanović et al., 2016). Regarding the research on protection carried out by Božičević, Štulhofer, Ajduković &Kufrin (2006), the results showed that more than 80% of participants know that the use of condom during sexual intercourse provides protection from HIV, but only 59.3% of boys and 46.1% of girls use condom during sexual intercourse. This indicates that there is a need for education in order to protect people from risky sexual behaviour and prevent sexual diseases.

When talking about the risks of sexual behaviours of young people, it is necessary to mention the term "sexual victimization", which means sexual experiences under some kind of coercion: physical force, blackmail or threat (Ybarra, Strasburger & Mitchell, 2014). The experience of sexual victimization in childhood can manifest in the future in two ways. The first way is through risky sexual behaviours like early entry into a sexual relationship, frequent changing of partners and not using protection, which can led to early pregnancies and contraction of sexual disease (Simon and Feirinig, 2008). The second way is the development of fear and avoiding sexual contact in the future as well as in sexual anxiety and negative reactions connected to any kind of sexual activity (Simon and Feiring, 2008).

---

5   According to Kirby and Lepore (2007) poverty is a risk factor for juvenile pregnancies because of low educational competence, high unemployment, high level of risky and criminal behaviours.

6   There are viral and bacterial sexual illnesses. Bacterial sexual illnesses include gonoria, chlamydia and syphilis, while virus sexual illnesses include HPV (*human papiloma virus*), genital herpes, hepatitis B and AIDS (*acquired immune deficiency syndrome*).

Aims, problems and research hypotheses

The goal of the research is to examine risky sexual behaviour, alcohol consumption and peer pressure in first year students at the University of Zagreb (the capital of Croatia).

According to the goal of the research, the following problems and hypotheses were defined:

1. Determine the correlation between frequency of alcohol consumption and risky sexual behaviour by first year students at the University in Zagreb.
H1: The expectation is that students who consume alcohol more frequently will have more involvement in risky sexual behaviour.

2. Determine the correlation between peer pressure and risky sexual behaviour among first year students at the University in Zagreb.
H2: The expectation is that students who experience more peer pressure will have more involvement in risky sexual behaviour.

Methodology

Sample

The participants are first year students at the University of Zagreb (N=222, 79.7% female students and 20.3% male students) studying at the department of philosophy, department of building and construction, and faculty of law. The average age of participants is 19.69 (min 18, max 25).

Measurements instruments

The survey consisted of 45 items in total. For the purpose of this research, there were three questionnaires:

1. Socio-demographic questions (gender, age, department of study and leisure time)

2a. Questionnaire concerning peer pressure developed by Lebedina-Manzoni and Ricijaš (2008) (=0, 89). The questionnaire consisted of 24 items and participants can chose from among five provided answers to express how much they think their behaviour is influenced by peer pressure. Higher result shows higher peer pressure exposure. Result on the scale can be between 24 and 120.

2b. Questionnaire about alcohol and drug consumption consisted of four questions taken from the questionnaire used in the *European School Survey Project on Alco-*

hol and Other Drugs ESPAD (2013) about the type of consumed alcoholic beverages, frequency of alcohol consumption and availability of alcohol beverages. Questions are designed to collect information on the use (frequency) of alcohol use in their lives and during the last 30 days. The response categories are '0', '1–2', '3–5', '6–9', '10–19', '20–39' and '40 or more'. Prevalence of any use (lifetime, last 30 days) and prevalence of experiencing any intoxication were also calculated ($\geq$ 1–2 times).

3. *Questionnaire covering risky sexual behaviour amoung youth* is made up of 11 questions taken from the original questionnaire developed by Štulhofer, A., Graham, C., Božičević, I., Kufrin, K. & Ajduković, D. (2007) about risky sexual behaviour frequency, protection, and frequent partner changing. Questions are simple and examine participant's age of first sexual experience, use of protection during sex, one-time sexual experiences and sex under the influence of alcohol.

Data collection and processing

Research was conducted through a web questionnaire constructed in the program Lime Survey, activated on 24 June, 2016 and active until 1 July 2016. The questionnaire was put on Facebook groups for first year students studying at the University of Zagreb.

The advantages of using web questionnaire are many: they are fast, simple and cheap to do, there is not obligation on the part of respondents, and they are interesting for young people. One of the most important disadvantages of using an online questionnaire is that participants do not see the researcher and cannot ask questions in case they need some additional information to be able to fully understand questions. Also, the researcher is not in a position to control the sample, for instance the questionnaire can be completed by someone who does not fulfil the criteria.

Participants were informed about the purpose of the research as well as the ethical principles that will be respected in the research (anonymity, respect, voluntary nature, group analysis of the data). Also, at the end of questionnaire there was contact by an NGO called *The Brave Telephone* (professionals who give psychological and social help to any children and youth who call) which they could call in case that they might feel uncomfortable by answering some of the questions. There was also a postal address of a person who they can contact to get feedback about the results of the research.

Regarding ethical dilemmas during the preparation of the research, what appeared was so called "trolling" (Cho and LaRose, 1999). Additionally, the questionnaire was put on the web pages that are used for the exchange of student materials, and this could be perceived by some of the students as a disturbance.

Data was processed through SPSS program by using descriptive statistic (arithmetic mean, standard deviation, mod, median, frequency) and Pearson's correlation.

Results and discussion

Leisure time of first year students in the capital of Croatia

Results about the leisure time of the participants show that most of the participants spend their leisure time with friends and/or partners (89.6%). Also, some of the students like to watch TV or play computer games (43.2%), go to a cafés, discos and parties (52.7%). Around half of the students like to sleep and rest in their leisure time (51.4%), some like to read books (28.8%) while 4.5% of the students gamble. Very few were involved in athletic activities, volunteering or art. The results are similar to earlier results about the leisure time of young people. This proves that youth today like to associate with peers, spend time on the Internet or play games and rest at home (Ilišin and Radin, 2002).

Alcohol consumption of first year students in the capital of Croatia

Regarding the consumption of alcoholic beverages by first year students, the results are extreme and show that 89.6% of students consume alcohol (only 10.4% do not consume any alcohol). In their lifetimes (Table 1), 61.7% of students had consumed alcohol 40 times or more, 16.2% of students had consumed alcohol 20 to 39 times in their life, while only 0.9% of students never consumed alcohol.

Regard the type of alcoholic beverages, our results show that students in the capital city of Croatia mostly drink beer, strong drinks and wine. In the last 30 days 62.6% of the students had consumed beer, 60.3% of students had consumed strong drinks and 59% had consumed wine (Table 2.).

Table 1. Lifetime Frequency of alcohol consumption

	Number of participants	%
Never	2	0.9%
1 to 2 times	6	2.7%
3 to 5 times	8	3.6%
6 to 9 times	5	2.3%
10 to 19 times	20	9.0%
20 to 39 times	36	16.2%
40 and more times	137	61.7%
Total	214	96.4%
I do not want to answer	8	3.6%
Total	222	100%

Table 2. Alcohol consumption in the last 30 days

	Number of participants	%
Beer		
Never	83	37.4%
1 to 2 times	49	22.1%
3 to 5 times	42	18.9%
6 to 9 times	28	12.6%
10 to 19 times	17	7.7%
20 to 39 times	2	0.9%
40 and more times	1	0.5%
Total for beer	222	100%
Wine		
Never	91	41.0%
1 to 2 times	74	33.3%
3 to 5 times	30	13.5%
6 to 9 times	19	8.6%
10 to 19 times	6	2.7%
20 to 39 times	0	0.0%
40 and more times	2	0.9%
Total for wine	222	100%
Strong drinks		
Never	87	39.2%
1 to 2 times	75	33.8%
3 to 5 times	36	16.2%
6 to 9 times	15	6.8%
10 to 19 times	6	2.7%
20 to 39 times	0	0.0%
40 and more times	3	1.4%
Total for strong drinks	222	100%

The results match some earlier research (Majdak, Novosel & Bagarić, 2018), which show that students do use (and misuse) alcoholic beverages more often that youth in general. Students who do not drink alcohol lack the social support necessary for the adjustment to student life.

Peer pressure among first year students in the capital of Croatia

The results about perceived peer pressure (Table 3) among first year students show that the lowest result is 25 and the highest result in our sample is 82 (min 24, max 120). The results indicate that some aspects of student's behaviour are influenced by peer pressure.

Table 3. Peer pressure

	N	Min	Max	Mean	Std. deviation
Total result about the peer pressure	209	25	82	45,36	12,244
Total n	209				

Earlier research (Majdak et al., 2018) show that students do notice more than average peer pressure (especially freshmen) and that peer pressure correlates with alcohol consumption.

Sexual relationships and risky sexual behaviour by first year university students in the capital of Croatia

Data about partners and relationships indicates that at the time research was conducted, 50% of participants were in intimate relationships while the other half (50%) did not have a partner.

Sexual intercourse was part of the lives of 72.1% of participants, and 27.9% did not have sexual intercourse. The earliest age for entering into a sexual relationship was 13, and the latest was 22. Most of the participants had their first sexual experience at the age of 18, while the average age for entering into a sexual relationship is 16.6 (Table 4.).

Table 4. The age of the first sexual experience

Age	Number of participants	%
13	1	0,5%
14	8	3,6%
15	11	5,0%
16	30	13,5%
17	38	17,1%
18	42	18,9%
19	18	8,1%
20	6	2,7%
22	1	0,5%
Total	167	75,2%
Missing	55	24,8%
TOTAL	222	100%

72.1% of participants use some sort of protection during sexual intercourse, while 27.9% do not use any sort of protection. The most used protection methods by students are condoms and contraception pills.

Regarding risky sexual relationships, in our sample 17.6% of participants had had a one-night stand in the last 12 months, and over the last 12 months 6.9% were having sex with a person who is 10 or more years older than they are.

Our data shows that 52.3% of participants never engage in sex under the influence of alcohol, 25.7% of participants rarely have sex under the influence of alcohol, 17.1% sometimes combine sex and alcohol and and 4.5% do this often. 11.7% of participants think that sex is better under the influence of alcohol or some other psychoactive substance because it allows them to be more relaxed and less focused on their physical appearance and therefore their sexual experience is better.

Alcohol consumption and risky sexual behaviour among first year students at the University of Zagreb

Our first research problem was to examine the correlation between alcohol consumption and risky sexual behaviour. The expectation was that there would be a positive correlation between alcohol consumption and risky sexual behaviours, or more precisely that students who consume alcohol more often will also enter into risky sexual relationships more often.

In this research, the only significance was found between two variables: frequency of alcohol consumption in the last 12 months and "having a one-night stand". The correlation is significant at a level of 5% (r = -0.264, p<0.05). The correlation is negative, which means that students who did consume more often alcohol in the last 12 months also had more one-time sexual experiences. In their research, Donenberg, Emerson, Bryand & King (2006) found that peers do influence alcohol consumption and this can contribute to risky sexual behaviours. Similar results were found by Chaney, Vail-Smith, Martin & Cremeens-Matthews (2016) about the correlation between youth alcohol consumption and risky sexual behaviour. The results of the research conducted by authors Castelo-Branco, Parera, Mendoza, Perez-Campos, Lete &CEA group (2014) show that 62.3% of participants think that alcohol relaxes and lowers psychological barriers for sexual encounters, while 40.7% think that alcohol consumption before sex is responsible for their not using protection.

Our results are only partly confirmed. The possible explanation is that in this research the participants were university student's (older young people, aged 18–25), which might indicate that they are also more experienced and more responsible compared to the general youth population.

Peer pressure and risky sexual relationship among first year students at the University of Zagreb

Our second research problem was to examine the correlation between peer pressure and risky sexual behaviour among first year students of the university in Zagreb, Croatia. The expectation was that there will be a significant correlation between peer pressure and risky sexual behaviour among first year students and that those students who experience more peer pressure will have more involvement in risky sexual behaviour.

In this research, we found significant correlation between peer pressure and risky sexual behaviour among first year students ($r = 0.279$, $p < 0.05$), which confirmed our hypothesis.

From earlier research, we know that youth form their behaviour because they want peers to like and accept them (Tome and Gaspar de Matos, 2012). Meta-analysis of research shows that perception of peer norms about sexuality strongly influences the decisions about sex made by youth. A perception of peer acceptance regard sexual behaviour and a perception that their peers do enter into sexual relationships strongly predicts the sexual activity of youth (Doornwaard, ter Bogt, Reitz & van den Eijnden, 2015). In the research of Potard, Courtois & Rusch (2008) the results show that sexual permissiveness of youth peers is connected to higher rates of sexual behaviours that they perceive as risky. Also, attitudes of peers about contraception influence youth attitudes about contraception. In their research, Jones, Biddlecom, Hebert & Milne (2011) show that youth mostly turn to peers for information about contraception and follow peer behaviour. Peers are the most important source of information for youth about sexuality (Epstein, Bailey, Manhart, Karl, Hill & Hawkins, 2014) and have an influence on first sexual relationships. Moreover, among other factors (e.g. family situation, sexual education) peers also influence risky sexual relationships (Epstein et al., 2014).

The correlations that we found in this research were low (although significant) which indicates that there is weak connection between peer pressure and risk sexual behaviours, as well as weak connection between alcohol consumption and risky sexual behaviours. This is understandable because there are many other factors which can also explain risky sexual behaviour among youth, which and should be considered in future research.

Conclusion

The intention of this research was to explore whether environment (mostly peers) influence risky sexual behaviour among young people. According to the theories of social learning, the individual is learning form the surroundings by observing others' behaviour (mostly those who are close to the individual). For youth, peers are very important factors (if not the most important) so our intention was to explore whether there is a correlation between alcohol consumption, peer influence and risky sexual behaviour among first year students at the University of Zagreb.

Our expectations were partly confirmed. Significant correlation was found between the frequency of alcohol consumption in the last 12 months and entering into sexual relationships lasting only one night. Students who consumed alcohol in the last 12 months more often engaged in "one-night stands". Regarding the correlation between peer influence and risky sexual behaviour, significant correlation was found between peer pressure and risky sexual behaviour (under the influence of alcohol). Youth who are under greater influence from their peers are more often enter into sexual relationships under the influence of alcohol. Earlier researches also confirmed that peer pressure is correlated with alcohol consumption in youth, especially among the university student population (Majdak et al., 2018.)

Our research results are in accordance with some earlier research, and also match theoretical explanations about youth behaviour. According to biological and psychoanalytical theories, it is important to keep in mind that youth are in a very sensitive period of their life when many changes in their body and mind are happening, and it is not easy for them to control their behaviour completely. According to psychosocial and ecological theories, youth behaviour and attitudes are formed by the influence of their important surroundings (mostly family and peers). According to learning theories, youth behaviour will be learned from their important surroundings. Our results confirmed that in the phase of adolescence, peers have an important influence on young people's attitudes and behaviours, but there are many other factors that also can influence risky sexual behaviour among young people. In future research, attention should be paid to the academic achievement of young people, their socio-economic status, and their relationships with parents.

These results show that in order to prevent risky sexual behaviours, more attention should be put on youth education. Although the ustudent population is a specific population, and probably more responsible than youth in general, prevention and education about the dangers of risky sexual behaviour is needed, as well as prevention of alcohol consumption. This is a task for the media, primary and secondary schools, universities, the social support system and healthcare system.

References

Bastašić, Z. (1995). *Pubertet i adolescencija*. Zagreb: Školska knjiga.

Castelo-Branco, C., Parera, N., Mendoza, N., Perez-Campos, E., Lete, I. & the CEA group (2014). Alcohol and drug abuse and risky sexual behaviors in young adult women, *Gynecological Endocrinology*, 30(8), 581–586.

Chaney, B.H., Vail-Smith, K., Martin, R.J. & Cremeens-Matthews, J. (2016). Alcohol use, risky sexual behaviour and condom possession among bar patons, *Addictive Behaviors*, 60, 32–36.

Cho, H. & LaRose, R. (1999). Privacy Issues in Internet Surveys, *Social Science Computer Review*,17(4), 421–434.

Dabo, J., Malatestrinić, Đ., Janković, S., Bolf Malović, M. & Kosanović, V. (2008). Zaštita reproduktivnog zdravlja mladih-model prevencije, *Medicina Fluminensis*, 44(1), 72–79.

Donenberg, G.R., Emerson, E., Bryand, F.B. & King, S. (2006). Does substance use moderate the effects of parents and peers on risky sexual behaviour?, *AIDS care*, 18(3), 194–200.

Doornwaard, S.M., ter Bogt, T.F.M., Reitz, E., van den Eijnden, R.J.J.M. (2015). Sex-Related Online Behaviors, Perceived Peer Norms an Adolescents' Experience with Sexual Behavior: Testing an Integrative Model, *PLOS ONE*, 10(6), 1–18.

Đepina, M. &Posavec, M. (2012). *Reproduktivno zdravlje mladih u Hrvatskoj.* Zagreb: Hrvatsko Društvo Obiteljskih Doktora.

Epstein, M., Bailey, J. A., Manhart, L. E., Karl G. Hill, K. G. & Hawkins, J. D. (2014). Sexual Risk Behavior in Young Adulthood: Broadening the Scope Beyond Early Sexual Initiation. *JOURNAL OF SEX RESEARCH*, 51(7), 721–730.

ESPAD (2013) The ESPAD validity study in four countries in 2013. http://www.espad.org/sites/espad.org/files/ESPAD-Validity-Study.PDF

Fingerson, L. (2005). Do Mothers' Opinions Matter in Teens' Sexual Activity? *Journal Of Familiy Issues, 26*(7), 947–974.

Hođić, A.& Bijelić, N. (2003). *Značaj roda u stavovima i seksualnom ponašanju adolescenata i adolescentica.* Zagreb: CESI.

Ilišin, V. & Radin, F. (2002). *Mladi uoči trećeg milenija.*Zagreb: Institut za društvena istraživanja.

Jones, R., Biddlecom, A., Hebert, L. & Milne, R. (2011). Teens Reflect on Their Sources of Contraceptive Information, *Journal of Adolescent Research*, 26 (4), 423–446.

Kuzman, M., Pejnović Franelić, I. & Pavić Šimetin, I. (2007). Spolno ponašanje adolescenata u Hrvatskoj i edukacija o zaštiti protiv HPV-a. *Medix, 72/73*, 79–83.

Kuzman, M. (2009). Adolescencija, adolescenti i zaštita zdravlja, *MEDICUS,* 18(2), 155–172

Lacković-Grgin, K. (2006). *Psihologija adolescencije.* Jastrebarsko: Naklada Slap

Lazarus, V.J., Sihvonen-Riemenschneider, H., Laukamm-Josten, U., Wong, F. & Ljiljestrand, J. (2010). Systematic Review of Interventions to Prevent the Spread of Sexually Transmitted Infections, Including HIV, Among Young People in Europe, *Croatian Medical Journal,* 51(1), 74–84.

Lebedina-Manzoni, M., Lotar, M. & Ricijaš, N. (2008). Podložnost vršnjačkom pritisku kod adolescenata- izazovi definiranja i mjerenja, *Ljetopis socijalnog rada,* 15(3) 401–419.

Majdak, M. Novosel, K. & Bagarić, A. (2018) Family acceptance, peer presure and alcohol abuse in young people. In: 5th International Multidisciplinary Scientific Conference on Social Sciences & Arts SGEM 2018, Conference Proceedings, Volume 5, Science and Art, Issue 6, (1) 59–70.

Raboteg-Šarić, Z., Sakoman, S. & Brajša-Žganec, A. (2002). Stilovi roditeljskog odgoja, slobodno vrijeme i rizično ponašanje mladih, *Društvena istraživanja Zagreb,* 58/59(2/3), 239–268.

Rajhvajn Bulat, L. (2011). *Okolinske i osobne odrednice seksualnog ponašanja adolescentica.* Zagreb: Filozofski fakultet.

Simon, A.V. & Feiring, C. (2008). Sexual Anxiety and Eroticisam Predict the Development of Sexual Problem sin Youth With a History of Sexual Abuse, *Sage Publications: Child maltreatment,* 13(2), 167–181.

Stevanović, R., Capak, K. & Benjak, T. (2016). *Hrvatski zdravstveno-statistički ljetopis za 2015. godinu.* Zagreb: Hrvatski zavod za javno zdravstvo.

Štulhofer, A., Jureša, V. & Mamula, M. (1999). Problematični užici: Rizično seksualno ponašanje u kasnoj adolescenciji, *Društveno istraživanje Zagreb,* 6(50), 867–893.

Štulhofer, A., Graham, C., Božičević, I., Kufrin, K. & Ajduković, D. (2007). HIV/AIDS-related knowledge, attitudes and sexual behaviors as predictors of condom use among young adults in Croatia, *International Family Planning Perspectives,* 33(2), 58–65.

Štulhofer, A. (2009). Sociokulturni i psihosocijalni aspekti rizičnog seksualnog ponašanja, *MEDICUS,* 18(1), 123–129.

Tome, G. & Gaspar de Matos, M. (2012). How can peer group influence the behavior of adolescents: Explanatory Model, *Global Journal of Health Science,* 4(2), 26–35.

Ybarra, L.M., Strasburger, C.V. & Mitchell, J.K. (2014). Sexual Media Exposure, Sexual Behavior and Sexual Violece Victimization in Adolescence, *Clinical Pediatric,* 53(13), 1239–1247.

Whitaker, J.D. & Miller, S.K. (2000). Parent-Adolescent Discussions about Seks and Condoms: Impact on Peer Influences of Sexual Risk Behavior, *Sage Publications: Journal of Adolescent Research,* 15(2), 251–273.

Knut M. Sten

In a Just Way: Decency and the Moral Dialogue

Abstract

The ultimate goal of this essay is to relate a discussion of decency to Amitai Etzioni's concept of "moral dialogs", Etzioni (2018). "The moral dialogue" is supposed to change the moral standing of social institutions. The sociologist and communitarian Amitai Etzioni is still very active at the age of 89, and he may be the most prominent sociologist at the moment regarding integrating moral discussions in sociology. A special issue of The Social Science Journal (2018) is dedicated to moral dialogs and commentaries. At the end of my essay, I propose a simple conceptual model of the social process, which has been named "the moral dialog". The elements are frames, norms of decency, critical mass and shaming, and the relations between the elements. I will not cover all these elements and relations in detail, due to lack of space of course, but also because I have at the moment not much to add to the discussions of frames, social movements and critical mass. It follows from that that I will concentrate on decency and shaming, although it is necessary as a starting point to make some remarks on the issue of normative sociology in general. What is it?

Normative sociology

In Abbott's (2018) Varieties of Normative Inquiry: Moral Alternatives to Politization in Sociology, he outlines four different ways of relating the normative side of sociology to its empirical side. This is what he calls two traditional ways, the first is often known as policy analysis, and the second an activist one. Policy analysis is characterized by a strong distinction between researching facts and drawing political conclusions – which is out of the sociological realm. In the activist perspective, these are two sides of the same coin, and traditionally this is research of the progressive camp. (Abbott calls the two approaches "dualist" and "monist", which is easily understood but not very illuminating). Abbott finds these two perspectives lacking in many respects, and he argues for two additional ones – which he put more faith into. The first is creating a pure normative sub-discipline (a "canonical" approach like political theory in political science, collective choice and welfare economics, etc.), and in addition to this more axiomatic approach he suggest a more inductive one in which you try to distill the moral significance from whatever happens and scrutinized it in terms of sociology. "Moral shocks" is an example, i.e. scandals in psychiatric treatment such as lobotomization without much moral concern – evoked in the public through the Jack Nicholson movie "One Flew over the Cuckoo's Nest" and other films. This odd practice has been extensively documented in Norwegian research, and sparked a moral debate (Tranøy, 1999). In the canonical approach, you usually start off by discussing some works considered as classics. In this essay I tie my discussions in large part to "A Decent Society" by Avishai Margalit (1998), and to the more inductive way of argumentation in Aimitai Etzioni's (2018) moral dialogues. As the leader of the communitarian network, Etzioni could also be classified as belonging to the activist camp.

A search for "normative sociology" on the net reveals three different answers or perspectives. The first is associated with a joke made by Robert Nozick, in Anarchy, State and Utopia (1974) where he claimed that "*normative* sociology, the study of what the causes of problems *ought to be*, greatly fascinates us all." The claim is that when we study social problems, there is often an almost irresistible temptation to study what we would *like* the cause of those problems to be (for whatever reason), and to the neglect of the actual causes. In Norway it has been a tendency to focus on gender (the social sex) and neglect the biological. Norwegian national television, with a sociologist who also is a journalist and comedian, made a series of programs entitled "Born So or Becoming So", much to the viewers amusement about sociologists arguing everything is social.

The second perspective is in the study of deviance, i.e. people living in circumstances different from mainstream circumstances. In disability research, there is much talk about normalization, which means creating ordinary lives for people in institutions, or living on the premises of the caring authorities and professions. The ultimate goal for treating criminals, drug addicts, etc. is the same: "normal" living like you and me. The moral issue is that it is shameful that not everybody has the opportunity to have an ordinary life. But who is to blame – the unfortunate person or a social system denying the opportunity?

The third perspective is an institutional one. The late sociologist James S. Coleman (1990) argued that sociology should contribute to institutional design. Not only describing how society functions in reality but also how it should function, according to some explicit values and goals. This will connect sociological theory to moral philosophy, political theory and welfare economics. Indeed Coleman (1966) suggested a social welfare function as a contribution to a long-running debate in economics. Todoroki (1998) discussed "A design of normative sociology based on the rational choice paradigm", which is also the paradigm chosen by Coleman (1990)

The position in this essay is similare to Coleman's – the confrontation of moral philosophical concepts with the sociologists' empirical position, but without Coleman's affinity for rational choice theory. There are other metatheoretical foundations to choose from, and one of them is an idea of cosmopolitanism. Cosmopolitanism is the ideology that all human beings belong to a single community, based on a shared morality. A person who adheres to the idea of cosmopolitanism in any of its forms is called a cosmopolitan or cosmopolite. As I see it, there are strong connections between a cosmopolitan metatheoretical foundation and a communitarian political perspective.

Kwame Anthony Appiah (2007) suggests the possibility of a cosmopolitan community in which individuals from different locations (physical, economic, etc.) enter relationships of mutual respect despite their differing beliefs (religious, political, etc.) A cosmopolitan community might be based on an inclusive morality. I regard ideas of decency and shame as cosmopolitan ones, in the sense that most cultures have ideas of decency and shame, not necessarily with the same content and quite often in contrast with each other, but nevertheless with the same kind of idea, and that could be the starting point of a moral dialogue. "The recent 'normative' and 'cosmopolitanism' turns in social science enhance social theory's capacity to contribute to the core debates about the connections between dignity, rights, justice and democracy. Sociologists' interest in the revival of 'social ethics' and in global problems translates into aspirations to construct a just world order which presupposes a strong commitment to the universal value of human dignity."

Decency is a core concept in this effort.

Decency and negative morality

Oxford English Dictionary (2018) suggest the following interpretations of decency:

Behaviour that conforms to accepted standards of morality or respectability, e.g. 'she had the decency to come'

Behaviour or appearance that avoids impropriety or immodesty, e.g. 'a loose dress, rather too low-cut for decency'

The requirements of accepted or respectable behavior, e.g. 'an appeal to common decencies'

Things required for a reasonable standard of life, e.g. 'I can't afford any of the decencies of life'

The origin is in 16th century (in the sense of 'appropriateness, fitness'): from Latin decentia, or decent, i.e. 'being fitting'. What is lacking in this short definition is of course the question of decency of a society and its institutions. I will have a proposal in this respect, as well as present what Margalit has suggested. For the moment we can dwell on the "classic" interpretation.

A classic in Norwegian sociology is Sverre Lysgård (1961) Arbeiderkollektivet (the collectivity of workers). Lysgård (1961) studied how workers established their sense of self, of the group and the morality of the group, and the decencies of the group. The same goes for sociologists such as Randy Hodson's (2001) "Dignity at Work" and Michele Lamont's (2000) "The Dignity of Working Men". The central focus of Hodson's book is the 'creative and purposive activities of employees to achieve dignity at work.' Her idea of dignity, interpreted as a fundamental part of achieving a life well-lived, and defined as the ability to establish a sense of self-respect and to enjoy the respect of others, refers to both inherent worth as well as to the dignity that people achieve through their actions. Hence, she wants the theory of justice to also 'extend beyond the distribution of rights and goods to examine institutionalized patterns of cultural value.'

Honneth (1995) is another author who does not see justice in terms of the language of redistribution. He is more concerned with intersubjectivity and the identity-based notion of recognition. While defining a universal morality in terms of respect and dignity, Honneth (1995) notes that a good society is a society in which individuals have a real opportunity for full self-realization and where common values ensure that no one is denied the opportunity to earn esteem for his or her contribution to the common good. In a study of my own about prisoners in an open jail, with the opportunity for education and work, open-minded interactions with the staff clearly contributed to their self-respect and will to change.

As has been said, a study of the question of a decent society should focus on its social institutions. Social institution range from those whose activities are publicly defined and controlled (e.g. courts, jails, banks, the postal system) to those whose activities are internally defined but publicly subsidized and regulated (like schools and hospitals) to self-generated but legally constrained civic associations between individuals whose interactions are subject to public concern and scrutiny (marriage, family, teacher-student)

There can be no decency without civility.

A decent society is one in which the decency of institutions and decency of human relationships prevails. The two do not necessarily coincide, and theyare not symmetrical. Where decent institutions are present, individuals are more likely to behave decently, though this connection is not so strong the other way around.

"A Decent Society" by Avishai Margalit (1998) stands to become canonical literature in a normative subdiscipline in sociology. Praise of the book is easily found on the Internet:

> *"Arguably the most important book on social justice published since John Rawls's 25 years ago ... Margalit shows that decency is a strong moral concept in its own right. A decent society strives to eliminate the institutional humiliation of its members, which robs them of their self-respect or control over their lives."* – Charles Leadbeater, New Statesman & Society

> *"This is a splendid book. It is an exacting account of the macro-ethics of political institutions and social practices that is also wonderfully attentive to the detail and nuance of everyday life. At its end, decency stands alongside justice as a distinctive moral idea."* – Michael Walzer

"A decent society," Avishai Margalit (1998) says, *"is one whose institutions do not [systematically] humiliate people."* He focuses on the *"concrete ... actual behavior of institutions,"* and not so much on the *"abstract rules or laws"* that define them.

"A civilized society is one whose members do not [typically] humiliate one another" (1998). He draws a distinction between decency and civility for heuristic, analytic purposes: those distinctions become blurred when he brings his analysis close to the phenomena. Humiliation is not necessarily experienced as a psychological feeling: it could be expressed in the conditions that objectively deny people self-respect. People can even be systematically humiliated without realizing it, and be so manipulated that one remains unaware. Sometimes the very awareness, and the outrage of experiencing the feeling of humiliation could be the seed of striving for self-respect.

Margalit's (1998) concern is to enhance understanding of the meaning and sensibility of the experience of humiliation, particularly in its institutional manifestations, for example denials of rights of citizenship to those who have a legitimate claim to them. From this analysis, he proposes a social ideal of decency as nonhumiliation.

Margalit has an interest in negative moral psychology, and in attempting to build normative reflection on this anatomy of vices and vulnerability. He wants to shape and constrain normative reflection through an analysis of evils and injuries. Put simply, what distinguishes his work from mainstream political theory and moral philosophy is his reflection on negative morality, the coinciding of a refined and acute moral sensibility and commitment and a "realistic" outlook through his many examples. This is not merely an external juxtaposition; rather, the moral sensibility and the concentration on evils mold each other.

Most moral philosophers and political theorists of this century have not given explicit attention to the analysis of negative moral concepts such as injustice, evil, vice, cruelty, humiliation, and so forth. Nor have they spent much time investigating the moral psychologies associated with these negative moral experiences. On the contrary, positive concepts such as *good*, *right*, *duty*, and *obligation* occupy the attention of moral philosophy. Interest in the significance of negative moral concepts and experiences remains very much the exception, in spite of the numerous horrors of our century.

Humiliation typically gives rise to reactive attitudes. Ideas of responsibility are connected to characteristic emotional responses. Responses to wrongdoing by others arise from the point of view of participants in interpersonal affairs.

We will take up a different perspective, an objective one, when we exempt people from evaluation, and understand them in terms of their responses to circumstances – especially shame as a reactive response.

Reactive responses sometimes lead to minimizing strategies, which ease the pain of some hurts. The humilator is not a responsive person, doing something inadvertently – the act as something that just happened.

Official humiliation gives rise to reactive attitudes. If someone is humiliated and others who could do something do nothing in response, the humiliated person will now have grounds for resentment, not least when she is effectively told that her experience of humiliation does not matter, that it is simply her problem.

There are criticism of Margalit's concept of humiliation, and at least four difficulties have been noted:

1. The extension of humiliation, as his list is very heterogeneous. Is there really an underlying concept that captures all these instances of maltreatment?

2. Three senses of humilitation – not been treated as humans, loss of basic control, rejecting a human from being a part of "the family of man". That these are three senses of the same thing is not convincing.

3. Restricting humiliation to institutional practice, not to relationships between individuals. There is a distinction between a macroethical and a microethical concept, wherein macro must also embrace the culturally patterned.

4. How do we decide cases where it is not widely obvious that there are sound reasons for diminished self-respect? This question becomes more acute when we turn to humiliation's symbolic character. Still, symbolism is subject to diverse and contending interpretations.

Negative morality may exercise a constraining and shaping influence on the identification of moral priorities in politics, and may form our understanding of the meaning of moral ideals as well as constrain our sense of their range of application in politics

As a disposition and mode of analysis, negative morality presents us with more direct access to the situations it aims to avoid than positive morality does to the goals it pursues. We do not know what a perfectly just society would be like to live in, but we do know – some of us know from everyday experience – what it is to live in an unjust, or cruel, or humiliating society. There is thus a cognitive reason for sometimes assigning priority to negative morality over elaborating a theory of respect: it is often easier to identify evils than it is to recognize and understand the good. Negative morality is not a moral doctrine on par with deontology or utilitarianism, but is better understood as a sensibility or ethos. Clearly, it accompanies and qualifies such doctrines.

Shame in a just society

Avishai Margalit draws important parallels between a decent society and a just society (1998). Ensuring an absence of humiliation in the way the institutions of a society deals with individuals marks the value of human beings as *ends* – their intrinsic worth. Conversely, where humiliation or shaming takes place, the shamed are rendered as inferior humans (Margalit, 1998). Shame and disgust are powerful emotions that can strip away dignity and respect when expressed in acts that humiliate. Moreover, these emotions can cause us to recoil from social interaction. Such human emotions are inappropriate guides for law and for the institutions of a society: 'the law must refuse to take part in active stigmatizing of vulnerable individuals and groups. But of course a decent society needs to go further, finding ways to protect the dignity of its members against shame and stigma through law' (Nussbaum, 2006).

A theory of justice needs two types of concepts, threshold concepts and distributional concepts. I will put forward recognition and decency as threshold concepts, and fittingness as the distributional concept. Recognition specifies if you are even a matter of concern in the distributional question. Typical is politics of assimilation, where you could have rights as a general citizen, but not as a member of a minority group – the minority doesn't officially exist. The case of ethnic minorities is a concern, for example the Lappish people in Norway had to learn Norwegian – there were no resources in schools to teach "Sami". Today they have a right to this; their language has been recognized as a language on equal terms with Norwegian. The sign-based languages of the deaf have achieved the same status.

The right to beg is another kind of issue. You are allowed to beg on the streets in Norway, and there are of course certain rules you have to consider, but in general you have a right to beg. The right to beg was the first social law from about 1200. Every man who could not earn any income because of sickness or disability, or had tried to get work but there was none, had the right to beg and he could not lawfully be prevented from doing so. You have to be recognized as a beggar, but if this was clearly the case then you have the right. This goes also for today. Begging is not a minority right, so for example being a gypsy doesn't create a right to beg. Begging is a more inclusive right, in spite of the fact that most of the beggars in Norway could very well be gypsy people from Eastern Europe. Misrecognition may indeed sometimes be a serious problem. It has been argued that the tendency to treat people in institutional settings (e.g. shopkeepers, tellers, bureaucrats, etc.) as background or as merely instrumental to our purposes is also instrumental in a failure to be aware of people as people with moral claims.

Twenty years ago, the king of Norway regretted the treatment of Sami: "The Norwegian state is founded on the territory of two people – Norwegians and Sami. Sami history is closely intertwined with Norwegian history. Today we must regret the injustice that the Norwegian state has previously inflicted on the Sami people through a hard anti-corruption policy." The words belong to King Harald and they were part of his speech when he officially opened the Sami Parliament in 1997. The king apologized for the injustice the Norwegian state's assimilation policy had on the country's Sami population. 20 years later – on the occasion of United Nations Day, Prime Minister Erna Solberg went a long way in the same direction as the king. Solberg mentioned the assimilation policy, which was maintained from the 18th century until modern times, as a black chapter in Norway's history.

Decency is also a threshold concept; it means too little or too much of a thing, too different or not in line with, according to a social standard. The limits are set by social norms and cultural values, and it is also a framing concept.

A famous picture is an iconic one from the history of care for the mentally disabled in Norway. It shows the doctor and director of a large institution, Ole B. Munch, talking to one of the patients. The patient is naked and tied by a foot to the wall; a group of other clients are spectators. The publishing of the picture raised a heated debate. Many argued that he should be ashamed of publishing a picture that is so humiliating for the patient. But the motive for Munch was to show, unmasked, the bad condition in institutional care. For a long time he had been asking for more resources, and in particular more people to care for patients who could hurt themselves as well as others. It is no doubt that the institution is humiliating the patient in the sense of Margalit, but it is possible that we should agree with Ole B. Munch, in that the biggest shame is that we allow this kind of care system to exist. Moreover, we don't know if the client thinks of the situation as humiliating, but we do know that most people seeing the picture feel that the system is in disgrace. Clearly, if we don't know we can always do a sociological survey. Whether or not this is an indicator of the decency of the society is better decided by people's feeling of shame concerning what the government does, rather than the feeling of the potential victim.

A decent society is a society where people are not ashamed of what their authorities do, or what their social institutions represent.

Social assistance and medical care, like the care for the mentally disabled, is often at the forefront of criticism of decency. Clearly there is a minimum level of decent care: Violation of norms of decency have the potential to elicit protest and initiate change by imposing shame on the responsible agencies. Often the violations of norms are made public by illustrating stories. This is on example:

For 60 years, Knut and Edith Lund lived as husband and wife. But when illness made it difficult to live at home, the cohabitation ended for the Lund couple. Now they sit alone in different nursing homes and miss each other. "I still hope we will have our last days together, we will not have much time left," Knut Lund (87) says. He, a retired accountant is sitting in his room at Nidarvoll Health Center and reflecting on a long life and a long marriage. His wife Edith is sitting in a similar room, but at another place. "We have no time to lose," he says. The newspapers tell stories of couples in the same situation. This mobilizes public opinion, and creates a critical mass that is not possible to look past for the politicians. Knut and Edith get to live together again, and the topic is made an issue in the coming national elections, paving the way for making it unlawful for local municipalities to split up married couples when they need care.

Another example demonstrates that it is not even necessary to have an outspoken opinion to conclude that the care is beyond the required minimum. It is easily anticipated, or in every way obvious.

In 2017 Oslo municipality is fined: A woman starved to death after moving home from a nursing home. The municipality of Oslo received a fine of 2 million NOK for providing inadequate health and care services. The municipality accepted the responsibility but negotiated the fine down to 1.5 million NOK (160,000 euro). This woman was not the only one to die – others have starved – and 60% of the elderly in care institutions suffer from malnutrition. There are also British reports that sat that nearly 1,200 people have starved to death in NHS hospitals because "nurses are too busy to feed patients". Additionally, for every patient who dies from malnutrition, four more have dehydration. In each of these countries, shave was expressed concerning the failure in terms of governance.

Richard J. Arneson (2006) says that shame, humiliation and disgust are negative states of mind that can be deployed as tools to induce desired behavior. Shame, humiliation and disgust are powerful motivators. A just society should not dispense with these tools, and these tools can be used against the authorities. As Margalit (1998) also notes, policy is implemented by humans.

Of course, the norms of decency can do just the opposite and help governance. The social norm inducing the egalitarian ethos is against greed and selfishness. This encourages the individual towards behavior that is not greedy and towards acts that draw attention to any excessive greed in others. This helps in creating at least somewhat social taxation systems.

The creation of social norms is an open question, but there are many examples where the authorities try to push norms, i.e pick up you own trash, don't leave plastic in the ocean. In Norway, the creation of a critical mass was helped by a particular event. A whale was captured and its stomach was full of plastic. The video clips and pictures of this whale were published in the news and shared extensively. It became a symbol.

This is an interesting British press release:

"*Record number of employers named and shamed for underpaying.*

From: Department for Business, Energy & Industrial Strategy and Margot James MP

15 February 2017

More than 350 employers have been named and shamed as the government publishes the largest ever list of national minimum and living wage offenders.

- More than 350 employers named for underpaying their workers the national minimum or living wage
- More than 15,500 of the UK's lowest paid workers receive back pay thanks to government investigations
- Employers who failed to pay National Living Wage named and shamed for the first time

The Department for Business, Energy and Industrial Strategy today named 359 businesses who underpaid 15,513 workers a total of £994,685, with employers in the hairdressing, hospitality and retail sectors the most prolific offenders."

Social norms are coarse-grained instruments. Arneson (2006) notes that if the enforcement falls disproportionately on those most sensitive to the norm, it will be sporadic and uneven. The person feeling shame thinks of himself as seen through the eyes of another, real or imagined, and feels being negatively judged according to a shared standard. Keep in mind that guilt is focusing on an act, and shame can be a consequence of guilt.

Consider "bad Samaritanism". A bad Samaritan does not provide emergency aid to persons in great need, and to a low cast or small risk to himself. Sometimes this is prohibited by law, for example you can't leave people after a car crash without doing something. But there is a more general norm of minimal decent Samaritanism (Arneson, 2006).

Many people react with disgust to sex between men, or are ashamed of thinking themselves in such activity. Nonetheless this does not excuse violence toward a person who is suggesting such sex, and this norm should not be mitigating nor aggravating in terms of punishing such violence.

Decent behavior induces non-violent behavior, but only according to a specific framing of the situation. The stabbing of Henry Vincent is a case in point. He was a burglar who broke into the house of an elderly couple. Defending your family is also decent framing, or isn't it? The male resident of the home stabbed Henry Vincent to death. Vincent's family and friends placed flowers and balloons opposite the scene in memory of Henry, but all of this was turned down by others. A commentary in the newspaper writes:

Everyone has a right to grieve, but in this case the family and their associates secured dozens of flowers and balloons on a fence opposite the heroic Osborn Brooks house with a clear intention to intimidate and send a message to an elderly man simply defending his home and disabled wife.

Yes, the stabbed criminal was a son and father, but his right to be treated as a normal member of society ended when he set out on a path of targeting the most vulnerable members of that society to satiate his own greed for getting something at the cost of other people. Henry Vincent's attitude was sick and depraved and that his family sees nothing wrong with that says much about them. They seem proud of him rather than hanging their heads in collective shame. It is gang mentality and is intended to intimidate not only Mr Osborn-Brooks but his neighbors too.

Many countries recognize that family shame is no defense for murder. An admirable example is the United Kingdom where, in 2002, 16 year old Hsehu Jones was stabbed to death by Abudullah Jones, her father, because she had a Christian boyfriend and had become "westernized". Her murder was one of 12 honor killings estimated by Scotland Yard to have taken place in the United Kingdom that year. Abdullah Jones was given a life sentence. Institutional violence is not beyond concepts of decency and shame.

The catastrophic situation in Aleppo has woken us up again in the face of a war that has lasted longer than the Second World War. Hundreds of thousands of people have been killed, while millions are on the run. A news commentary read:

And Norway has the strictest asylum and refugee policy in Europe. Thousands of Norwegians gathered to express their compassion for the people of Syria and other countries in crisis, but also in frustration over the inaction of their own leaders. Several well-known Norwegians spoke for a more humane Norwegian policy when the torch arrived at the Storting tonight. "I do not know what to do other than to be proud of continuing to shout about goodness and humanism. That we are the ones who hope everyone understands what kind of crisis this is and that it's not a shame to know the feelings it awakes."

Shaming policy-makers is not uncommon. Here are two examples:

Radiohead frontman Thom Yorke has led the charge in slamming Theresa May for attempting to form a government with the DUP, Northern Ireland's Democratic Unionist Party. Due to the DUP's past of opposing same sex marriage and abortion, as well climate change denial, a number of figures from the world of music, entertainment and politics have hit out at the Tories – with Yorke saying "not my government – have you no shame?"

At least 79 people died or went missing after a large fire in the municipal apartment block in the UK known as Grenfell Tower. Hundreds of people lived in the 24 story high block, which was engulfed in flames last Wednesday night. In the days after the fire, there was a tense atmosphere, with demonstrations being held in several places in London over the weekend. On Friday, hundreds of people entered the Kensington District Council, while shouting their frustration with the authorities. "We want justice! You should be ashamed of yourselves! Murderers!"

The moral dialogue

Moral dialogs are social processes through which people form new shared moral understandings (SMU). The dialogs could be passionate and disorderly, but a characteristic is that it is the subject of talks at home, at the workplace, in the media, etc.

The case of the whale with the stomach full of plastic is an example, which sparked off an increase in the interest in plastic polluting the ocean. Moral dialogs often do lead to profound changes in the moral positions shared by a great number of people.

Central to Etzionis (2000) idea of the moral dialogue is also his concept of the megalogue; by that he means that a moral question has been a question shared by almost everybody – a subject of talk at home, at work, in the media and so on. For this to happen it is obvious that it should be embedded in a frame known to most. Discussing a decent dress code, for example whether it's okay to wear a miniskirt to church, requires an understanding of the prevailing dress code (e.g. in the church). This is about frames and framing, a term borrowed from Erving Goffman's (1974) frame analysis. The concept is rooted in the symbolic interactionist and constructionist principle that meanings do not naturally or automatically attach themselves to the objects, events, or experiences we encounter, but they arise, instead, through interpretive processes mediated by culture. Frames contribute to this interpretive work by performing three core functions as outlined by David Snow et al. (1986) and Benford and Snow (2000):

First they *focus attention* by punctuating or bracketing what is relevant and what is irrelevant, what is "in-frame" and what is "out-of-frame", in relation to the object of orientation.

Second, they function as *articulation mechanisms* in the sense of tying together the various punctuated elements of the scene so that one set of meanings rather than another is conveyed, or, in the language of narrativity, one story rather than another is told.

Third, frames often perform a *transformative function* by reconstituting the way in which some objects of attention are seen or understood as relating to each other or to the actor.

Norms of decency are interpretations of frames, and because of this they have the potential to create megalogues. This transforms routine grievances or misfortunes into injustices or mobilizing grievances, and by the reconfiguration of aspects of one's biography, as commonly occurs in both political and religious conversion.

Framing, within the context of social movements, refers to the signifying work or meaning construction engaged in by movement adherents (e.g. leaders, activists, and rank-and-file participants) and other actors (e.g. adversaries, institutional elites, media, social control agents, and countermovements) relevant to the interests of movements and the challenges they mount in pursuit of those interests. Following Snow et al. (1986), and given the focusing, articulation, and transformative functions of frames, it is arguable that how we see, what we make of, and how we act toward the various objects of orientation depends on how they are framed. Etzioni's idea of the megalogue is useful, but it is somewhat diffuse. It creates the common ground for change, but doesn't answer the question of: How much? What is the tipping point? The idea of the critical mass (Oliver et.al, 2003) does just this. The advantage of critical mass theory is that it not only focuses on tipping points, but

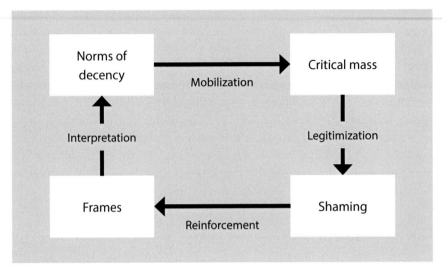

Chart 1: The moral dialog

more generally allow us to see decency norms as public goods, and from there the production functions of decency when there is interdependence between the actors. This will be a gateway into more formal analysis of the production of norms, initiated by Oliver et al. (2001), Coleman (1990) and others – but is not of concern to provide more details in this essay.

A comprehensive theory has been illustrated in the figure to follow. Norms of decency are embedded in cultural frames; the decency norm is an interpretation of these cultural rules. Violations of decency can spark mobilization, which turn into a critical mass. The critical mass must be of sufficient magnitude and composition to legitimize actions of shaming. Shaming reinforces the frames that give rise to the decency norms.

This model could be used with different focus, in this essay I have focused on decency and shaming. From that perspective, we could consider frames and the critical mass as intervening variables. On the contrary, it is possible to focus on the frames and the critical mass, then the norms of decency and shaming as intervening variables.

We could also say that frames and norms of decency are the social cognitive part, and the critical mass and shaming the action part. The general model is quite flexible.

Many of my examples could be understood in the light of this model. This model also illustrates what Amitai Etzioni has called "moral dialogues".

From this vantage point, mobilizing grievances are seen neither as naturally occurring sentiments nor as arising automatically from specifiable material conditions, but as the result of interactively based interpretation or signifying work. The verb framing conceptualizes this signifying work, which is one of the activities that social movement leaders and participants, as well as their adversaries, do on a regular basis.

The case study in Etzioni's (2000) essay is the changed moral status of same-sex marriage in the US. The same approval has happened in Norway and many countries. Mobilization for change must achieve a critical mass of support before the change can take place. The study of moral dialogs are often done retrospectively, although this should not be mandatory (more studies of ongoing processes where the outcome is uncertain would be welcome), the methodology seems clear enough. One needs to start with a baseline, what was the moral understanding before the dialog changed them. Next one should identify sociological starters that lead to the initiation, and the sometimes-crucial role of dramatization. The closure is the milestone of the process, and the associated significant sociological consequences revealed in new shared values, law and behavior. James Jaspers describes what here is referred to as "starters" using the term "moral shocks" which occur when an unexpected event or piece of information raises such a sense of outrage in a person that she becomes inclined toward action, whether or not she has acquaintances in the movement.

On May 23, 1914 a steamship arrived in the western city of Vancouver carrying 376 Sikhs, Hindus and Muslims, who were hoping to immigrate to Canada. Most of the passengers were refused entry and had to stay on board the vessel for two months. The ship was obliged to return to India where many of the passengers were killed or imprisoned. The government of Canada formally apologized in the House of Commons in 2016 for its role in the incident, citing the cruel, discriminatory laws of the day and the pain and suffering of the passengers.

In a news release from the government, they say that at a time when Canada is celebrating its 150th anniversary as a nation "we must member this dark chapter in Canadian history and the tragedy that can result from prejudice and intolerance.

Many have discovered that shaming has enormous power when used by human-rights organizations as their principal lever for social change, especially when applied to governments and institutions that are guilty of "shameless" behavior.

"The Shame of the Cities" is a book written by American author Lincoln Steffens and published in 1904. It reports on the workings of corrupt political machines in several major US cities, along with a few efforts to combat them. It is considered one of several early major pieces of muckraking journalism. Muckcracking journalism has been the source of many scandals and the shameful governance that is revealed.

Though Steffens' subject was municipal corruption, he did not present his work as an exposé of corruption; rather, he wanted to draw attention to the public's complicity in allowing corruption to continue. Steffens tried to advance a theory of city corruption: corruption, he claimed, was the result of "big business men" who corrupted city government for their own ends, and "the typical business man" – average Americans – who ignored politics and allowed such corruption to continue. He framed his work as an attempt "to sound for the civic pride of an apparently shameless citizenship" by making the public face their responsibility in the persistence of municipal corruption.

References

Abbott, Andrew (2018): Varieties of Normative Inquiry: Moral Alternatives Politization in Sociology. Am. Soc. 49: 158–180.

Appiah, Kwame Anthony (2007): Cosmopolitanism: Ethics in a World of Strangers. W.W Norton & Company.

Arneson, Richard J (2006): Shame, Stigma, and Disgust in the Decent Society. The Journal of Ethics.

Benford, Robert D, David A Snow (2000): Framing Processes and Social Movements. An Overview and Assesment. Annu. Rev. Sociol. 26: 611–39.

Coleman, James S. (1990): Foundations of Social Theory. The Belknap Press.

Coleman, James S. (1966): The possibility of a Social Welfare Function American Economic Review 55: 1105–1122.

Etzioni, Amitai (2001): On Social and Moral Revival. The Journal of Political Philosophy 9: 356–371.

Etzioni, Amitai (2018): Moral dialogs. The Social Science Journal 55: 6–18.

Etzioni, Amitai (2000): Moral Dialgues. Public Perspective March/April 27–30.

Fjermeros, Halvor (1998): Om hundre år er allting glemt? 100-års jubileumsskrift for Emma hjorts hjem 1898–1998 Bærum kommune/Emma Hjorts hjem museum.

Goffman, Erving (1974): Frame analysis: An essay on the organization of experience. Northeastern Univ. Press.

Hodson, Randy (2001): Dignity at work Cambridge Univ. Press.

Honneth, Axel (1995): The Struggle for Recognition: The Moral Grammar of Social Conflicts Polity Press.

Lamont, Michell (2002): The Dignity of Working Men. Harvard Univ. Press.

Lysgård, Sverre (1961): Arbeiderkollektivet: en studie i de underordnedes sosiologi Universitetsforlaget.

Maibom, Heidi L.(2010): The descent of Shame. International Phenomenological Society 80: 566–594.

Margalit, Avishai (1998) The Decent Society Harvard Univesity Press.

Nozick, Robert (1974): Anarchy, State and Utopia. Basic Books.

Nussbaum, Martha C. (2006): Hiding from Humanity. Disgust, Shame, and the Law.

Oliver, Pamela E., Jorge Cadena-Roa, Kelley D. Strawn (2003) Emerging trends in the study of protest and social movement. Political Sociology 12: 213–244.

Oliver, Pamela E., Gerald Marwell (2001): Whatever Happened to Critical Mass Theory? A Retrospective and Assessment. Sociological Theory 19: 292–311.

Oxford English Dictionary (2018): Decency.

Schumaker, Paul (2018): Amitai Etzioni: Comunitarian Centrist and Principled Pluralist. The Social Science Journal 55: 4–5.

Silver, Hilary (2018): Moral dialogues and normative change. The Social Science Journal 55: 19–22.

Snow, David A. et al. (1986): Frame Alignment Processes, Micromobilization and Movement Participation American sociological Review 51: 464–481.

Social Science Journal (2018) Special issue on the moral dialgue.

Streeck, Wolfgang (2003): Social Science and Moral Dialogue. Critical Forum: Toward a New Socio-Economic Paradigm. Socio-Economic Review, Vol. 1: 126–129.

Tangney, June Price (1996): Conceptual and methodological issues in the assessment of shame and guilt. Behav. Res. Ther. 9: 741–754.

Todoroki, Makoto (1998): A design of normative sociology based on the rational choice paradigm International Journal of Japanese Sociology 7: 85–104.

Tranøy, Joar (1999): "Til pasientens beste": Behandling, makt og pasientprotest i norsk psykiatri, Forlaget Forum.

Maria Ozanira da Silva e Silva (Universidade Federal do Maranhão, UFMA)

Income Transfer Programs as a Strategy Against Poverty in Latin America: Reality and Limits[1]

Abstract

Latin America is one of the most unequal regions in the world. It has a large income and property concentration and a weak and disintegrated work market. In this context, the economic crisis of the 90's in the last century favored the intervention of the state to protect the increasingly poor population. A survey, bibliographical and documentary investigation developed by researchers from Brazilian, Argentinian and Uruguayan Universities, in 2012, found a high prevalence of Conditional Income Transfer Programs (PTRC) in the Social Protection System among the Latin America Countries. These programs are directed at fighting poverty on the continent. This article in intended to contextualize and provide an overview of the PTRC that are implemented in Latin America. It points out who is their target population, the objectives, the coverage areas, the acceptance criterion for access and inclusion, criterion for exclusion from the programs, the requirements for families to remain in the programs, the benefits and the possible impacts. The discussion tries to also highlight the contribution and weakness to meet the central objective of the Income Transfer Program in Latin America, which aims to fight poverty and extreme poverty.

Introduction

From the 1930s up to the middle 1990s, social protection in Latin America was based on small-scale programs dispersed throughout different countries, with advances and steps backwards in each country. The relevant trait was that they were short-lived, with consequent impacts that were insufficient to change the social pic-

---

1   This article was presented at the 20th Biennial International Symposium of International Consortium for Social Development (ICDS 2017) (Croatia, July 7–11, 2017) and contains partial results of studies developed with the support of Fundação Coordenação de Aperfeiçoamento de Pessoal de Nível Superior (CAPES) and of Conselho Nacional de Desenvolvimento Científico e Tecnológico (CNPq), Brazilian Government agencies aimed at training resources education and research. It is a research project that contains an exploratory study on Conditioned Income Transfer Programs (i.e. PTRC – Programas de Transferência de Renda Condicionada) which are implemented in Latin American and the Caribbean, and a comparative study conducted by three PTRC: Bolsa Família (Brazil), Nuevo Régimen de Asignaciones Familiares – AFAM-P.E. (Uruguay) and Asignación Universal por Hijo para la Protección Social (Argentina) and was submitted to and approved through the following official notices: *Programa CAPES PPCP – Edital CGCI n. 072/2010 – MERCOSUL and Edital Universal CNPq n. 14/2011.*

ture, which was marked by poverty and inequality. This configuration has undergone changes since the second half of the 1990s, highlighting the implementation and dissemination of the Conditioned Income Transfer Programs (PTRC). However, this shift has not yet been able to significantly change the social picture in the region and achieve a system of social protection that ensures rights. In other words, it is not yet possible to speak of passing from a concept focused on the needy to a concept that considers people whose rights are assured by providing sufficient and quality services, going beyond immediate assistance to sustainable social protection (Silva, 2014).

The PTRC option is located at a juncture of a rise in social costs with the acknowledgment by governments of the need to adopt an option of social intervention focusing on poverty and extreme poverty, underscoring the relevance of social development as an impetus for economic development. The models adopted focus on individual capitalization, seeking to combine the fight against poverty with the struggle against inequality and promotion of social cohesion. The proposal is to offer social services and programs of assistance aiming to break down the contradiction among the principles of universality of rights and rationality of focalization (Comisión Económica para América Latina y el Caribe [CEPAL], 2009).

From the perspective indicated, the PTRCs in Latin America are founded on technical-ideological concepts, the most noteworthy references of which are the theoretical categories of poverty, human capital, social capital and focalization.

Therefore, beginning in the second half of the 1990s, the most mportant point in the field of social protection in Latin America and the Caribbean has been the PTRC, which proposed to transfer income to families or individuals over the short term and to contribute over the middle and long term, to raising the human capital of the new generations by fulfilling the conditionalities that underscore the requirement to attend school and seeking assistance from the basic health care system, especially children, adolescents and women who are part of these programs.

The present text proposes to present general indications about the socioeconomic and political context that has promoted the creation and development of the PTRC, as a privileged strategy of a policy to deal with poverty in Latin America that began in the 1990s. It situates the PTRC in the field of non-contributive social protection, highlights and clarifies the problems surrounding the dimensions that qualify these programs and points to structural limits to deal with extreme poverty on this continent.

The socioeconomic and political context of the rise and development of income transfer programs in Latin America

Beginning at the end of the 1960s, the world's capitalist economy underwent an inflection whose clearest symptoms were the deceleration of the growth rate of industrial production, the retraction of the value of international trade and a concomitant financial expansion unprecedented in the history of this production system.

These manifestations expressed one more structural crisis of capital, caused by the drop in the profit rate, in a context of worsening inter-capitalist competition worldwide, and of exhaustion of the Taylorist-Fordist productive and technological paradigm.

In this context and in response to the crisis, a set of transformations occurred that extrapolated the productive base and reached the other spheres of society, shaping a process of capitalist restructuring on a global scale. Indeed, as a substitute for the Fordist regimen of accumulation, a regimen of flexible accumulation gained space, whose implications went well beyond the introduction of technological and organizational innovations in the basic units that form the structure of the capitalist system, affecting the dominant standard of economic and social regulation and even the very form of state organization. All of this was favored by a political context marked by the end of the Cold War and the rise to power of conservative parties and governments in the central capitalist countries, creating space to disseminate and apply neoliberal thinking (Lima, 2002).

Focusing on the analysis of the Latin America region, which is the subject of this reflection, the world crisis that began at the end of the 1960s, the great social transformations that occurred during the 1970s and the following years, in the context of globalization of the markets and internationalization of the capital, the *foreign debt crisis* and the presence of strong macroeconomic imbalances in the region, in the 1980s, under the management of the central countries and multilateral agencies imposed the adoption of new measures of economic policy management by the peripheral countries.

The guidelines of economic policies aiming to protect the adjustment for Latin America are clearly defined in the document called *Washington Consensus*, which was supported by international agencies and by the central countries that were the drivers of globalization. This document includes the series of reforms that the state-run economies of Latin America were to apply to attract private capital again, after the devastating debt of the 1980s, the *lost decade*, as it is called in the literature.

The restructuring inspired by neoliberal thinking had major consequences in the Latin American region. Always bearing in mind the specificities of each country, there is no doubt that the privatization process, fiscal adjustment, flexibility of the labor-capital relationship, opening the market and deterioration of the natural and energy resources and of the public services had a significant impact on the different countries in the region, summarized by a growing mass of impoverished people with job insecurity.

Indeed, Latin America was meeting the end of the 20th century with almost half of its population in a situation of poverty, and considered as one of the most unequal regions in the world. In fact, the neoliberal adjustment policies in Latin America, overlaying the historically and structurally accumulated social heritage, worsened the situation of social crisis in the region, with a considerable increase in unemployment rates. Between 1990 and 2002, the mean rate of unemployment in Latin America had increased from 4.5% to 11.1% (CEPAL & Organización Internacional del Trabajo [OIT], 2011).

The changes in the job market had profound consequences for social protection. This is because, given the characteristics of the Latin American social systems, remunerated work and, in particular, access to formal jobs is the link *par excellence* for access to social protection in matters of social security, and to a lesser extent to matters involving health.

In the first decade of the 21st century, in Latin America – with its heterogeneities and complexities – a few inflections occurred in relation to the final decades of the 20th century. In a context of economic growth and changes in the politics of several countries in the region, improvements of a few social indicators were recorded centrally in terms of poverty, indigence, inequality and unemployment rates. The improvement of the indicators of poverty and inequality was in part a response to the economic growth, the positive effect of which was the creation of new jobs and, in part, the recovery from the loss of real salary that occurred in the 1990s and the significant increase of national minimum wages.

At the same time these changes were occurring, under the rule of sectors of the left that rose to power in several countries in the region in the decade of 2000, there was criticism about the direction of neoliberal reforms. In this context, two general approaches began to coexist regarding social policy: one related to the systemic competitiveness in which concepts such as human capital and intergenerational transmission of poverty become relevant; another linked to the focus on rights and guarantees of citizenship and sustained by the international pacts and treaties assumed by the states. These approaches are not mutually exclusive, even if the second has become more visible in recent years (Cecchini & Martínez, 2011).

In reality, it should be mentioned that based on this scenario, the implementation of PTRC proliferates in several countries of the region. Its objective, in the speeches given by the heads of state and their executives and formulators of social policies is to *eradicate poverty*. However, behind this discourse it can be clearly perceived that these programs are the result of impositions caused by internal and external restrictions. The internal ones are the alignment of state public expenditures because of the redefinition of the role of the state, and the macroeconomic governance required by the structural adjustment, and the external ones are materialized in the commitments signed by the heads of state, both at the First Meeting of the Americas, promoted by the Organization of American States (OAS), held in 1994 in Miami, and in the Millennium Development Goals (MDG) for the regions, established in September 2000, the main goal being the eradication of poverty.

Considering the most recent juncture, particularly since the second decade of the 2000s, there has been an inflection in the economic and political situation, following the specificities of the Latin American countries, but the decline and recession of the economies can be highlighted, with increased unemployment and precarious jobs and the reduction of income from work. These indicators rose significantly during the 1990s and in the first decade of the 2000s. In the field of politics, the number of conservative governments explicitly allied to the interests of large capital has been increasing on this continent, so thatat this point, prioritization of the fight against poverty appears to have been given a secondary role. Centrality has been attributed to the structural adjustments and labor and social service reforms, the objective of which is essentially to deconstruct rights achieved by the working classes. An outstanding example in this field is the Brazilian case, in which a presidential election by popular vote was overturned to create conditions to engender a congress that can approve any reform, even it takes away the most elementary rights of workers and of the poor population. In this context the social programs, and among these the income transfer programs, no longer receive the same priority that marked the 1990s when they were implemented in various countries in Latin America.

Indicating and problematizing the central dimensions of the characterization of the PTRC in Latin America

The central dimensions of the PTRC in Latin America are essentially its evolution, the target population, its objectives and coverage of its target public, the entry and removal criteria, the monetary and non monetary benefits, and finialy the management, implementation and expected impacts.

Some details about those aspects are provided below.

Evolution of the PTRC

Referring to the evolution of the PTRC, Cecchini and Madariaga (2012) emphasized that in 19 countries of Latin America and the Caribbean, the coverage of this program grew from 5.7%, in 2000 to 19.3% of the total population of these countries in 2010. In the same period, the PTRC recorded an increase in relation to the gross domestic product (GDP) from 0.19% in 2000 to 0.40% in 2010, growing at a much slower rate than the expansion of the programs.

Exploratory research performed in 2012, based in information from documents and sites of the programs, developed by researchers from Brazilian, Argentinian and Uruguayan universities identified PTRC distributed throughout 18 countries of Latin America and the Caribbean[2], and it should be kept in mind that some of

---

2   The countries and year of founding of the programs were Honduras (1990), Mexico (1997), Ecuador (1998), Colombia (2000), Jamaica, (2001), Chile (2002), Brazil (2003), El Salvador (2005, 2009), Peru (2005), Paraguay (2005), Dominican Republic (2005), Panama (2006), Trindad and Tabago (2007), Uruguay (2008), Bolivia (2009), Argentina (2009) and Guatemala (2012).

the programs have more than one component, sometimes considered independent programs. Furthermore, this does not include Nicarágua, which implemented an income transfer program from the year 2000 to 2006. It also should be considered that we limited the list of programs to those that maintain conditionalities, and thus did not include major income transfer programs such as the Benefit of Continuing Provision (BPC – Benefício de Prestação Continuada) of Brazil, which is aimed at the elderly and people with special needs.[3]

The exploratory study made it possible to systematize a general profile of the PTRC in Latin America and the Caribbean based on dimensions and respective qualifiers, constructed by the reality of the program enabling initial problem clarification, as indicated below.

As a mobilizing axis to create and implement the PTRC, we can highlight as *junctural determinations*: the economic crisis of the 1980s and 1990s; the need to increment human capital to cover the new demands of globalized capitalism; the development of a new social security network, represented by strengthening the non-contributive social assistance directed at the poor and impoverished, maintaining the contributive social insurance for workers. Regarding this aspect, the PTRC originated from pilot experiences, transformation of developing income transfer programs or other programs focusing on poor families, all of which were generated based on the need to increase the income of the poor populations, as well improvement of the conditions of food, health care and education of children and adolescents.

The target public, the objectives and the coverage of the PTRC

As to the *target public*, the public in focus were children, the elderly, the unemployed, pregnant or breastfeeding women, and people with special needs. Although they have less prevalence: indigenous people, populations displaced due to an emergency situation or expelled due to conflicts, *quilombola* families of African descent, the homeless and families with members in a situation of child or slave labor, or extremely poor people living in the urban environment, and also in rural areas. We also emphasize that the great majority of the programs refer to families and not to individuals as their target public, and that the latter are chosen based on variables related to the economic situation of the families, especially income. The most widely used procedures to select them are forms or spreadsheets filled out by computerized systems, interviews, home visits to choose and follow up with families and see whether the inclusion criteria are still present or not.

As to the *objectives*, these are connected to poverty, extreme poverty or vulnerability and social exclusion. The outstanding general objectives are: overcoming or

---

3   A more complete characterization and problem description are found in the book Silva (2014).

relieving intergenerational poverty and the formation of human capital, expressed by a broad, varied set of intentions, positioned in a strategy to deal with poverty, such as providing minimum income, food, offers of services, especially education, health, professional qualifications and work opportunities. There are also programs guided by specific objectives, directed at given target groups such as children and adolescents or pregnant women.

If the *reach* and *coverage* are considered, the reach of the PTRC is predominantly national, although the majority develop progressive implementation or pilot experiences and do not cover the entire territory of the respective country. Other programs are directed at specific population groups as was already mentioned: children, adolescents, pregnant and breastfeeding women, indigenous people and others. Moreover, others prioritize certain groups such as rural populations or group of people who live pockets of poverty. A lack of resources also limits the expansion of many programs.

The entry and removal criteria for the PTRCs

As to *entry criteria*, there is an indication of a direct connection to the target public, that is, the entry criteria were the poor and extremely poor.

Here we should make a brief incursion regarding focalization. We emphasize that we do not consider focalization and universalization as strictly opposite fields, and we also do not restrict focalization to residualism. That is because we adopt a perspective that we call progressive/distributive, which indicates the possibility of focalization being considered positive discrimination (Silva, 2001, 2014). However, this does not appear to be the concept adopted by the PTRC in Latin America. The use of means testing is outstanding, with control and even invasion of the private life of the target population, although the use of differentiated procedures has been indicated, giving greater importance to the formation of *information systems on a national or local level* to be used as a source of data to select the beneficiaries of social programs; *home visits* to confirm the information provided; *interviews* to obtain information and fill out question forms; *participation of the state with involvement of civil society*. As regards the entry criteria, we find the use of a broad set of variables to size and classify the population at levels or lines of poverty, including a few programs that utilize the construction of classification indexes, although variable income is determinant for the selection of the beneficiaries. *Geographic criteria* were also used prior to the selection of the beneficiaries, prioritizing populations that live in urban or rural areas, for instance; the requirement of signing *statements of agreement; corroborative documents* regarding the information provided and assistance restricted to the population who are citizens of that country.

Analyzing the procedures to select the target public, the complexity and sophistication of procedures should be highlighted. They are extended to the follow-up and control of the conditionalities, with complexification and technification of the field of social assistance, changes in the institutional management transforming the use of the technology to control the human factor in order to minimize randomness in the name of efficiency, so that techniques and computerization of professional work in the field of assistance become outstanding dimensions on the management of the social programs used to standardize the practices and mechanisms of management and control of professional work, and furthermore to control the lives of the beneficiaries of social programs (Garrido, 2012).

Considering the continuation in and removal of the PTRC beneficiaries from the program, most of the programs underscore the loss of conditions of eligibility and the lack of compliance with the conditionalities as the main reasons to suspend or remove the public that uses them. Some establish a time limit for the beneficiaries to stay in the programs or emphasize periodic or continuous review proceedings.

About the *conditionalities, follow up and sanctions* for non-compliance, these imply a commitment of the families or individuals to fulfilling the demands that are mainly in the field of education and health, essential components to form the human capital of future generations, as the approach emphasized by the PTRC and a responsibility of the state for the offer of services. A few programs present conditions in the field of work (professional training and insertion into the work market) and personal and family formation along with capacity-building.

The conditionalities are not a consensus, and for instance in the literature on the largest PTRC in Latin America, the *Bolsa Familia* of Brazil, three different concepts are identified: conditionalities as access and expansion of rights; conditionalities as the denial of rights and conditionalites as a political issue and conservative moralistic imposition (Silva, Guilhon, & Lima, 2013).

In order to follow the conditionalities, the use of sophisticated information systems was identified; involvement of public agencies and society and, regarding sanctions for non-compliance, there are a variety of situations that locate the conditionalities as weak, strong and conditionality systems (Cecchini & Martínez, 2011; Cecchini, 2013). Outstanding among them are a warning, followed by suspension and even removal from the program; few programs associate informative and educational work with the process of following up and controlling the conditionalities, and few refer to the deficiencies or to the non-offer of services related to the conditionalities by the state as reasons for this non-compliance. Here we have the risk of establishing the triad of conditionalities/punishement/blaming the most vulnerable.

Monetary and non-monetary benefits of the PTRC

Regarding the *monetary benefits* and *forms of payment*, a variety of values and modalities were identified: transfers to families, to the elderly, to people with special needs and to children or adolescents; periodical transfer; transfers of a single amount assigned per family or per person; values with staggered amounts. It was also found that the payments were done mostly monthly, but also quarterly, every two months or as a lump sum. The agentcies that paid out the most important benefits were: public or accredited private banks; mobile cashiers, networks of automatic cash points or self-service terminals, lottery agencies, transport companies, authorized payment points, post offices and the executive agency itself, and the forms of payment are transfers to bank accounts; cash and check to beneficiary signing a receipt; pre-paid cards; bonuses or tickets; wide use of electronic magnetic cards, some with sophisticated devices to control what items are being purchased, since there are programs that restrict the use of money transfers to a given list of items and explicitly forbid the purchase of others, especially alcoholic beverages and cigarettes.

It was underscored that mothers are the person of preference to receive the monetary benefit.

Besides the *monetary benefits*, the PTRC in Latin America highlight as the axis of the programs the non-monetary benefit, represented by complementary actions directed at the beneficiaries as a complement to the money transfer, in close relationship with the fulfillment of conditionalities in the field of health, education, food/nutrition and work (professional training, insertion into the work market and development of productive actions). Other actions are citizenship (identity cards), strengthening of family formation or education, human development, infrastructure, housing and others.

Management, implementation and expected impacts of the PTRC

Regarding *management and implementation* of the PTRC, outstanding fundamental aspects were: decentralization of most national experiences down to the local level, that is, the national programs are implemented at the level of each municipality; systematic inclusion of practices to follow up and evaluate the beneficiaries by some programs, above all to follow the conditionalities and results and impacts of the programs and the practice of involving entities from the community and users in the implementation of some programs.

As to the expected impacts of the PTRC in Latin American, according to Cecchini and Madariaga (2012), the most significant are: reduction of power and social inequality and the formation of human capital, focusing on education, health and nutrition. Thus the authors consider among the changes regarding the indicators of human capacities: access to school and to the health services, the effects of education focused on increased school enrollment, although no impacts on learning have been proven; in health and nutrition they mention the increased coverage of verifying the growth of children and on preventive medical examinations, but the results vary in terms of if the impacts on the state of health and nutrition of the children are considered. As to the indicators of poverty, regarding the users and the indexes of poverty at a national level, the authors underscore that the repercussions of income transfer in the beneficiary families can be sustainable over the short term, but even so, vary according to the size of the program. On the other hand, the impacts of transfers on the indicators of poverty on a national level underscore that the information about positive effects comes from countries where these programs are wide-ranging and the amount transferred is significant, such as Argentina, Brazil, Ecuador, Jamaica and Mexico. It was highlighted that the sustainability over time of the effects of poverty and inequality reduction, beyond the duration of the programs requires the integregation of the PTRC with other social promotion programs.

Possible impacts on consumption, based on evaluations in five countries (Brazil, Colombia, Mexico, Nicaragua and Paraguay,) showed that the families' consumption has risen, especially as to the diversity of foods consumed, although they are not always healthier food, and also buying clothes for the children.

Regarding the generation of income and insertion into jobs, the conclusions of the study mentioned emphasized that the beneficiaries generally do not manage to be inserted sustainably into the formal job market, i.e. informal jobs continue to be the most feasible possibility for most of the poor and vulnerable families that are in the PTRC. On the other hand, since child labor is given a different treatment by the programs in the region, the results achieved vary. About expected impacts related to *empowerment* of the beneficiary families as a whole or of some of their members there are more doubts than answers. The analysis of the PTRC allowed the identification of the foundationals limits to achieve this empowerment. Regarding this aspect, we underscore that the beneficiary is formed by families or individuals who live in a situation of poverty, extreme poverty and vulnerability, in societies marked by the exploitation and division of classes, where the opportunities are unequally distributed; the monetary transfer is very low, and therefore insufficient to cover the basic needs of the families. Furthermore, the number of people served by most PTRC in Latin America leaves a great number of poor without the protection of non-contributive social assistance, and the non-monetary benefits or complementary actions offered, even in the field of education, health, nutrition and work are insufficient to serve the public they are meant for, and above all, they are in most cases low quality services. Other than these basic limits, we find few references in the study to what can be called empowerment. The most often identified mentions are expressions of mere expectations, limited to subjective intentionalities.

Conclusion

The study of the PTRC in Latin America shows that it is not a single model, and the programs are marked by the economic, sociopolitical and institutional reality of each country. Furthermore, diversity was found in the coverage of the target population and in the volume of resources aimed at these programs, so that countries with less human development are those that have the least coverage.

It is important to point out that the proposals of the PTRC in Latin America are based essentially on four main theoretical categories: poverty, theory of human capital, theory of social capital and focalization, which guide the objectives, the target public and the process of implementing these programs.

Considering the poverty category, evidence of a multidimensional conception in the formulation of the objectives, the inclusion criteria, the conditionalities and the development of the non-monetary benefits have been identified. Thus, poverty is considered the expression of a set of deficiencies, lacks, absences and, outstandingly, lack of income. However, no consideration of the structural dimension of poverty was found, ignoring that in the capitalist society poverty is the opposite of wealth, a product of exploitation that determines how society is organized to produce and distribute the wealth that is socially generated. Thus, the individual is considered responsible for their poverty and for overcoming intergenerational poverty, instituting the ideology of accountability and stigmatization.

The ideas of the theory of human capital are duly articulated with the theoretical concept of poverty formulated by Sen (1992, 2000), who believes that poverty will only be overcome when privation is surpassed by the offer of opportunities that will enable the insertion of individuals into the labor market and maintaining an income; access to education, to health and basic social services that will allow them a decent life, an assumption that guides the formulation of conditionalities as the central element in the constitution of the PTRC in Latin America. From this perspective, the ideas of the theory of human capital are largely present in the discourses and proposals of the PTRC. The assumption is that human work, formaized by education, becomes one of the most important instruments to expand economic productivity. In order to support this orientation, education takes on an essential technicist and mistifying connotation. It assumes the enhancement of the value of economic development and the development of the individual, of capital and of oneself.

Thus, education is seen as a potentiator of the working and production capacity, and the investment in human capital is considered profitable for the development of nations and the mobility of individuals. Consequently, education is reduced to its potential as an instrument for work and for production. It is a *solution* to reduce inequalities between developed and developing countries, and between individuals, widely disseminated throughout Latin American countries and the Third World by international agencies (Frigotto, 2010).

Thus, the instrumental concept of the theory of human capital that guides the PTRC in Latin America contributes to intensifying the concept of making the poor responsible for their situation of poverty and for overcoming this situation. From this perspective, the state has the task of making opportunities available, including education for all, considered the fundamental condition to raise the capacities of the human factor, generating what has been called in economic literature their *employability*. It is also the state that must create and guarantee the operation of the skill-building mechanisms, and to individuals with skills the responsibility of inserting themselves and maintaining themselves in the labor market in order to guarantee overcoming intergenerational poverty, which is the strategic objective of the PTRC.

Complementing the theory of human capital is the theory of social capital, the central idea of which emphasizes *social cohesion* as a mobilizing factor of society. Thus, social capital consists of shared rules and values to promote cooperation. It emerges from practice, within the sphere of cultural standards of each society, instituting forms of establishing trust to consolidate *solidary and cooperative actions* among the poor, enabling the *empowerment* and participation of poor communities to consolidate their social capital. This concept of *social capital* is an important mechanism to solve social conflicts and generate potentials to break the *vicious cycle* of reproduction of poverty and intergenerational transmission of *incapacities*, potentiating resources generated by the community and family networks.

The concept of focalization, as a foundation of the PTRC in Latin America, is also integrated with the concept of poverty, both of them constituting central qualifiers in providing the foundation and implementation of the PTRC.

The need to focus on poor and extremely poor segments comes from the criticism regarding the high costs of universal policies, largely driving the PTRC in Latin America since the 1990s, with the support of international financial agencies as a minimalist social policy. The justification is to obtain greater efficiency from the scarce resources, raising the impact by concentrating the programs on higher risk populations.

Finally, the PTRC that are being developed in Latin America are programs oriented by focusing on poor, extremely poor and vulnerable families. Each program adopts its own mechanisms to implement the focalization, although all articulate focalization with conditionalities using sophisticated information technologies, with a growing technification of the field of assistance, moving these programs even further to a neoliberal and conservative conception of focalization.

Articulating poverty, human capital, social capital and focalization as the foundations of the PTRC in Latin America, there is a reinforcement of the representation of the poor based on individual attributes, underscoring their lack of capacities to make use of opportunities and their *negative* behaviors. Consequently, there is a concept of poverty seen as a matter of individual and family deficiencies that does not take into account their structural causes. Hence, overcoming intergenerational poverty, which is the aim of the PTRC in Latin America, would be achieved by providing opportunities that generate human capital and by processes that can mobilize and develop social capital to add to cooperation in the poor communities.

References

Cecchini, S., & Madariaga, A. (2012). *Programas de Transferência Condicionadas: balance de la experiência reciente em América Latina y el Caribe* (Cuadernos de la CEPAL, 95). Santiago de Chile: Naciones Unidas.

Cecchini, S., & Martínez, R. (2011). *Protección social inclusiva en América Latina: una mirada integral, un enfoque de derechos.* Santiago de Chile: CEPAL.

Comisión Económica para América Latina y el Caribe. (2009). *Panorama Social de América Latina, 2009.* Santiago de Chile: Author. Retrieved from www.eclac.cl [01.04.2017].

Comisión Económica para América Latina y el Caribe, & Organización Internacional del Trabajo. (2011). *Coyuntura Laboral em América Latina y el Caribe.* Santiago de Chile: Author.

Frigotto, G. (2010). *Educação e a crise do capitalismo real* (6th ed.). São Paulo: Cortez.

Garrido, M. L. V. (2012). *La reconfiguración del campo assistencial: el caso del Plan de Equidad de Uruguay* [Mimeo]. Montevideo.

Lima, V. F. S. de A. (2002, Julho/Dezembro). Reforma do Estado e Controle Social: limites e possibilidades da descentralização e do terceiro setor. *Revista de Políticas Públicas*, 6 (2), 127.

Sen, A. (1992). Sobre conceptos y medidas de pobreza. *Comércio Exterior*, 42 (4), 310–322.

Sen, A. (2000). *Desenvolvimento com liberdade.* São Paulo: Companhia das Letras.

Silva, M. O. da S. e (Coord.). (2001). *O Comunidade Solidária: o não enfrentamento à pobreza no Brasil.* São Paulo: Cortez.

Silva, M. O. da S. e (Coord.). (2014). *Programas de Transferência de Renda na América Latina e Caribe.* São Paulo: Cortez.

Silva, M. O. da S. e, Guilhon, M. V. M., & Lima, V. F. S. de A. (2013, Junho). As Condicionalidades e o Índice de Gestão Descentralizada (IGD) enquanto Dimensões Centrais do Bolsa Família (BF): uma incursão na realidade do Programa no Maranhão. *Cadernos de Pesquisa*, 1(1). Retrieved from www.gaepp.ufma.br.

Authors

Auferbauer, Martin

PhD., lecturer and resarcher at the University College of Teacher Education Styria (Pädagogische Hochschule Steiermark). Research areas: sociology of education, inclusion, multiprofessional cooperation in the field of social work and education.

martin.auferbauer@phst.at

Babic, Marina Milic

Assistant Professor, at the Department of Social Work, Faculty of Law, University of Zagreb. Research areas: Counseling in social work, human rights, green social work, migrant children and families, children with disabilities, gestalt therapy in practice.

marina.milic.babic@pravo.hr

Baturina, Danijel

PhD., postdoctoral researcher, Department for Social Policy, Faculty of Law, University of Zagreb. Research areas: third sector, social innovation, social entrepreneurship, social policy.

danijel.baturina@pravo.hr

Berc, Gordana

Associate professor at the University of Zagreb, Faculty of Law, Department of Social Work. Research areas: family and youth, psychosocial support (counselling), family community services, social work in education.

gordana.berc@gmail.com

Bežovan, Gojko

PhD., full professor, Department for Social Policy, Faculty of Law, University of Zagreb. Research areas: civil society, welfare mix, social innovation, social polic

gojko.bezovan@pravo.hr

Buchner, Thomas

Senior researcher at the SOS Children's Villages, Department for Research and Development. Research areas: youth welfare work and statistical data analysis.

thomas.buchner@sos-kinderdorf.at

Findenig, Ines

Senior researcher at the SOS Children's Villages, Department for Research and Development. Research areas: child and youth welfare, generations, volunteering movements, social-participation and social-pedagogical frameworks & developments.

ines.findenig@sos-kinderdorf.at

Grytbakk, Anne

Assistant Professor. Masters degree in Social work; Department of Social Work, NTNU, NO-7491 Trondheim, Norway, Research area; My Life Education and My life cooperation; Co-production with children in child welfare and education.

anne.grytbakk@ntnu.no

Heimgartner, Arno

Universitätsprofessor, Mag. Dr.; Work area Social pedagogy; Department of Educational Sciences; University of Graz; Research Area: Social Pedagogy; Children and Youth Help Services, Youth Work, School Social Work, Volunteering, Empirical Research methods and concepts.

arno.heimgartner@uni-graz.at

Hyrve, Geir

PhD., associate professor at Norwegian University of Science and Technology, Department of Social Work. Research areas: Utilization-focused evaluation, organizations and social change and child and youth welfare.

geir.hyrve@ntnu.no

Isaksen, Joachim Vogt

Researcher at the Norwegian University of Science and Technology, Department of social work, with a specialization within sociology. Reserch areas: child protection, migration, and health sociology.

joachim.v.isaksen@ntnu.no

Isaksen, Lasse Skogvold

Assistant Professor at the Sør-Trøndelag University College, Faculty of Health and Social Science, Department of Applied Social Science. Research areas: Education policy, social pedagogic and schooling for children in residential care.

lasse.s.isaksen@ntnu.no

Klinger, Sabine

Post-doc University assistant with specialization in Social Pedagogy at the Department for Educational Sciences at the University of Graz. Research areas: gender-reflexive social pedagogy, migration and forced displacement, digitalization and social work.

sabine.klinger@uni-graz.at

Kolstad, Hans

Independent researcher and philosopher. He is a government grant holder appointed by the Norwegian Government. Research areas: European continental philosophy, philosophical analysis, theories of knowledge and values, and political and social philosophy.

kolstad@mail.dk

Krasniqi, Vjollca

PhD., sociologist. She teaches at the Faculty of Philosophy, University of Prishtina, in Kosovo. Research areas: gender, social policy, nation and collective memory, peace-building and post-war reconstruction.

vjollca.krasniqi@uni-pr.edu

Leko, Zrinka

Master of Social Work, Department of children, youth and family, Social Welfare Centre Vinkovci. Research areas: youth with behavioural problems, risk sexual behaviour of youth.

zrinka0112@hotmail.com

Majdak, Marijana

PhD., Associate professor, University of Zagreb, Faculty of Law, Department of Social Work. Research areas: children and youth with behavioural problems, youth in conflict with the law, social work with perpetrators of criminal acts, interpersonal communication, supervision.

marijana.majdak@pravo.hr

Matančević, Jelena

PhD., assistant professor, Department for Social Policy, Faculty of Law, University of Zagreb. Research areas: civil society, welfare mix, social innovation, social policy.

jelena.matancevic@pravo.hr

McPherson, Jane

Assistant Professor and Director of Global Engagement at the University of Georgia (USA) School of Social Work. Research areas: human rights practice; migration; maternal/child health; social work education.

janemcphers@gmail.com

Ozanira, Maria da Silva e Silva

PhD. in Social Work; professor of the Graduate Program in Public Policies at Universidade Federal do Maranhão. Research areas: Social Work, Poverty, Policies Focused on Poverty.

maria.ozanira@gmail.com

Pezerovic, Alma

Save the Children. Research areas: human rights, work in emergencies, migration and forced displacement, children and youth, unaccompanied children.

pezerovic.alma@yahoo.com

Liljana Rihter

Ph.D; Work area: assistant professor and researcher at Faculty of Social Work, University of Ljubljana, Slovenia; Research area: methods and models of evaluation of social protection programmes, vulnerable groups, dementia, working poor, precarious work, analysis and assessment of effects of programmes in the social protection field, needs-assessment, and poverty.

liljana.rihter@fsd.uni-lj.si

Skauge, Berit

Department manager in Child Welfare services in Trondheim Municipality and phd student at the Department of Social Work, Norwegian University of Science and Technology (NTNU). Research areas: Child participation, social work, collaborative relations, child welfare.

berit.skauge@ntnu.no

Sten, Knut M.

Assistant professor at the Sør-Trøndelag University college, Faculty of Health and Social Sciences, Department of Applied Social Science. Research areas: Transactional analysis – the microfoundation of sociology, caring, social science modelling.

knut.m.sten@ntnu.no

Sundby, Roar

associate professor, sociologist; Department of Social Work, NTNU, NO-7491 Trondheim, Norway; Research area; My Life Education and My life cooperation; Co-production with children in child welfare and education.

roar.sundby@ntnu.no.

Svetlik, Ivan

Professor of Human Resources at the Faculty of Social Sciences, University of Ljubljana. Research areas: human resources development and management, eduation and training, social development.

ivan.svetlik@fdv.uni-lj.si

Soziale Arbeit – Social Issues

hrsg. von Univ.-Prof. Mag. Dr. Arno Heimgartner (Universität Graz) und
FH-Prof. Dr. Maria Maiss (Fachhochschule St. Pölten GmbH)

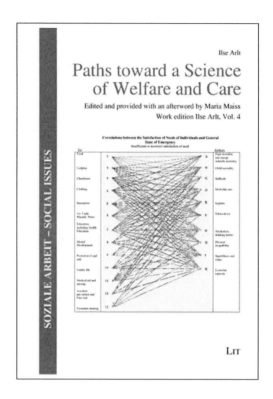

LIT Verlag Berlin – Münster – Wien – Zürich – London

Auslieferung Deutschland / Österreich / Schweiz: siehe Impressumsseite

Martin Riesenhuber
Drogengebrauch bei Jugendlichen von „normalem" zu „riskantem" Konsum
Schritte einer Diagnostik auf sozialpädagogischer Ebene
Bd. 16, 2013, 360 S., 34,90 €, br., ISBN 978-3-643-50454-8

Arno Heimgartner; Ulrike Loch; Stephan Sting (Hg.)
Empirische Forschung in der Sozialen Arbeit
Methoden und methodologische Herausforderungen
Bd. 15, 2012, 328 S., 29,90 €, br., ISBN 978-3-643-50359-6

Sylvia Leitner; Ulrike Loch, Stephan Sting unter Mitarbeit von Rita Schrabeck
Geschwister in der Fremdunterbringung
Fallrekonstruktionen von Geschwisterbeziehungen in SOS-Kinderdörfern aus der Sicht
von Kindern und Jugendlichen
Bd. 14, 2011, 216 S., 24,90 €, br., ISBN 978-3-643-50344-2

Maria Anastasiadis; Arno Heimgartner; Helga Kittl-Satran; Michael Wrentschur (Hg.)
Sozialpädagogisches Wirken
vol. 13, 2011, 408 pp., 29,90 €, br., ISBN 978-3-643-50342-8

Bettina Messner; Michael Wrentschur (Hg.)
Initiative Soziokultur
Diskurse. Konzepte. Praxis
Bd. 12, 2011, 192 S., 19,90 €, br., ISBN 978-3-643-50256-8

Ilse Arlt – (Auto)biographische und werkbezogene Einblicke
Werkausgabe Ilse Arlt, Band 3. Herausgegeben von Maria Maiss und Silvia Ursula Ertl
Bd. 11, 2011, 176 S., 19,90 €, br., ISBN 978-3-643-50254-4

LIT Verlag Berlin – Münster – Wien – Zürich – London
Auslieferung Deutschland / Österreich / Schweiz: siehe Impressumsseite

Ilse Arlt
Die Grundlagen der Fürsorge
Werkausgabe Ilse Arlt, Band 1. Herausgegeben und mit einem Nachwort versehen von
Maria Maiss
Bd. 10, 2010, 288 S., 19,90 €, br., ISBN 978-3-643-50182-0

Manuela Brandstetter; Marina Schmidberger; Sabine Sommer (Hg.)
Die Funktion „verdeckter Kommunikation"
Impulse für eine Technikfolgenabschätzung zur Steganographie
Bd. 9, 2010, 184 S., 19,90 €, br., ISBN 978-3-643-50128-8

Waltraud Gspurning; Arno Heimgartner; Sylvia Leitner; Stephan Sting
Soziale Qualität von Nachmittagsbetreuungen und Horten
Bd. 7, 2010, 232 S., 24,90 €, br., ISBN 978-3-643-50121-9

Bernhard Haupert; Sigrid Schilling
Fall- und Biografiearbeit in der Sozialen Arbeit
Eine Einführung
Bd. 6, 2019, ca. 88 S., ca. 18,90 €, br., ISBN 978-3-643-80037-4

Peter Pantucek; Dieter Röh (Hg.)
Perspektiven Sozialer Diagnostik
Über den Stand der Entwicklung von Verfahren und Standards
Bd. 5, 2009, 480 S., 34,90 €, br., ISBN 978-3-643-50074-8

Ilse Arlt
Wege zu einer Fürsorgewissenschaft
Werkausgabe Ilse Arlt, Band 2. Herausgegeben und mit einem Nachwort versehen von
Maria Maiss
Bd. 4, 2010, 152 S., 19,90 €, br., ISBN 978-3-643-50059-5

Arno Heimgartner
Komponenten einer prospektiven Entwicklung der Sozialen Arbeit
Bd. 3, 2009, 448 S., 29,90 €, br., ISBN 978-3-8258-9828-1

Konstanze Wetzel (Hg.)
Ganztagsbildung – eine europäische Debatte
Impulse für die Bildungsreform in Österreich
Bd. 2, 2006, 200 S., 14,90 €, br., ISBN 3-8258-9333-2

Arno Heimgartner (Ed.)
Face of Research on European Social Development
Community Work, Civil Society, and Professionalisation of Social Work
vol. 1, 2006, 384 pp., 34,90 €, pb., ISBN 3-8258-8984-X

LIT Verlag Berlin – Münster – Wien – Zürich – London
Auslieferung Deutschland / Österreich / Schweiz: siehe Impressumsseite